Jamaican Cookbook

250 Classic Recipes Made Easy And Modern
Techniques For An Unrivaled Cuisine

Elizabeth A. Schultz

INTRODUCTION

Jamaican cuisine is a fusion of cooking techniques, flavors, and spices influenced by the island's diverse population of Amerindians, Africans, Irish, English, French, Portuguese, Spanish, Indians, Chinese, and Middle Easterners. Crops imported to the island from tropical Southeast Asia also have an impact. All of these plants are now growing in Jamaica. There is a vast range of seafood, tropical fruits, and meats to choose from.

Some Jamaican meals are adaptations of cuisines that were brought to the island from other parts of the world. These are frequently tweaked to include fresh ingredients and spices from the area. Others are unique or hybrid, and they have emerged locally. Curry goat, fried dumplings, ackee, and saltfish are all popular Jamaican cuisines. Popular items include Jamaican patties, pastries, breads, and beverages.

Emigrants from the island exported Jamaican cuisine to other countries, especially during the twentieth century, as Jamaicans sought economic possibilities in other countries.

As a result of waves of enslavement, African food emerged on the island, such as Callaloo from the Angolan dish "Calulu." West African peoples also brought the fruit of Jamaica's most popular meal, ackee, to the island. The first Europeans to arrive on the island were the Spaniards, who brought foods like vinegary escovitch fish (Spanish escabeche), which was introduced by Spanish Jews. Later, the Jamaican patty, a pasty-styled turnover packed with spiced meat, could be said to have been influenced by Cornish. As a result of indentured labourers who replaced slaves after independence brought their own culinary abilities, more Chinese and East Indian influences can be found in Jamaican food, such as Roti and Curry Goat (especially curry, which Jamaican chefs sometimes use to season goat meat for special occasions). In the 1500s, Portuguese Jews who had escaped the inquisition brought salted codfish, which is currently used in the national dish Ackee and saltfish, but it was also a mainstay for enslaved Africans as a long-lasting, economical protein.

Rastafarian influences can be found in Jamaican food, but not exclusively. Rastafarians follow a vegetarian diet and have added a variety of distinctive vegetarian dishes to Jamaican cuisine. Rastafarians abstain from eating pork. Pork, on the other hand, is a popular dish in Jamaica. Pork stew and jerk pork are two of the most popular preparations. Some people even believe in cooking with little or no salt, which is known as the 'Ital' method.

TABLE OF CONTENTS

RECIPES

1. PLANTAIN TARTS

Prep: 25 mins

Cook: 40 mins

Additional: 6 hrs

Total: 7 hrs 5 mins

Servings: 25

Ingredients
Pastry:

- 2 cups all-purpose flour
- 1 tsp salt
- ¼ cup cold butter, cut into 1/2 inch pieces
- 3 tbsps shortening, chilled and diced
- 1 egg, beaten
- 1 tbsp ice-cold water

Filling:

- 3 very ripe (black) plantains
- ¼ cup white sugar
- 1 tsp vanilla extract
- 1 tsp grated nutmeg
- 2 drops red food coloring (Optional)
- 1 egg white, beaten
- white sugar for decoration

Directions

1. Combine the flour and salt in a mixing bowl to make the pastry. Rub in the butter and shortening until completely combined, and the mixture resembles sand. Stir the egg and water into the flour mixture until a dough forms, then knead the dough for a few turns to bring it together. Wrap tightly in plastic wrap and chill for 3 hours.
2. Plantains should be peeled and cut into thirds while the dough is chilling. Fill a small saucepan halfway with water. Bring to a simmer and steam until the plantains are cooked, around 5 to 10 minutes depending on how ripe they are. When the plantains are soft, drain the water and mash them with sugar, vanilla, nutmeg, and red food coloring. Allow to cool before serving.
3. Preheat the oven to 350 ° Fahrenheit (175 ° C).
4. On a lightly floured surface, roll out the dough to a thickness of 1/4 inch. Using a 4 or 5-inch round cookie cutter, cut into circles. Fill each circle with a small amount of the plantain filling,

then fold in half to form a half-moon shape. Brush the tarts with beaten egg white and sugar before placing them on a baking pan.

5. Bake for 20 to 25 minutes, or until golden brown, in a preheated oven. Before serving, allow the tarts to cool to room temperature.

Nutrition Facts

Per Serving:

107 calories; protein 1.7g; carbohydrates 17.1g; fat 3.8g; cholesterol 12.3mg; sodium 112.2mg.

2. OXTAIL

Prep: 30 mins

Cook: 3 hrs 15 mins

Total: 3 hrs 45 mins

Servings: 6

Ingredients

- 2 ½ pounds oxtail
- 1 tbsp Worcestershire sauce
- 1 tbsp soy sauce
- 1 tbsp salt
- 1 tbsp white sugar
- 1 tbsp garlic and herb seasoning (such as Spike®)
- 1 tsp browning sauce (such as Grace®)
- ¼ tsp ground paprika
- ¼ tsp ground cayenne pepper
- ¼ tsp ground black pepper
- 2 tbsps vegetable oil
- 2 carrots, thinly sliced
- 2 stalks celery, thinly sliced
- 1 onion, chopped
- 4 garlic cloves, minced
- 3 cups low-sodium beef broth
- 1 bunch fresh thyme
- 1 sprig fresh rosemary
- 1 bay leaf
- 2 tbsps unsalted butter

Directions

1. In a small dish, place the oxtail. In a small bowl, mix together Worcestershire sauce, soy sauce, salt, sugar, garlic and herb spice, browning sauce, paprika, cayenne pepper, and black pepper. Marinade both sides of the oxtail and pour off the excess.
2. In a big, deep skillet, heat the vegetable oil over medium-high heat. 3 minutes per side, sear oxtail in high oil until golden brown. Place on a small plate to cool.
3. In the same skillet, cook carrots, celery, onion, and garlic until softened, about 5 minutes. Bring to a boil the beef broth, thyme, rosemary, and bay leaf. Add the oxtail and its juices, as well as the butter. Reduce heat to low, cover, and cook for 3 hours, or until oxtail is fork soft.
4. Increase the heat to high and remove the cover from the skillet. Cook, stirring periodically, for about 5 minutes, or until sauce reduces and thickens.

Nutrition Facts

Per Serving:

361 calories; protein 32.3g; carbohydrates 9.4g; fat 22g; cholesterol 114.1mg; sodium 1583.3mg.

3. MUDSLIDE

Prep: 15 mins

Total: 15 mins

Servings: 4

Yield: 4 servings

Ingredients

- 1 cup crushed ice
- ½ cup pina colada mix
- ½ cup rum
- 2 cups caffeinated pepper-type soda (such as Dr Pepper)

Directions

1. In a blender, combine the ice, pina colada mix, and rum; blend until smooth and free of icy lumps, about 10 minutes. Divide the mixture across four glasses. Fill each glass with 1/2 cup pepper-type soda.

Nutrition Facts

Per Serving:

149 calories; protein 0.1g; carbohydrates 20.4g; fat 0.7g; sodium 17.2mg.

4. CABBAGE

Prep: 20 mins

Cook: 20 mins

Total: 40 mins

Servings: 6

Yield: 6 servings

Ingredients

- 1 head cabbage
- 2 tbsps olive oil, or as needed
- 1 small onion, thinly sliced
- ½ chopped green bell pepper
- 1 green onion, sliced
- 2 sprigs fresh thyme
- 1 whole Scotch bonnet chile pepper
- 1 tsp salt (Optional)
- 1 cup shredded carrots
- ¼ cup white vinegar
- 2 tbsps white sugar

Directions

1. Peel the cabbage's stiff outer leaves, core the head, and shred the cabbage.
2. In a large skillet, heat the olive oil over medium-high heat; then increase the heat to high. Cook, turning frequently, until the onion, green bell pepper, and green onion have softened in the heated oil, about 5 minutes. Combine the onion mixture with the thyme, Scotch bonnet pepper, and salt.
3. Combine the shredded cabbage and carrots with the onion mixture in a skillet, cover, and decrease heat to medium-low. Cook, turning occasionally, until cabbage has softened, about 10 minutes. Uncover skillet and whisk vinegar and sugar into cabbage mixture; cook and stir for an additional 3 minutes, or until cabbage is soft. Before serving, remove the Scotch bonnet pepper and thyme sprigs.

Nutrition Facts

Per Serving:

121 calories; protein 3g; carbohydrates 19.2g; fat 4.8g; sodium 437mg.

5. JAMAICAN TEN SPEED

Prep: 5 mins

Total: 5 mins

Servings: 2

Yield: 2 rocks glasses

Ingredients

- 1 fluid ounce melon liqueur
- 1 fluid ounce vodka
- 1 fluid ounce coconut flavored rum
- 3 fluid ounces cranberry juice
- 3 fluid ounces pineapple juice

Directions

1. In a cocktail shaker with ice, combine the melon liqueur, vodka, rum, cranberry juice, and pineapple juice. Cover and shake until the shaker is frosted on the outside. To serve, strain into cold martini glasses.

Nutrition Facts

Per Serving:

161 calories; protein 0.2g; carbohydrates 21.7g; fat 0.1g; cholesterol 0mg; sodium 7mg.

6. CURRY POWDER

Prep: 10 mins

Cook: 10 mins

Total: 20 mins

Servings: 36

Ingredients

- ¼ cup whole coriander seeds
- 2 tbsps whole cumin seeds
- 2 tbsps whole mustard seeds
- 2 tbsps whole anise seeds
- 1 tbsp whole fenugreek seeds
- 1 tbsp whole allspice berries
- 5 tbsps ground turmeric

Directions

1. In a skillet, toss together the coriander seeds, cumin seeds, mustard seeds, anise seeds, fenugreek seeds, and allspice berries. About 10 minutes over medium heat, toast the spices until the color darkens somewhat and they are quite aromatic. Allow the spices to cool to room temperature before removing them from the skillet. In a spice grinder, combine the spices and turmeric. Keep at room temperature in an airtight container.

Nutrition Facts

Per Serving:

12 calories; protein 0.5g; carbohydrates 1.8g; fat 0.5g; sodium 1.6mg.

7. GINGER BEER

Prep: 15 mins

Additional: 3 days

Total: 3 days

Servings: 16

Ingredients

- 4 quarts boiling water
- 3 cups white sugar, divided
- ½ pound ginger root with skin, grated
- ½ cup honey
- ½ cup lime juice
- 1 cup fresh brewers' yeast

Directions

1. 1/2 cup boiling water should be removed and set aside to cool to lukewarm.
2. In a big plastic container, combine the remaining boiling water, 2 cups sugar, ginger, honey, and lime juice.
3. In a separate basin, combine 1/2 cup lukewarm water, 1 cup sugar, and yeast. Allow 5 minutes for the yeast to soften and produce a creamy paste before stirring into the ginger mixture. Cover the container and set it aside for three days. Remove the foam from the top, filter the liquid, and transfer the ginger beer to clean storage containers to cool.

Nutrition Facts

Per Serving:

213 calories; protein 3.4g; carbohydrates 52.5g; fat 0.2g; sodium 19.2mg.

8. APPLE PIE

Prep: 25 mins

Cook: 50 mins

Additional: 15 mins

Total: 1 hr 30 mins

Servings: 8

Ingredients

- 1 pastry for a 9-inch double crust pie, divided
- 8 cups peeled, cored, and sliced sweet, firm apples
- ½ cup firmly packed light brown sugar
- ¼ cup molasses
- ¼ cup dark corn syrup
- 3 tbsps cornstarch
- 1 tsp rum-flavored extract
- 1 tsp vanilla extract
- ½ tsp ground cinnamon
- ¼ tsp ground nutmeg
- 1 tbsp caramel syrup, or to taste

Directions

1. Preheat the oven to 425 ° Fahrenheit (220 ° C). 1 pie crust should be used to line the bottom of a deep-dish pie plate.
2. In a large mixing bowl, combine the apples, brown sugar, molasses, corn syrup, cornstarch, rum extract, vanilla extract, cinnamon, and nutmeg. Combine all of the ingredients in a large mixing bowl and pour over the crust. Place the top crust on top. Slits should be cut into the dough, and the edges should be crimped. Wrap aluminum foil around the bottom and sides of the pie pan.
3. Bake for 50 minutes to 1 hour in a preheated oven until the crust is golden brown. Allow it cool for 15 to 20 minutes before serving with a drizzle of caramel syrup on top.

Nutrition Facts

Per Serving:

424 calories; protein 3.1g; carbohydrates 71.1g; fat 15.2g; sodium 258.9mg.

9. CORNMEAL PORRIDGE

Prep: 5 mins

Cook: 15 mins

Additional: 5 mins

Total: 25 mins

Servings: 1

Ingredients

- 1 cup water
- 1/3 cup cornmeal
- ¼ cup whole milk
- ¼ cup coconut milk
- 3 tbsps white sugar
- ½ tsp vanilla extract
- ½ tsp salt
- ¼ tsp ground nutmeg
- ¼ tsp ground cinnamon
- 2 tbsps raisins (Optional)

Directions

1. In a blender, blend together the water, cornmeal, whole milk, coconut milk, white sugar, vanilla extract, salt, nutmeg, and cinnamon until smooth.
2. In a saucepan, bring the mixture to a boil, whisking occasionally, until it begins to thicken, about 5 minutes. When sluggish bubbles appear, turn down the heat. Stir frequently for about 5 minutes, or until the sauce is as thick as you like it. Toss in the raisins.
3. Remove from heat, cover, and set aside for 5 minutes before serving.

Cook's Notes:

You can also use a NutriBullet(TM) to combine the cornmeal mixture or shake it well in a tight container.

Nutrition Facts

Per Serving:

536 calories; protein 7.1g; carbohydrates 95.7g; fat 15.2g; cholesterol 6.1mg; sodium 1207.5mg.

10. BURGERS

Prep: 2 mins

Cook: 15 mins

Total: 17 mins

Servings: 6

Ingredients

- 2 tbsps olive oil
- 2 ¼ cups chopped onion
- 3 cloves garlic, minced
- 1 habanero pepper, chopped
- 1 ½ tbsps grated fresh ginger root
- 1 tsp salt
- ¾ tsp ground allspice
- ¾ tsp ground nutmeg
- 2 ¼ cups cooked black beans, rinsed and drained
- 2 ¼ cups cooked long-grain white rice
- 2 ½ cups dry bread crumbs
- 6 hamburger buns, split

Directions

1. In a large skillet, heat 1 tbsp of olive oil over medium heat. Cook and stir for a few minutes after adding the onions and garlic. Continue to simmer until the habanero pepper is soft. Remove from the heat and place in a mixing basin. Combine the beans, rice, and bread crumbs in a mixing bowl. Add ginger, salt, allspice, and nutmeg to taste. Using your hands, thoroughly combine the ingredients. Make 6 patties out of the mixture.
2. In a large skillet, heat the remaining oil over medium-high heat (you can use the same one). Fry the patties for about 10 minutes total, until browned on both sides. Serve with your favorite toppings on buns.

Nutrition Facts

Per Serving:

531 calories; protein 17.5g; carbohydrates 92.6g; fat 9.7g; sodium 1307.4mg.

11. FRIED SNAPPER

Prep: 10 mins

Cook: 15 mins

Total: 25 mins

Servings: 2

Ingredients

- 1 (1 1/2 pound) whole red snapper, cleaned and scaled
- salt and freshly ground black pepper to taste
- 1 quart vegetable oil for frying
- 1 tsp vegetable oil
- ½ white onion, sliced
- 1/8 tsp minced garlic
- ½ large carrot, peeled and cut into thin strips
- 1 sprig fresh thyme, leaves stripped
- 1 allspice berry, cracked
- ¼ habanero pepper, seeded and minced
- ¼ cup white vinegar
- 1 tbsp water
- ¾ tsp salt
- 1 pinch brown sugar

Directions

1. Cut three small slits on either side of the fish after patting it dry. Season with salt and pepper on both sides.
2. In a large skillet, heat 1 quart oil over medium-high heat until it smokes. Carefully insert the fish in the pan and cook for 5 minutes per side, or until browned and crisp. Remove the fish and place it on a dish lined with paper towels.
3. In a large skillet, heat 1 tsp oil over medium-high heat. Cook and stir for 1 to 2 minutes after adding the onion, garlic, and carrot to the pan. Continue cooking until onions have softened and liquid has decreased, about 5 minutes, with thyme, allspice, habanero pepper, vinegar, water, salt, and sugar.
4. Serve the fish with the onion mixture spooned on top.

Nutrition Facts

Per Serving:

770 calories; protein 70.3g; carbohydrates 4.9g; fat 50.9g; cholesterol 124.8mg; sodium 1035.7mg.

12. JERKED PORK LOIN CHOPS

Prep: 30 mins

Cook: 15 mins

Additional: 8 hrs

Total: 8 hrs 45 mins

Servings: 8

Ingredients

- ½ (12 ounce) bottle lager style beer
- 3 fluid ounces dark rum
- ¼ cup molasses
- ¼ cup soy sauce
- ¼ cup lime juice
- 2 tbsps minced garlic
- 2 tbsps minced ginger
- 1 scotch bonnet chile pepper, minced
- 2 tsps chopped fresh thyme
- 2 tsps chopped fresh marjoram
- 1 ½ tsps ground allspice
- 2 tsps ground cinnamon
- 1 tsp ground nutmeg
- 2 bay leaves
- 8 (6 ounce) pork loin chops
- koshar salt and cracked black pepper to taste

Directions

1. In a mixing bowl, combine the beer, rum, molasses, soy sauce, and lime juice. Add the garlic, ginger, scotch bonnet pepper, thyme, and marjoram and stir to combine. Add allspice, cinnamon, nutmeg, and bay leaves to taste. Put the pork chops in a zip-top bag and pour the marinade over them. Refrigerate for at least one night.
2. Heat up an outdoor grill to medium. Remove the pork chops from the marinade, place them on a platter, and set aside to cool for 15 to 20 minutes while the grill heats up.
3. Season the chops with kosher salt and freshly cracked black pepper to taste. Grill the chops until a thermometer placed in the center registers 145 ° F on both sides (63 ° C). Allow 5 minutes for the pork chops to rest before serving to allow the juices to redistribute.

Nutrition Facts

Per Serving:

323 calories; protein 28.4g; carbohydrates 11.7g; fat 14.3g; cholesterol 80.6mg; sodium 639.4mg.

13. BROWN STEW CHICKEN

Prep: 40 mins

Cook: 1 hr 20 mins

Additional: 12 hrs

Total: 14 hrs

Servings: 8

Ingredients
For the Marinade:

- 1 tbsp minced habanero pepper
- 2 tbsps fresh thyme leaves, chopped
- 4 cloves garlic, minced
- 2 tsps minced fresh ginger root
- ½ cup sliced green onions, divided
- 2 tbsps packed dark brown sugar
- 1 tsp freshly ground black pepper
- 2 tsps kosher salt
- 1 tsp smoked paprika
- ½ tsp ground allspice
- 1 tbsp cider vinegar
- 8 (5 ounce) bone-in, skin-on chicken thighs

For the Rest:

- 3 tbsps olive oil, divided
- 1 large yellow onion, diced
- 1 pinch kosher salt
- 1 tbsp brown sugar
- 4 cups chicken broth
- 1/3 cup ketchup
- 2 each bay leaves
- 1 cup sliced carrot
- 1 cup bell peppers, mini sweet peppers

Directions

1. In a large mixing bowl, whisk together the habanero, thyme, garlic, ginger, light portions of green onions, brown sugar, black pepper, kosher salt, smoked paprika, allspice, and vinegar for the marinade.
2. Cut 2 slashes perpendicular to the bone, about 1 inch apart, into the skin side of each thigh, cutting all the way down to the bone. Toss the chicken thighs in the marinade until they are well coated. Wrap the chicken in plastic wrap and place it in the refrigerator for 12 hours or overnight. Toss many times during the marinating time if feasible.
3. Remove the chicken from the marinade and set it aside. Scrape any remaining marinade bits from the chicken into the bowl and set aside for later.
4. In a large, deep, heavy-bottomed pan or Dutch oven, heat 2 tbsps oil over medium-high heat until almost blazing hot. Working in batches if required, add the chicken and brown well on both sides, about 5 minutes. Remove all of the browned chicken to the marinade bowl and set aside.
5. Over medium-high heat, preheat the same pan. Add the onion and a pinch of salt, and cook until golden brown in the fat, 3 to 5 minutes. 3 to 5 minutes more, add 1 tbsp brown sugar and simmer until everything caramelizes and turns a dark brown.
6. Bring the chicken stock, ketchup, and bay leaves to a boil in the pan. Add the carrots, bell peppers, and reserved marinade to the browned chicken thighs.
7. Reduce the heat to medium-low and cook, stirring occasionally, for 1 to 1 1/2 hours, or until the chicken is cooked and no longer pink in the center and the sauce has reduced and thickened, scraping any excess oil that rises to the surface and basting the chicken with the sauce as needed. Taste and adjust as needed.

Chef's Notes:

1. You may marinate the chicken for as little as 4 hours, but the longer the better.
2. If desired, diced tomatoes can be substituted for ketchup. You can make this with any seasonal vegetables you desire.
3. Remove the chicken and keep it warm while the sauce continues to simmer if the chicken becomes tender before the sauce decreases. If the sauce thickens and reduces before the chicken is tender, add a splash of water and boil until the chicken is done.
4. Use 1 tbsp of brown sugar in the marinade if you want a less sweet flavor profile.

Nutrition Facts

Per Serving:

343 calories; protein 25.4g; carbohydrates 13.8g; fat 20.2g; cholesterol 91.3mg; sodium 1318.6mg.

14. RICE

Prep: 15 mins

Cook: 30 mins

Total: 45 mins

Servings: 2

Ingredients

- 1 tbsp vegetable oil
- ½ large onion, sliced
- ½ red apple, cored and sliced
- 1 pinch curry powder
- 1 cup water
- 2/3 cup brown rice
- 1 tsp dark molasses or treacle
- 1 small banana, sliced
- 1 tbsp unsweetened flaked coconut

Directions

1. In a saucepan, heat the oil over medium heat. Cook and mix in the onion and red apple until the onion is translucent. Stir in the water and season with curry powder. Add the rice and molasses, cover, and cook over low heat for 30 minutes, or until the rice is soft and the water has been absorbed.
2. Toss in the banana, then top with the coconut. Before serving, reheat for a few moments over low heat.

Nutrition Facts

Per Serving:

398 calories; protein 6.1g; carbohydrates 71.6g; fat 10.7g; sodium 11.1mg.

15. CURRY CHICKEN

Prep: 20 mins

Cook: 30 mins

Total: 50 mins

Servings: 6

Ingredients

- ¼ cup curry powder, divided
- 2 tbsps garlic powder
- 1 tbsp seasoned salt
- 1 tbsp onion powder
- 2 tsps salt
- 1 sprig fresh thyme, leaves stripped
- 1 pinch ground allspice, or more to taste
- salt and ground black pepper to taste
- 2 ¼ pounds whole chicken, cut into pieces
- 3 tbsps vegetable oil
- 3 cups water
- 1 potato, diced
- ½ cup chopped carrots
- 2 scallions (green onions), chopped
- 1 (1 inch) piece fresh ginger root, minced
- 1 Scotch bonnet chile pepper, chopped, or to taste

Directions

1. In a large mixing bowl, combine 2 tbsps curry powder, garlic powder, seasoned salt, onion powder, salt, thyme leaves, allspice, salt, and pepper. Coat the chicken in the curry mixture until it is wet and clings to the chicken.
2. 2 to 3 minutes over high heat, heat oil and 2 tbsps curry powder in a large cast-iron pan until oil is hot and curry powder changes color. Reduce the heat to medium and add the chicken to the hot oil mixture. In a skillet, combine the water, potato, carrots, scallions, ginger, and chilli pepper.
3. Allow chicken to cook undisturbed for the last 15 minutes of cooking, 30 to 40 minutes, until it is no longer pink in the center and the gravy has thickened. A thermometer implanted near the bone in the thickest section of the thigh should read 165 ° F. (74 ° C). Remove the chicken to a serving dish and continue to thicken the gravy over low heat, uncovered (if needed). Chicken should be served with gravy.

Cook's Note:

Allowing the curry to cook correctly is essential for curried chicken. Make sure your curry has had enough time to cook before serving.

Try a meatless version by substituting vegetables for the chicken.

I normally use a little more than half of a scotch bonnet pepper, but some are hotter than others.

Nutrition Facts

Per Serving:

348 calories; protein 27.8g; carbohydrates 13.8g; fat 20.3g; cholesterol 102.5mg; sodium 1353.2mg.

16. CURRIED GOAT

Prep: 15 mins

Cook: 1 hr 44 mins

Additional: 1 hr

Total: 2 hrs 59 mins

Servings: 8

Ingredients

- 2 pounds goat stew meat, cut into 1-inch cubes
- 2 fresh hot chile peppers, seeded and chopped
- 2 tbsps curry powder
- 2 cloves garlic, minced
- 1 tsp salt
- 1 tsp ground black pepper
- 3 tbsps vegetable oil
- 1 onion, chopped
- 1 rib celery, chopped
- 2 ½ cups vegetable broth
- 1 bay leaf
- 3 potatoes, peeled and cut into 1-inch chunks, or more as desired

Directions

1. In a mixing bowl, combine the goat meat, chile pepper, curry powder, garlic, salt, and black pepper. Cover and chill for 1 hour to overnight to enable flavors to mingle.
2. Remove the goat meat combination from the bowl and blot dry with a paper towel, keeping the marinade. In a stockpot, heat the vegetable oil over medium-high heat. Cook the meat in

batches, 5 to 6 minutes per batch, browning on all sides. Place the meat on a platter. Cook and stir the onion and celery in the stockpot until the onion begins to brown, about 4 to 6 minutes.

3. Brown the goat meat and add it to the onion mixture. Combine the leftover marinade, vegetable broth, and bay leaf in a large mixing bowl. Bring to a boil, then reduce to a low heat and cook for 1 hour. Stir in the potatoes and continue to cook for another 35 to 45 minutes, or until the potatoes and beef are soft.

4. Remove the stockpot from the heat, skim off the fat on the surface, and discard the bay leaf.

Cook's Notes:

If preferred, replace the veggie broth with homemade stock or water.

The hotter the chilli pepper you use, the hotter the dish will be.

The goat can be replaced with lamb or pork.

Instead of rice, we like to serve this with bruschetta.

For dessert, we like to serve this dinner with Slow Cooker Tapioca.

Nutrition Facts

Per Serving:

238 calories; protein 21.9g; carbohydrates 20.1g; fat 7.8g; cholesterol 53.2mg; sodium 509.3mg.

17. SPICE BREAD

Prep: 25 mins

Cook: 1 hr 5 mins

Additional: 1 hr

Total: 2 hrs 30 mins

Servings: 20

Ingredients
Batter:

- 3 ¼ cups all-purpose flour
- 5 tsps baking powder
- 3 tsps ground cinnamon
- 2 tsp ground nutmeg
- ½ tsp ground allspice
- 1 pinch salt

- 1 egg
- 1 cup milk
- 1/3 cup beer (such as Heineken®)
- 1 ¾ cups brown sugar
- ½ cup melted butter
- 1 tsp browning sauce
- 1 tsp vanilla extract
- 1 tsp lime juice
- 1 cup raisins

Glaze:

- ½ cup brown sugar
- ½ cup water

Directions

1. Preheat the oven to 325 ° Fahrenheit (165 ° C). 2 8x4-inch loaf pans, greased
2. In a mixing dish, combine the flour, baking powder, cinnamon, nutmeg, allspice, and salt; set aside. In a mixing bowl, whisk together the egg, milk, beer, and 1 3/4 cup brown sugar until the brown sugar is completely dissolved. In a large mixing bowl, combine the butter, browning sauce, vanilla essence, and lime juice. Combine the flour and raisins in a mixing bowl. Stir until there are no dry lumps left. Pour the batter into the loaf pans that have been prepped.
3. Bake for 1 hour in a preheated oven, or until a toothpick inserted in the center comes out clean.
4. In a small saucepan, combine 1/2 cup brown sugar and the water when the bread is almost done. Bring to a boil over high heat and cook for 5 minutes, or until the sugar is thick and syrupy. When the bread is done, drizzle the glaze over it and bake for an additional 5 minutes. Cool for 5 minutes in the pans before transferring to a wire rack to cool fully.

Nutrition Facts

Per Serving:

245 calories; protein 3.2g; carbohydrates 46.9g; fat 5.4g; cholesterol 22.5mg; sodium 147.3mg.

18. RUM PUNCH

Prep: 10 mins

Total: 10 mins

Servings: 8

Ingredients

- 2 ½ cups pineapple juice
- 2 ½ cups orange juice
- 1 cup 151 proof rum (such as Bacardi®)
- ½ cup dark rum (such as Meyer's®)
- ¼ cup coconut-flavored rum (such as Malibu®)
- ¼ cup fresh lime juice
- 3 tbsps grenadine syrup
- 1 orange, sliced
- 1 lime, sliced
- 1 lemon, sliced

Directions

1. In a punch bowl, combine pineapple juice, orange juice, 151 proof rum, black rum, coconut-flavored rum, lime juice, and grenadine syrup. Slices of orange, lime, and lemon should be floating in the punch.

Nutrition Facts

Per Serving:

254 calories; protein 1.6g; carbohydrates 30g; fat 0.9g; cholesterol 4.5mg; sodium 10mg.

19. OXTAIL WITH BROAD BEANS

Prep: 30 mins

Cook: 45 mins

Total: 1 hr 15 mins

Servings: 4

Ingredients

- 1 pound beef oxtail, cut into pieces
- 1 large onion, chopped
- 1 green onion, thinly sliced
- 2 cloves garlic, minced
- 1 tsp minced fresh ginger root
- 1 scotch bonnet chile pepper, chopped
- 2 tbsps soy sauce
- 1 sprig fresh thyme, chopped
- ½ tsp salt
- 1 tsp black pepper
- 2 tbsps vegetable oil
- 1 ½ cups water
- 1 cup canned fava beans, drained
- 1 tsp whole allspice berries
- 1 tbsp cornstarch
- 2 tbsps water

Directions

1. Combine the oxtail, green onion, garlic, ginger, chile pepper, soy sauce, thyme, salt, and pepper in a mixing bowl. In a large skillet, heat the vegetable oil over medium-high heat. In a skillet, sauté the oxtail until it is evenly browned, about 10 minutes. 1 1/2 cup water should be added to a pressure cooker. Cook for 25 minutes at high pressure, then turn off the heat and remove the cover according to the manufacturer's instructions.
2. Bring to a simmer over medium-high heat with the fava beans and allspice berries. Stir the cornstarch into the simmering oxtail with 2 tsps water. Cook for a few minutes, stirring occasionally, until the sauce has thickened and the beans are cooked.

Cook's Note

In step 1, a slow cooker can be used instead of a pressure cooker. Simply add the browned oxtail to the slow cooker with the water and cook on low for 10 hours or high for 6 hours. Step 2 should be completed as directed.

Nutrition Facts

Per Serving:

425 calories; protein 38.8g; carbohydrates 17.6g; fat 22.4g; cholesterol 124.8mg; sodium 1088.6mg.

---

20. SPINACH SOUP

Prep: 30 mins

Cook: 20 mins

Total: 50 mins

Servings: 8

Ingredients

- 3 tbsps olive oil
- 1 onion, chopped
- 2 stalks celery, chopped
- 4 cloves garlic, minced
- 2 tbsps fresh ginger root, minced
- 1 tbsp turbinado sugar
- 2 tsps sea salt
- ¼ tsp ground turmeric
- ¼ tsp ground allspice
- ¼ tsp ground nutmeg
- 2 potatoes, peeled and diced
- 4 cups chopped zucchini
- 6 cups vegetable stock
- 1 pinch cayenne pepper
- 1 cup chopped fresh spinach
- ½ red bell pepper, minced

Directions

1. In a big pot over medium heat, heat the oil. Combine the onion, celery, garlic, ginger, and sugar in a mixing bowl. Cook for 5 minutes, or until the onion is soft. Add salt, turmeric, allspice, and nutmeg to taste. In a large mixing bowl, combine the potatoes and zucchini, then pour in the vegetable stock. Bring to a boil, then reduce to a low heat and continue to cook for 10 minutes, or until the potatoes are cooked.

2. Remove the soup from the heat and season with cayenne pepper before adding the spinach. Blend the soup with a hand blender until it is completely smooth. Serve with a red bell pepper garnish.

Nutrition Facts

Per Serving:

124 calories; protein 2.6g; carbohydrates 16.7g; fat 5.8g; sodium 666.9mg.

21. JERK DRY RUB

Prep: 15 mins

Total: 15 mins

Servings: 832

Ingredients

- 1 ½ cups allspice
- 8 cups salt
- 5 ½ cups garlic powder
- 4 cups white sugar
- 1 cup chipotle chile powder
- ½ cup ground cloves
- 2 cups dried thyme leaves
- 2 cups ground black pepper
- 4 cups cayenne pepper
- 1 cup ground cinnamon

Directions

1. In a large mixing bowl, combine allspice, salt, garlic powder, sugar, chipotle powder, cloves, thyme, black pepper, cayenne pepper, and cinnamon. Mix everything together until it's completely smooth. Keep it in an airtight container.
2. To use, rub 1 1/2 tsps of spice mix into the meat of your choice each serving. Allow at least an hour for the flavors of the rub to enter the meat for optimal results.

Nutrition Facts

Per Serving:

10 calories; protein 0.3g; carbohydrates 2.4g; fat 0.1g; sodium 0.9mg.

22. JAMAICAN PATTIES

Prep: 25 mins

Cook: 40 mins

Total: 1 hr 5 mins

Servings: 36

Ingredients

- 3 pounds lean ground beef
- 2 cups seasoned bread crumbs
- 1 (28 ounce) can tomato sauce
- 1 bunch (1-inch) pieces green onions
- ¼ cup soy sauce
- ¼ cup Maggi™ liquid seasoning
- 1 tbsp salt
- 1 tbsp pepper
- 1 tsp vinegar-based hot pepper sauce
- 2 recipes pie crust pastry
- 2 eggs
- ¼ cup water

Directions

1. Combine the ground beef, bread crumbs, tomato sauce, green onions, soy sauce, Maggi seasoning, salt, pepper, and spicy sauce in a large mixing bowl. It's possible that you'll have to use your hands. Remove from the equation.
2. Preheat oven to 425 ° Fahrenheit (220 ° C).
3. Using a big coffee can, roll out the pie crust dough to 1/8 inch thickness and cut into 6 inch circles. Fold the circle in half to produce a half circle with a heaping tbsp or slightly more of the meat mixture in the center. Place the pies on baking pans and crimp the edges together with the tines of a fork. At this time, the pies can also be frozen. In a small bowl, whisk together the egg and water with a fork. Brush the egg wash all over the pies' tops.
4. In a preheated oven, bake for 30 to 40 minutes, or until golden brown. If you're baking frozen pies, add 10 minutes to the baking time.

Nutrition Facts

Per Serving:

215 calories; protein 9.9g; carbohydrates 15.6g; fat 12.5g; cholesterol 33.3mg; sodium 667.1mg.

23. ME CRAZY CHILI

Prep: 15 mins

Cook: 30 mins

Total: 45 mins

Servings: 12

Ingredients

- 1 ½ pounds ground round
- 1 tsp olive oil
- 1 ½ cups chopped onion
- 2 cloves garlic, crushed
- 2 ½ cups chopped yellow bell pepper
- 1 tbsp ground cumin
- 1 tbsp hot paprika
- 1 tbsp chile powder
- 2 tsps white sugar
- ½ tsp salt
- ¼ tsp ground cloves
- 2 (14.5 ounce) cans stewed tomatoes
- 1 (15 ounce) can kidney beans, drained
- 1 (15 ounce) can black beans, drained
- 1 (15 ounce) can cannellini beans
- 1 (6 ounce) can tomato paste
- 2 tbsps balsamic vinegar
- 1/3 cup chopped fresh cilantro

Directions

1. In a big, deep skillet, place the ground round. Cook until uniformly browned over medium-high heat. Drain the water and set it aside.
2. Cook over medium-high heat in a large Dutch oven coated with cooking spray. Cook the onion and garlic in olive oil in a hot pan until the onion is soft. Cook until the yellow pepper is soft. Cumin, paprika, chili powder, sugar, salt, and cloves are used to season. Stir in the kidney beans, black beans, and cannellini beans, as well as the stewed tomatoes. Fill the container halfway with water. Bring to a boil, then add the meat and tomato paste and cook for another 5 minutes. Bring to a boil, then reduce to a low heat for 30 minutes.
3. Remove from the fire, mix in the vinegar, and sprinkle with fresh cilantro before serving.

Nutrition Facts

Per Serving:

225 calories; protein 16.3g; carbohydrates 23g; fat 8.1g; cholesterol 39.5mg; sodium 551.4mg.

24. VEGETARIAN JAMAICAN JERK BURRITO

Prep: 20 mins

Cook: 10 mins

Additional: 30 mins

Total: 1 hr

Servings: 8

Ingredients

- ¾ cup Jamaican jerk marinade, divided
- 5 tbsps lime juice, divided
- 5 cloves garlic, minced
- 4 pinch ground black pepper, or to taste
- 5 cups pressed and cubed extra-firm tofu
- cooking spray
- 2 cups diced jicama
- 1 cup diced pineapple
- 2 cups prepared rice
- 1 (15 ounce) can black beans, rinsed and drained
- 8 (8 inch) low-fat flour tortilla
- ½ cup shredded Monterey Jack cheese
- ½ cup salsa
- ½ cup sour cream

Directions

1. In a mixing bowl, combine 1/2 cup marinade, 1/4 cup lime juice, garlic, and black pepper; pour into a large resealable plastic bag. Toss in the tofu, coat it in the marinade, squeeze out the air, and seal the bag. Refrigerate for 30 minutes after marinating.
2. Drain the tofu and toss out the marinade.
3. Cook over medium-high heat in a large skillet coated with cooking spray. Cook for 4 minutes, stirring regularly, until tofu begins to brown; remove to a basin. Bring the skillet back up to medium-high heat.

4. In a large skillet, heat the jicama, pineapple, remaining 1/4 cup marinade, and 1 tbsp lime juice until heated, about 2 to 3 minutes. Return the tofu to the skillet and cook, stirring constantly, for another 2 minutes, or until cooked through.
5. Fill each tortilla with 1/3 cup tofu mixture in the center. Evenly distribute rice, black beans, and cheese on each plate.
6. Fold two opposing ends together to overlap the filling's edges. Wrap one of the tortilla's opposing edges around the filling and roll to form a burrito. Salsa and sour cream go on top of each tortilla.

Nutrition Facts

Per Serving:

386 calories; protein 17g; carbohydrates 58.4g; fat 11g; cholesterol 12.6mg; sodium 1242.8mg.

25. TORTILLA SOUP

Prep: 20 mins

Cook: 20 mins

Total: 40 mins

Servings: 8

Ingredients

- 3 skinless, boneless chicken breast halves
- 8 cups water
- 8 tsps chicken bouillon granules
- 1 cup chopped carrot
- ¼ tsp ground allspice
- ½ tsp chopped fresh thyme
- 1/8 tsp ground cinnamon
- 1 tbsp chopped fresh ginger
- 1 tbsp minced garlic
- 1 cup chopped tomato
- 1 cup coconut milk
- 1 tsp hot pepper sauce
- 1 cup shredded mozzarella cheese
- 2 cups crispy tortilla strips
- 2 limes, cut into wedges

Directions

1. Preheat the grill for medium heat, whether it's outside or inside. 6 to 8 minutes per side on the grill, or until browned and cooked through. Remove the burgers from the grill and chop them into bits.
2. Combine the chicken, water, bouillon, and carrot in a big pot. Add spices, thyme, cinnamon, ginger, and garlic to taste. Bring to a boil, then reduce to a low heat and continue to cook for 10 minutes, or until carrots are soft. Combine the tomato, coconut milk, and hot pepper sauce in a mixing bowl. Bring to a boil, but not to a boil.
3. Top with shredded mozzarella cheese and tortilla strips and serve in bowls. Lime wedges should be used to squeeze juice into the soup.

Nutrition Facts

Per Serving:

196 calories; protein 14.6g; carbohydrates 10.6g; fat 11.3g; cholesterol 34.5mg; sodium 540.4mg.

26. FRUIT CAKE

Prep: 20 mins

Cook: 1 hr 30 mins

Total: 1 hr 50 mins

Servings: 12

Ingredients

- 2 cups butter
- 2 cups white sugar
- 9 eggs
- ¼ cup white rum (Optional)
- 1 tbsp lime juice
- 1 tsp vanilla extract
- 1 tbsp almond extract
- 1 grated zest of one lime
- 2 pounds chopped dried mixed fruit
- 2 cups red wine
- 1 cup dark molasses
- 2 ½ cups all-purpose flour
- 3 tsps baking powder
- ½ tsp ground nutmeg
- ½ tsp ground allspice

- ½ tsp ground cinnamon
- 1 pinch salt

Directions

1. Preheat the oven to 350 ° Fahrenheit (175 ° C). 2 - 9-inch round cake pans, greased and floured
2. Cream the butter and sugar together in a large mixing basin until light and creamy. In a separate bowl, whisk together the eggs, rum, lime juice, vanilla, almond essence, and lime zest. Combine the mixed fruit, wine, and molasses in a mixing bowl. Flour, baking powder, nutmeg, allspice, cinnamon, and salt should all be sifted together. Carefully fold into the batter, taking care not to over-mix. Pour into the pans that have been prepared.
3. Bake for 80 to 90 minutes in a preheated oven, or until a knife inserted in the center comes out clean. Allow to cool for 10 minutes in the pan before turning out onto a wire rack to cool completely.

Notes

Fruits should be steeped in wine for at least 3 weeks or boiled in wine for optimal results.

Use a variety of dried fruits, such as currants, golden raisins, prunes, and dried cherries, or any dried fruit of your choice.

To keep the cake moist, brush it with more wine or rum as needed.

Nutrition Facts

Per Serving:

862 calories; protein 9.6g; carbohydrates 124.2g; fat 35.1g; cholesterol 220.8mg; sodium 418.4mg.

27. FRIED DUMPLINGS

Prep: 10 mins

Cook: 10 mins

Total: 20 mins

Servings: 6

Ingredients

- 4 cups all-purpose flour
- 2 tsps baking powder
- 1 ½ tsps salt
- ½ cup butter
- ½ cup cold water
- 1 cup vegetable oil for frying

Directions

1. Combine the flour, baking powder, and salt in a large mixing bowl. Rub in the butter until it is in small pea-sized pieces. 1 tbsp at a time, add water until the dough is moist enough to form a ball. The dough should have a solid texture. Knead for a few minutes.
2. In a big heavy skillet, heat the oil over medium heat until it is hot. Break out pieces of dough and form into patties, similar to flat biscuits. Place just enough dumplings in the pan to avoid overcrowding. Cook until golden brown on both sides, about 3 minutes per side. Before serving, remove from the pan and drain on paper towels.

Nutrition Facts

Per Serving:

472 calories; protein 8.8g; carbohydrates 64g; fat 19.8g; cholesterol 40.7mg; sodium 855.1mg. F

28. BEEF PATTIES

Prep: 50 mins

Cook: 30 mins

Total: 1 hr 20 mins

Servings: 10

Ingredients

- 2 cups all-purpose flour
- 1 ½ tsps curry powder
- 1 dash salt
- ¼ cup margarine
- ¼ cup shortening
- 1/3 cup water
- 2 tbsps margarine
- 1 pound ground beef
- 1 small onion, finely diced
- 1 tsp curry powder
- 1 tsp dried thyme
- 1 tsp salt
- 1 tsp pepper
- ½ cup beef broth
- ½ cup dry bread crumbs
- 1 egg, beaten

Directions

1. Preheat the oven to 400 ° Fahrenheit (200 ° C). Combine flour, 1 1/2 tsps curry powder, and a pinch of salt in a large mixing basin. 1/4 cup margarine and 1/4 cup shortening, cut in until mixture resembles coarse crumbs. Stir in the water until the mixture comes together in a ball. Form the dough into a log and cut it into ten parts. Each part should be rolled into a six-inch circular (about 1/8 inch thick). Remove from the equation.

2. In a skillet over medium heat, melt margarine. Cook until the onion is tender and transparent. Add the ground beef and mix well. 1 tsp curry powder, 1 tsp thyme, 1 tsp salt, and pepper Cook, tossing regularly, until the beef is evenly browned. Combine the beef broth and bread crumbs in a mixing bowl. Simmer until all of the liquid has been absorbed. Remove the pan from the heat.

3. Fill each pastry round with the same quantity of filling. To make a half circle, fold over and push the edges together. Brush the tops of each burger with beaten egg and push the edges with a fork.

4. Bake for 30 minutes, or until golden brown, in a preheated oven.

Nutrition Facts

Per Serving:

371 calories; protein 11.9g; carbohydrates 24.3g; fat 24.9g; cholesterol 57.2mg; sodium 466.9mg.

29. RUNAWAY BAY JAMAICAN CHICKEN

Prep: 30 mins

Cook: 30 mins

Additional: 1 day

Total: 1 day

Servings: 6

Ingredients

- 1 large red onion
- 3 cloves garlic
- 1 habanero pepper, seeded
- 1 tbsp fresh ginger root
- ¼ cup olive oil
- ¼ cup brown sugar
- 3 tbsps red wine vinegar
- 3 tbsps orange juice concentrate, thawed
- 2 tsp soy sauce
- 3 tsps ground cinnamon
- ½ tsp ground nutmeg
- ¼ tsp ground cloves
- ½ cup chopped cilantro
- ½ tsp salt and pepper to taste
- 6 skinless, boneless chicken breast halves

Directions

1. Combine onion, garlic, habanero pepper, and ginger in a food processor. Pulse until all of the components are finely minced. Combine the olive oil, brown sugar, vinegar, orange juice concentrate, soy sauce, cinnamon, nutmeg, cloves, cilantro, salt, and pepper in a large mixing bowl. Combine the marinade and the chicken in a container. Refrigerate overnight, covered.
2. Preheat an outside grill to medium heat and brush the grate gently with oil.

3. Cook for 10 minutes per side on the grill, or until the chicken is no longer pink and the juices run clear.

Note

The full amount of marinade ingredients is included in the nutrition facts for this dish. The amount of marinade used varies depending on marinating duration, ingredients, cooking style, and other factors.

Nutrition Facts

Per Serving:

279 calories; protein 25.3g; carbohydrates 17g; fat 12g; cholesterol 67.2mg; sodium 308.7mg.

30. JERKED CHICKEN

Prep: 10 mins

Cook: 20 mins

Additional: 8 hrs

Total: 8 hrs 30 mins

Servings: 4

Ingredients

- ½ green onion, minced
- ¼ cup orange juice
- 1 tbsp minced fresh ginger root
- 1 tbsp minced jalapeno peppers
- 1 tbsp lime juice
- 1 tbsp soy sauce
- 1 clove garlic, minced
- 1 tsp ground allspice
- ¼ tsp ground cinnamon
- ½ tsp ground cloves
- 1 ½ pounds boneless, skinless chicken thighs

Directions

1. In a resealable container, combine green onion, orange juice, ginger, jalapeno, lime juice, soy sauce, garlic, allspice, cinnamon, and cloves. To blend, seal the container and shake it vigorously. Add the chicken and toss to coat; set aside for 8 hours to marinate.

2. Preheat an outside grill to medium heat and brush the grate gently with oil. Remove the chicken and set aside the marinade.
3. Cook chicken on a hot grill for 12 to 15 minutes, flipping halfway through, until no longer pink in the center and juices run clear. At least 170 ° F should be read on an instant-read thermometer inserted into the center (77 ° C).
4. Meanwhile, in a small saucepan, bring the reserved marinade to a boil. Reduce heat to low and cook, uncovered, for 5 minutes, or until slightly thickened. Drizzle the sauce over the cooked chicken.

Nutrition Facts

Per Serving:

247 calories; protein 29.2g; carbohydrates 3.6g; fat 12.2g; cholesterol 105mg; sodium 324.6mg.

31. JAMAICAN-SEASONED SAUTEED SWAI FILLETS

Prep: 10 mins

Cook: 10 mins

Total: 20 mins

Servings: 5

Ingredients

- 1 tbsp olive oil
- 2 tbsps butter
- 1 tbsp Jamaican jerk seasoning
- 1 tsp salt
- 5 (3 ounce) fillets swai fish

Directions

1. In a skillet, heat the olive oil over medium heat and add the butter. Season the swai fish evenly with Jamaican jerk flavor and salt.
2. Cook until salmon flakes easily with a fork, 3 to 4 minutes per side, in a single layer in the skillet, cooking in batches if necessary.

Cook's Notes:

Make sure the oil does not get too hot or it will splatter. Heat should be kept at a medium-low to medium level.

If required, add up to 1 tbsp butter to the oil between batches.

Nutrition Facts

Per Serving:

169 calories; protein 12.5g; carbohydrates 0.8g; fat 12.7g; cholesterol 54.6mg; sodium 814.9mg.

32. JAMAICAN TURKEY SANDWICH

Prep: 35 mins

Cook: 6 hrs

Total: 6 hrs 35 mins

Servings: 6

Ingredients
Pulled Turkey:

- ½ cup chopped celery
- 1/3 cup chopped green onion
- 1 (2 pound) skinless, boneless turkey breast, cut into 8 ounce chunks
- ½ cup juice from canned pineapple
- ¼ cup sweet chile sauce
- 3 tbsps distilled white vinegar
- 2 tbsps water
- 1 tbsp beef bouillon granules
- 2 tsps garlic powder
- 6 canned pineapple rings

Coleslaw Topping:

- ¼ cup mayonnaise
- 1 tbsp lemon juice
- 2 tbsps chopped fresh parsley
- ½ cup chopped onion
- 2 cups chopped cabbage
- 1 cup shredded Cheddar cheese
- salt and black pepper to taste
- 6 Kaiser rolls, split

Directions

1. In the bottom of a slow cooker, layer the celery and green onions; on top, layer the turkey chunks. Pour over the turkey the pineapple juice, sweet chile sauce, vinegar, water, beef bouillon, and garlic powder. On top of the turkey chunks, arrange the pineapple rings.
2. Cook on low for 6 to 7 hours, or until the turkey easily pulls apart.
3. Meanwhile, combine the mayonnaise, lemon juice, parsley, and onion in a mixing dish to form the coleslaw. Season with salt and pepper after adding the cabbage and Cheddar cheese. While the turkey cooks, cover and chill.
4. Shred the turkey with two forks after it's tender. To serve, place some shredded turkey and a pineapple ring on a Kaiser roll and top with coleslaw.

Nutrition Facts

Per Serving:

524 calories; protein 49.4g; carbohydrates 42.8g; fat 16.5g; cholesterol 132.5mg; sodium 808.5mg.

33. JERK SHRIMP IN FOIL

Prep: 15 mins

Cook: 15 mins

Total: 30 mins

Servings: 4

Ingredients

- 1 cup soy sauce
- ¾ cup distilled vinegar
- 1 medium white onion, coarsely chopped
- ¼ cup extra-virgin olive oil
- 4 green onions, coarsely chopped
- 2 tbsps dried thyme
- 2 habanero peppers, stemmed
- 1 tbsp brown sugar
- 1 tbsp ground nutmeg
- 1 tsp ground allspice
- 1 tsp ground cloves
- 1 pound uncooked medium shrimp, peeled and deveined
- heavy duty aluminum foil

Directions

1. Preheat the grill to medium-high.

2. To make the jerk seasoning, combine together soy sauce, vinegar, onion, olive oil, green onions, thyme, habanero peppers, sugar, nutmeg, allspice, and cloves in a food processor for about 15 seconds.
3. Form a bowl out of foil. Pour in enough jerk seasoning to coat the prawns. Preheat the grill and place the foil bowl on it. Seal the top but leave a tiny gap. Grill for about 10 minutes, tossing regularly, until pink. Put the shrimp in a medium mixing bowl.
4. In a small saucepan over medium heat, cook the remaining sauce for 2 to 3 minutes. Pour the sauce over the shrimp.

Nutrition Facts

Per Serving:

299 calories; protein 23.6g; carbohydrates 15.3g; fat 16.2g; cholesterol 172.6mg; sodium 3814mg.

34. JAMAICAN JERK CHICKEN

Prep: 20 mins

Cook: 1 hr

Additional: 2 hrs

Total: 3 hrs 20 mins

Servings: 6

Ingredients

- 6 skinless, boneless chicken breast halves - cut into chunks
- 4 limes, juiced
- 1 cup water
- 2 tsps ground allspice
- ½ tsp ground nutmeg
- 1 tsp salt
- 1 tsp brown sugar
- 2 tsps dried thyme
- 1 tsp ground ginger
- 1 ½ tsps ground black pepper
- 2 tbsps vegetable oil
- 2 onions, chopped
- 1 ½ cups chopped green onions
- 6 cloves garlic, chopped
- 2 habanero peppers, chopped

Directions

1. In a medium mixing dish, place the chicken. Lime juice and water should be added to the mix. Remove from the equation.
2. Combine allspice, nutmeg, salt, brown sugar, thyme, ginger, black pepper, and vegetable oil in a blender or food processor. Blend till almost smooth, then add onions, green onions, garlic, and habanero peppers.
3. Pour the majority of the marinade mixture into the bowl with the chicken, reserving a small quantity to use as a basting sauce while the chicken is cooking. Cover and marinate for at least 2 hours in the refrigerator.
4. Preheat a medium-hot outside grill.
5. Using a brush, coat the grill grate in oil. On a prepared grill, cook the chicken slowly. Turn regularly and baste with the remaining marinade mixture as needed. Cook until desired doneness is reached.

Nutrition Facts

Per Serving:

221 calories; protein 28.8g; carbohydrates 13.3g; fat 6.4g; cholesterol 68.4mg; sodium 473.9mg.

35. SALTFISH FRITTERS (STAMP AND GO)

Prep: 1 hr

Cook: 20 mins

Additional: 1 day

Total: 1 day

Servings: 6

Ingredients

- 6 ounces dried salted cod fish
- cold water, to cover
- 1 cup all-purpose flour
- 1 tsp baking powder
- 2 tsps ground black pepper
- ½ cup water
- 1 large tomato, chopped
- 2 green onions, chopped
- vegetable oil for frying

Directions

1. To rehydrate the cod and remove excess salt, soak it in cold water overnight (or see Cook's Note).
2. Any bones and skin should be removed. Set aside the fish after flaking and shredding it into small pieces.
3. In a large mixing basin, sift together the flour, baking powder, and pepper. Combine the chopped tomatoes, green onions, and flaked fish in a mixing bowl. Stir add 1/2 cup water until everything is well combined.
4. In a big heavy skillet, heat 1/4 inch of oil over medium heat. Drop rounded spoonfuls of batter into the skillet once the oil is heated. Cook until golden brown and crisp on both sides, about 5 minutes per side. Serve immediately after draining on paper towels.

Nutrition Facts

Per Serving:

232 calories; protein 20.4g; carbohydrates 18.1g; fat 8.3g; cholesterol 43.1mg; sodium 2079.4mg.

36. DAD'S KICKIN' JAMAICAN WINGS

Prep: 25 mins

Cook: 2 hrs

Additional: 8 hrs

Total: 10 hrs 25 mins

Servings: 8

Ingredients

- 3 tbsps Jamaican jerk seasoning blend
- 3 tbsps vegetable oil
- 3 cloves garlic, diced
- 1 (1 inch) piece peeled fresh ginger, diced
- 1 bunch green onions, chopped
- 12 slices pickled jalapeno peppers
- 4 pounds chicken wings

Directions

1. In a blender, combine the jerk seasoning, oil, garlic, ginger, green onions, and jalapeno slices and blend until smooth and thick. Dip the wings in the mixture and place them on baking pans

in a single layer. Using the remaining mixture, evenly coat the wings. Refrigerate for 8 hours or overnight, covered in aluminum foil.

2. Preheat the oven to 300 ° Fahrenheit (150 ° C).
3. In a preheated oven, bake wings for 2 hours.

Nutrition Facts

Per Serving:

230 calories; protein 16g; carbohydrates 4.4g; fat 16.4g; cholesterol 47.7mg; sodium 646.6mg.

37. BACON-WRAPPED JAMAICAN JERK PORK TENDERLOIN

Prep: 15 mins

Cook: 45 mins

Total: 1 hr

Servings: 4

Ingredients

- 2 tbsps brown sugar
- 2 tbsps Jamaican jerk seasoning
- 1 tsp ground paprika
- 1 tsp ground thyme
- ½ tsp dried oregano
- ½ tsp seafood seasoning (such as Old Bay®)
- 1 pinch crushed red pepper, or to taste
- 1 (1 1/2 pound) pork tenderloin
- 4 slices bacon, or more to taste
- 1 tbsp olive oil, or more as needed
- ½ medium sweet onion, diced

Directions

1. Preheat the oven to 375°F (190°C) (190 ° C).
2. In a mixing bowl, combine brown sugar, jerk seasoning, paprika, thyme, oregano, seafood flavor, and crushed red pepper; massage all over the tenderloin generously. Wrap the bacon around the meat and fasten with toothpicks. Place in a loaf pan or casserole dish and lightly coat with oil. Any residual spice rub should be sprinkled on top, followed by some diced onion and the remaining onion.
3. 45 to 60 minutes in a preheated oven, uncovered, until pork is slightly pink in the center. At least 145 ° F should be read on an instant-read thermometer put into the center (63 ° C).

Cook's Note:

You can substitute vegetable oil for olive oil and seasoned salt for Old Bay (R).

Nutrition Facts

Per Serving:

268 calories; protein 30.3g; carbohydrates 10.9g; fat 11g; cholesterol 83.6mg; sodium 996.6mg.

38. SPIKED CHICKEN AND RICE

Prep: 15 mins

Cook: 30 mins

Total: 45 mins

Servings: 3

Ingredients

- ½ cup uncooked long-grain white rice
- 1 cup water
- 3 tbsps vegetable oil
- ¼ cup butter
- 3 skinless, boneless chicken breast halves
- 3 fluid ounces dark rum
- 1 (6 ounce) can broiled-in-butter-style sliced mushrooms
- 2 ½ tbsps chicken bouillon granules
- 2 tsps garlic powder
- 2 tsps ground black pepper
- 1 (14 ounce) can coconut milk
- 1 small banana, sliced

Directions

1. Bring the rice and water to a boil in a pot. Reduce to a low heat setting, cover, and cook for 20 minutes.
2. In a skillet over medium-high heat, heat the oil and melt the butter. Cook for 6 to 8 minutes per side, or until juices run clear, in a skillet.
3. Pour rum over the chicken and serve. Carefully light the rum on fire using a long match. Mix the mushrooms, bouillon granules, garlic powder, pepper, and coconut milk into the skillet after the flames have died down. Reduce heat to low and cook for 10 minutes, or until well heated.

4. Serve the chicken and mushroom combination over rice that has been cooked. Serve with banana slices on top.

Nutrition Facts

Per Serving:

916 calories; protein 34.8g; carbohydrates 42.9g; fat 61.9g; cholesterol 113.3mg; sodium 1322.2mg.

39. BANANA BREAD

Prep: 45 mins

Cook: 1 hr

Additional: 1 hr

Total: 2 hrs 45 mins

Servings: 24

Ingredients

- 2 tbsps unsalted butter, softened
- 2 tbsps cream cheese
- 1 cup white sugar
- 1 egg
- 2 cups all-purpose flour
- 2 tsps baking powder
- ½ tsp baking soda
- 1/8 tsp salt
- 1 cup mashed overripe bananas
- ½ cup milk
- 2 tbsps dark rum, or rum flavoring
- ½ tsp lime zest
- 2 tsps lime juice
- 1 tsp vanilla extract
- ¼ cup chopped toasted pecans
- ¼ cup flaked coconut

Topping

- ¼ cup brown sugar
- 2 tsps unsalted butter
- 2 tsps lime juice

- 2 tsps dark rum, or rum flavoring
- 2 tbsps chopped toasted pecans
- 2 tbsps flaked coconut

Directions

1. Preheat the oven to 375 ° Fahrenheit (190 ° C). Grease two 8x4 inch loaf pans lightly.
2. In a large mixing bowl, cream together 2 tbsps melted butter and cream cheese until frothy. Slowly beat in the sugar until it is fully combined. Mix in the egg thoroughly. In a separate basin, sift together the flour, baking powder, baking soda, and salt. Combine the bananas, milk, 2 tbsps rum, lime zest, lime juice, and vanilla essence in a separate bowl and whisk well. 1/3 of the flour mixture should be poured into the butter and mixed thoroughly. 1/2 of the mashed bananas should be added at this point. Continue with another third of the flour, then the remaining banana mixture, and then the final 1/3 of the flour. 1/4 cup pecans and 1/4 cup coconut flakes should be folded in.
3. Fill the loaf pans halfway with the batter and bake for one hour, or until a toothpick inserted in the center comes out clean. Cool for 10 minutes in the pan before removing and cooling completely on a wire rack.
4. Prepare the topping by combining the brown sugar, remaining butter, lime juice, and 2 tbsps of rum in a small saucepan over medium-high heat once the banana bread has been removed from the oven. Bring to a simmer, stirring frequently, for one minute, or until the sugar has dissolved and the mixture is smooth. Take the pan off the heat and add 2 tsps pecans and 2 tbsps coconut. While the loaves are still warm, spoon this topping over them. When the loaf cools, the topping will stiffen slightly.

Nutrition Facts

Per Serving:

131 calories; protein 1.9g; carbohydrates 22g; fat 3.8g; cholesterol 12.9mg; sodium 92mg.

40. JERK SAUCE

Prep: 15 mins

Total: 15 mins

Servings: 4

Ingredients

- 1 bunch green onions, chopped
- ½ cup peanut oil
- ½ cup vinegar
- 3 tbsps ground allspice
- 3 habanero peppers
- 1 (1 inch) piece fresh ginger, peeled
- 5 cloves garlic, peeled
- 5 limes, juiced
- ¼ cup dark brown sugar
- 2 tbsps chopped fresh thyme
- 2 tbsps soy sauce
- 2 tbsps ketchup
- 1 tbsp whole black peppercorns
- 1 tbsp ground cinnamon

Directions

1. In a blender, combine the green onions, peanut oil, vinegar, allspice, habanero peppers, ginger, garlic, lime juice, brown sugar, thyme, soy sauce, ketchup, peppercorns, and cinnamon.

Nutrition Facts

Per Serving:

355 calories; protein 2.6g; carbohydrates 29.2g; fat 27.7g; sodium 553.3mg.

41. INSTANT POT® JAMAICAN RICE AND BEANS

Prep: 15 mins

Cook: 27 mins

Additional: 10 mins

Total: 52 mins

Servings: 6

Ingredients

- 1 tbsp vegetable oil
- 3 skinless, boneless chicken breasts, cut into bite-sized pieces
- 1 cooking onion, diced
- 3 cloves garlic, minced
- 2 cups chicken broth
- 1 (15 ounce) can black beans, drained
- 1 ½ cups long-grain rice
- 1 (8 ounce) can corn, or to taste
- 1 cup coconut milk
- 1 tbsp Scotch bonnet hot sauce, or to taste
- 2 tsps ground thyme
- 2 tsps kosher salt
- 2 tsps ground black pepper
- 2 tsps brown sugar
- 1 tsp allspice

Directions

1. Select the Saute function on a multi-functional pressure cooker (such as an Instant Pot®). Pour in the oil. 1 to 2 minutes until chicken, onion, and garlic are aromatic; do not brown garlic.
2. In a large mixing bowl, combine the broth, black beans, rice, corn, coconut milk, spicy sauce, thyme, black pepper, brown sugar, and allspice. Close the lid and secure it. Close the vent and select high pressure. Set a 15-minute timer. Allow 10 minutes for the pressure to rise.
3. 10 to 40 minutes after applying pressure, use the natural-release method according to the manufacturer's recommendations. Remove the lid by unlocking it.

Cook's Note:

Feel free to use 2 bay leaves in place of thyme, if you prefer.

Nutrition Facts

Per Serving:

454 calories; protein 22.2g; carbohydrates 63.9g; fat 12.9g; cholesterol 34.3mg; sodium 1512.7mg.

42. INSTANT POT JAMAICAN CHICKEN CURRY

Prep: 15 mins

Cook: 20 mins

Additional: 15 mins

Total: 50 mins

Servings: 6

Ingredients

- 2 tbsps ghee
- 1 medium onion, chopped
- 1 tbsp minced garlic
- 1 tbsp minced fresh ginger
- 2 tbsps Jamaican curry powder
- 1 fresh jalapeno pepper, seeded and sliced
- ¼ tsp ground thyme
- 1 pinch salt and ground black pepper to taste
- 2 cups chicken broth
- 1 ½ pounds boneless, skinless chicken thighs, cut into 3 pieces each
- 2 medium potatoes, peeled and cubed
- 1 pound baby carrots
- 3 cups steamed basmati rice

Directions

1. Select the Saute function on a multi-functional pressure cooker (such as an Instant Pot®). Ghee should be heated. Cook, stirring occasionally, until the onion begins to turn clear, about 2 to 3 minutes. Cook, stirring constantly, until the garlic is aromatic, about 1 minute. Combine the Jamaican curry powder, jalapeño, thyme, salt, and pepper in a large mixing bowl.
2. Scrape the browned bits from the bottom of the inner pot and pour in 1/4 cup chicken broth. Stir in the chicken, potatoes, and carrots until they are well covered in the spices and seasonings. Pour in the rest of the chicken broth. Close the lid and secure it.
3. Set the timer for 6 minutes and select high pressure according to the manufacturer's recommendations. Allow for a 10- to 15-minute build-up of pressure.
4. For 10 minutes, release pressure using the natural-release method as directed by the manufacturer. Using the quick-release approach, slowly release pressure for around 5 minutes. Remove the lock and

Cook's Note:

The island curry adds spice to the peppers used in the meal. I used a sliced, seeded jalapeño because we enjoy mild curry. Choose a serrano pepper or, for the truly bold, a Scotch Bonnet pepper if you have a more experimental palette.

Nutrition Facts

Per Serving:

330 calories; protein 22g; carbohydrates 22.7g; fat 16.7g; cholesterol 83.6mg; sodium 542.4mg.

43. HOT BANANA SALSA

Prep: 30 mins

Total: 30 mins

Servings: 24

Ingredients

- 1 large firm banana, peeled and diced
- ½ cup red bell pepper, seeded and diced
- ½ cup green bell pepper, seeded and diced
- ½ cup yellow bell pepper, seeded and diced
- 3 tbsps chopped fresh cilantro
- 2 green onions, chopped
- 2 tbsps fresh lime juice
- 1 tbsp brown sugar
- 2 tsps minced fresh ginger root
- 2 tsps olive oil
- 1 tsp minced habanero pepper
- salt to taste

Directions

1. Season with salt and combine the banana, red pepper, green pepper, yellow pepper, cilantro, green onion, lime juice, brown sugar, ginger, olive oil, and habanero pepper in a bowl. Within 1 hour, serve.

Nutrition Facts

Per Serving:

14 calories; protein 0.2g; carbohydrates 2.6g; fat 0.4g; sodium 0.9mg.

44. GRILLED JAMAICAN JERKED PORK LOIN CHOPS

Prep: 30 mins

Cook: 15 mins

Additional: 8 hrs

Total: 8 hrs 45 mins

Servings: 8

Ingredients

- ½ (12 ounce) bottle lager style beer
- 3 fluid ounces dark rum
- ¼ cup molasses
- ¼ cup soy sauce
- ¼ cup lime juice
- 2 tbsps minced garlic
- 2 tbsps minced ginger
- 1 scotch bonnet chile pepper, minced
- 2 tsps chopped fresh thyme
- 2 tsps chopped fresh marjoram
- 1 ½ tsps ground allspice
- 2 tsps ground cinnamon
- 1 tsp ground nutmeg
- 2 bay leaves
- 8 (6 ounce) pork loin chops
- koshar salt and cracked black pepper to taste

Directions

1. In a mixing bowl, combine the beer, rum, molasses, soy sauce, and lime juice. Add the garlic, ginger, scotch bonnet pepper, thyme, and marjoram and stir to combine. Add allspice, cinnamon, nutmeg, and bay leaves to taste. Put the pork chops in a zip-top bag and pour the marinade over them. Refrigerate for at least one night.
2. Heat up an outdoor grill to medium. Remove the pork chops from the marinade, place them on a platter, and set aside to cool for 15 to 20 minutes while the grill heats up.
3. Season the chops with kosher salt and freshly cracked black pepper to taste. Grill the chops until a thermometer placed in the center registers 145 ° F on both sides (63 ° C). Allow 5 minutes for the pork chops to rest before serving to allow the juices to redistribute.

Nutrition Facts

Per Serving:

323 calories; protein 28.4g; carbohydrates 11.7g; fat 14.3g; cholesterol 80.6mg; sodium 639.4mg.

45. BEANS AND RICE DISH

Prep: 5 mins

Cook: 2 hrs 30 mins

Total: 2 hrs 35 mins

Servings: 6

Ingredients

- 1 ¼ cups dry kidney beans
- 1 cup coconut milk
- 1 sprig fresh thyme
- 1 tsp minced garlic
- 1/8 cup chopped green onions
- 1 hot red chile pepper, sliced
- 2 ¼ cups uncooked brown rice

Directions

1. In a large saucepan, combine the beans and coconut milk; simmer for 2 hours on low heat.
2. Simmer for 7 minutes after adding the thyme, garlic, onions, and 3 slices chile pepper. Bring to a boil with the rice. Reduce heat to low, cover, and cook for 25 minutes, or until rice is soft and liquid has been absorbed.

Nutrition Facts

Per Serving:

407 calories; protein 13.8g; carbohydrates 67.5g; fat 9.9g; sodium 12.2mg.

46. CABBAGE IN WINE SAUCE

Prep: 5 mins

Cook: 20 mins

Total: 25 mins

Servings: 4

Ingredients

- ½ cup water
- ½ medium head cabbage, cored and cut into wedges
- 1 ear corn
- ½ cup butter, melted
- 1/8 cup dry vermouth or white wine
- ½ tsp minced shallots
- 2 large cloves garlic, minced
- salt and black pepper to taste
- crushed red pepper flakes to taste

Directions

1. Fill a big saucepan halfway with water. Remove the leaves from the cabbage and set them in a steamer basket. Place the basket in the water-filled pot. Bring to a boil over medium heat, then remove the ear of corn and lay it on top of the cabbage. Steam for 15 to 20 minutes, or until corn is soft, covered. Remove the basket from the saucepan and set aside to cool.
2. Cut the ear of corn into four pieces and combine with the cabbage in a serving bowl. Combine the butter, vermouth, shallots, garlic, salt, pepper, and red pepper flakes in a mixing bowl; pour over the cabbage and toss to evenly coat. Divide the salad among four dishes and top with a piece of corn on each.

Nutrition Facts

Per Serving:

279 calories; protein 3g; carbohydrates 15.3g; fat 23.6g; cholesterol 61mg; sodium 190.4mg.

47. BOSCOBEL BEACH GINGER CAKE

Prep: 30 mins

Cook: 45 mins

Total: 1 hr 15 mins

Servings: 12

Ingredients

- 1 cup butter
- 1 ¼ cups packed brown sugar
- 4 eggs
- ¼ cup grated fresh ginger root
- 1 tsp vanilla extract
- 1 cup milk
- 2 ½ cups all-purpose flour
- 4 tsps baking powder
- 4 tsps ground ginger
- 1 ½ tsps ground cinnamon
- ½ tsp salt
- 2 tbsps confectioners' sugar for dusting

Directions

1. Preheat the oven to 350 ° Fahrenheit (175 ° C). A 9-inch Bundt pan should be greased and floured. Combine the flour, baking powder, ginger, cinnamon, and salt in a sifter. Remove from the equation.
2. Cream the butter and brown sugar together in a large mixing mixer until light and creamy. One at a time, beat in the eggs, then toss in the shredded ginger root and vanilla extract. Alternately add the flour mixture and the milk, mixing just until combined. Pour the batter into the pan that has been prepared.
3. Bake for 45 to 50 minutes in a preheated oven, or until a toothpick inserted in the center of the cake comes out clean. Allow to cool for 10 minutes in the pan before turning out onto a serving platter. Before serving, lightly dust with confectioners' sugar.

Nutrition Facts

Per Serving:

362 calories; protein 5.7g; carbohydrates 46g; fat 17.7g; cholesterol 104.3mg; sodium 364.9mg.

48. MILD HOT TAMARIND SAUCE

Prep: 20 mins

Cook: 45 mins

Total: 1 hr 5 mins

Servings: 50

Ingredients

- 1 quart water
- 12 pods tamarind (skin removed), broken into pieces
- 1 habanero pepper, stemmed and chopped (wear gloves)
- 2 cloves garlic, chopped
- salt and freshly ground black pepper to taste
- 1 tbsp brown sugar
- ¼ cup cilantro leaves
- 1 lime, juiced
- 1 tbsp white vinegar

Directions

1. Fill a pot halfway with water and add the tamarind pods, habanero pepper, garlic, salt, and black pepper. Bring to a boil, then reduce to a low heat and continue to cook until the tamarind pods begin to break down and the seeds appear. Brown sugar should be added to the mixture. As the pods cook, press them against the pan's side with a slotted spoon to help extract the pulp. Seeds should be discarded.
2. Continue to cook, stirring frequently, until the tamarind mixture thickens to the consistency of tomato soup, about 40 minutes. Stir in the cilantro, lime juice, and vinegar to the sauce and cook for another 1 to 2 minutes, or until the cilantro has wilted.
3. Pour the sauce through a fine mesh strainer, pushing the pulp and solids as much as possible through the mesh. Scrape the outside of the strainer into the residual sauce and discard the leftover almost-dry particles (about a hand full).

Nutrition Facts

Per Serving:

15 calories; protein 0.2g; carbohydrates 3.8g; sodium 3.3mg.

49. SWEET AND SPICY JERK SHRIMP

Prep: 20 mins

Cook: 15 mins

Total: 35 mins

Servings: 4

Ingredients

- 1 ½ pounds large shrimp in shells
- 1 (20 ounce) can pineapple slices packed in 100% juice, drained, and cut into 2-inch pieces
- 2 red bell peppers, cut into thin strips
- 1 large red onion, sliced
- 1 jalapeno pepper - halved lengthwise, seeded, and sliced
- 2 tbsps olive oil
- 1 tbsp Jamaican jerk seasoning
- ½ cup chopped fresh cilantro
- 2 cups hot cooked brown rice
- 1 lime, cut into wedges

Directions

1. Preheat oven to 425 ° Fahrenheit (220 ° C). Two 10x15-inch baking pans should be lined with foil.
2. Remove the shells and devein the shrimp, keeping the tails on if desired. Clean the shrimp by rinsing them and patting them dry.
3. In a large mixing bowl, gently combine shrimp with pineapple, bell peppers, red onion, jalapeño, oil, and jerk seasoning. Divide the mixture between the two pans that have been prepared.
4. Roast for 15 minutes in a preheated oven until the shrimp are opaque.
5. Serve with brown rice and lime wedges, garnished with cilantro.

Cook's Note:

Thaw frozen shrimp before using.

Nutrition Facts

Per Serving:

455 calories; protein 31.4g; carbohydrates 61.1g; fat 9.4g; cholesterol 258.9mg; sodium 647.5mg.

50. JERK CHICKEN AND PASTA

Prep: 15 mins

Cook: 30 mins

Additional: 1 hr

Total: 1 hr 45 mins

Servings: 4

Ingredients

- 4 skinless, boneless chicken breast halves
- 5 tsps jerk paste
- 4 (12 ounce) package uncooked egg noodles
- 4 tbsp olive oil
- 4 clove garlic, minced
- 4 cup chicken stock
- 4 tbsp jerk paste
- ½ cup dry white wine
- ¼ cup chopped fresh cilantro
- 2 limes, quartered
- salt and pepper to taste
- ½ cup heavy whipping cream
- 4 sprigs fresh cilantro, for garnish

Directions

1. Place each breast half in a shallow dish and rub with 1/2 tsp jerk paste. Refrigerate for at least 1 hour after covering.
2. Preheat the grill to medium-high. Bring a large saucepan of lightly salted water to a boil, then cook the egg noodles until al dente, about 6 to 8 minutes.
3. Grease the grill grate lightly. Grill the chicken for 8 to 10 minutes per side, or until the juices run clear.
4. Meanwhile, in a large saucepan over medium heat, heat the olive oil and sauté the garlic for one minute. Combine the chicken stock, 1 tbsp jerk paste, white wine, cilantro, lime juice, salt, and pepper in a mixing bowl. Bring to a boil, then lower to a low heat and add the heavy cream. Cook, stirring constantly, until the mixture thickens, about 5 minutes. Don't let it come to a boil.
5. Toss the cooked egg noodles with the cream sauce in a large pot. To serve, divide the noodles among four dishes and top with grilled chicken. Serve with a sprig of cilantro and 1/4 lime juice on top of each serving.

Nutrition Facts

Per Serving:

595 calories; protein 37.3g; carbohydrates 59.6g; fat 25.2g; cholesterol 168.9mg; sodium 205.2mg.

51. BIRRIA RECIPE

Prep: 20 mins

Cook: 3 hrs 15 mins

Additional: 5 mins

Total: 3 hrs 40 mins

Servings: 12

Ingredients

- 5 dried Anaheim chile peppers, stemmed and seeded
- 5 guajillo chile peppers, stemmed and seeded
- water to cover
- ¼ onion
- 1 tbsp mixed spices, or more to taste
- 1 tbsp salt, or to taste
- 3 pounds cubed beef stew meat
- 6 bay leaves

Directions

1. Fill a pot halfway with water and bring to a boil with the Anaheim and guajillo peppers. Reduce heat to medium-low and cook for 15 minutes, or until vegetables are soft. Remove the saucepan from the heat and set it aside to cool for 5 minutes.
2. In a blender, combine the chiles, water, onion, mixed spices, and salt. Blend until the sauce is completely smooth.
3. In a large saucepan, combine stew meat, sauce, and bay leaves; simmer over medium-low heat for 3 to 5 hours, or until meat is extremely soft.

Tip

Aluminum foil keeps food wet, guarantees consistent cooking, keeps leftovers fresh, and is simple to clean.

Nutrition Facts

Per Serving:

159 calories; protein 21.3g; carbohydrates 2.7g; fat 6.6g; cholesterol 59.9mg; sodium 630.4mg.

52. JAY'S JERK CHICKEN

Prep: 15 mins

Cook: 30 mins

Additional: 4 hrs

Total: 4 hrs 45 mins

Servings: 4

Ingredients

- 6 green onions, chopped
- 1 onion, chopped
- 1 jalapeno pepper, seeded and minced
- ¾ cup soy sauce
- ½ cup distilled white vinegar
- ¼ cup vegetable oil
- 2 tbsps brown sugar
- 1 tbsp chopped fresh thyme
- ½ tsp ground cloves
- ½ tsp ground nutmeg
- ½ tsp ground allspice
- 1 ½ pounds skinless, boneless chicken breast halves

Directions

1. Combine the green onions, onion, jalapeño pepper, soy sauce, vinegar, vegetable oil, brown sugar, thyme, cloves, nutmeg, and allspice in a food processor or blender. For around 15 seconds, mix everything together.
2. Coat the chicken in the marinade in a medium mixing bowl. Refrigerate for 4 to 6 hours or overnight in the refrigerator.
3. Preheat the grill to high.
4. Grease the grill grate lightly. Cook the chicken for 6 to 8 minutes on the preheated grill, or until the juices flow clear.

Note

The full amount of marinade ingredients is included in the nutrition facts for this dish. The amount of marinade used varies depending on marinating duration, ingredients, cooking style, and other factors.

Nutrition Facts

Per Serving:

385 calories; protein 39.2g; carbohydrates 15.4g; fat 18.2g; cholesterol 96.9mg; sodium 2797.7mg.

53. AIR FRYER JERK PORK SKEWERS WITH BLACK BEAN AND MANGO SALSA

Prep: 30 mins

Cook: 10 mins

Total: 40 mins

Servings: 4

Ingredients
Jamaican Jerk Seasoning:

- 2 tbsps white sugar
- 4 ½ tsps onion powder
- 4 ½ tsps dried thyme, crushed
- 1 tbsp ground allspice
- 1 tbsp ground black pepper
- 1 ½ tsps cayenne pepper, or to taste
- 1 ½ tsps salt
- ¾ tsp ground nutmeg
- ¼ tsp ground cloves
- ¼ cup shredded coconut
- 1 (1 pound) pork tenderloin, cut into 1 1/2-inch cubes
- 4 each bamboo skewers, soaked in water for 30 minutes, drained
- 1 tbsp vegetable oil
- 1 mango - peeled, seeded, and chopped
- ½ (15 ounce) can black beans, rinsed and drained
- ¼ cup finely chopped red onion
- 2 tbsps fresh lime juice
- 1 tbsp honey
- 1 tbsp chopped fresh cilantro
- ¼ tsp salt
- 1/8 tsp ground black pepper

Directions

1. In a small bowl, combine sugar, onion powder, thyme, allspice, black pepper, cayenne pepper, salt, nutmeg, and cloves for seasoning mix. Transfer the rub to a small airtight container, saving 1 tbsp for the pork in a separate bowl. Stir in the coconut with the remaining 1 tbsp spice.
2. Preheat the air fryer to 350 ° Fahrenheit (180 ° Celsius) (175 ° C).
3. Using skewers, thread pork slices. Brush the pork with oil and season it all over with the seasoning combination before placing it in the air frying basket.
4. Cook for 5 to 7 minutes in a preheated air fryer until an instant read thermometer put in the thickest part of the meat registers 145°F (63°C).
5. In a medium mixing basin, mash 1/3 of the mango. Combine the remaining mango, black beans, red onion, lime juice, honey, cilantro, salt, and pepper in a mixing bowl. Along with the pork skewers, serve salsa.

Cook's Note:

For the seasoning mix, paprika can be substituted for cayenne pepper. Instead of preparing your own jerk seasoning, you can buy store-bought jerk seasoning.

Nutrition Facts

Per Serving:

313 calories; protein 22.3g; carbohydrates 34.6g; fat 10.8g; cholesterol 49.1mg; sodium 1268.4mg.

54. CARIBBEAN SLAW

Prep: 20 mins

Additional: 1 hr

Total: 1 hr 20 mins

Servings: 8

Ingredients

- ½ head green cabbage, shredded
- 1 red bell pepper, thinly sliced
- ½ red onion, thinly sliced
- 2 carrots, peeled and shredded
- 1 mango - peeled, seeded, and diced
- ½ cup fresh cilantro, chopped
- 1/3 cup nonfat plain yogurt
- 2 tbsps reduced-fat mayonnaise
- 1 tbsp prepared yellow mustard
- 1 tbsp apple cider vinegar
- 1 tsp agave nectar
- salt and black pepper to taste
- 1 dash habanero hot sauce, or more to taste

Directions

1. In a large mixing bowl, combine the cabbage, red bell pepper, red onion, carrots, mango, and cilantro.
2. In a small mixing bowl, combine the yogurt, mayonnaise, mustard, cider vinegar, agave nectar, salt, pepper, and spicy sauce; pour over the cabbage mixture and toss to coat. Allow the slaw to marinade for at least 1 hour in the refrigerator to allow the flavors to meld.

Nutrition Facts

Per Serving:

61 calories; protein 2.1g; carbohydrates 13.1g; fat 0.6g; cholesterol 0.2mg; sodium 94.5mg.

55. CARROT RECIPE

Prep: 5 mins

Cook: 12 mins

Total: 17 mins

Servings: 4

Ingredients

- 4 cups grated carrots
- 2 cups milk
- 1 cup white sugar
- 1 tbsp butter
- ½ cup cashew halves
- ½ cup raisins
- 1 pinch ground cardamom (Optional)

Directions

1. Combine carrots and milk in a saucepan over medium heat. Bring to a boil, then reduce to a low heat and cook for 10 minutes, or until most of the milk has evaporated. Stir add the sugar and cook until the mixture is completely dry. To keep it from burning, keep stirring constantly. Remove the pan from the heat.
2. In a skillet over medium heat, melt the butter. Add the cashews and raisins to the pan and cook until the cashews are golden brown. Spread the carrot mixture on top. For a fragrant finish, sprinkle ground cardamom on top.

Note

Although some individuals purée their carrots, shredded carrots have a wonderful texture.

Nutrition Facts

Per Serving:

486 calories; protein 8.4g; carbohydrates 88.3g; fat 13.6g; cholesterol 17.4mg; sodium 258.3mg.

56. ROASTED TOMATILLO AND GARLIC SALSA

Prep: 10 mins

Cook: 30 mins

Total: 40 mins

Servings: 20

Ingredients

- 1 pound fresh tomatillos, husks removed
- 1 head garlic cloves, separated and peeled
- 3 fresh jalapeno peppers
- 1 bunch fresh cilantro
- ½ cup water, or as needed
- salt and pepper to taste

Directions

1. Preheat the broiler in the oven. On a baking sheet, arrange the whole garlic cloves, tomatillos, and jalapenos. Place under the broiler for a few minutes to cook. To avoid developing a bitter flavor, remove garlic cloves as soon as they are toasted. Continue to roast the jalapenos and tomatillos, tossing them regularly, until they are evenly browned. Allow to cool before serving. The charred parts of the tomatillos and peppers should not be removed. They give the dish a wonderful flavor.
2. In a blender, combine the peppers, tomatillos, garlic, and cilantro. If required, add a little water to the mixture to make it easier to blend. To taste, season with salt and pepper. Refrigerate until ready to serve.

Nutrition Facts

Per Serving:

13 calories; protein 0.5g; carbohydrates 2.5g; fat 0.3g; sodium 2mg.

57. STUFFING RECIPE

Prep: 1 hr

Cook: 30 mins

Total: 1 hr 30 mins

Servings: 12

Ingredients

- 1 cup water
- 2 ½ cups uncooked wild rice
- ½ cup butter
- 1 pound ground pork sausage
- 2 ½ cups chopped onions
- 2 cups chopped celery
- 2 ½ cups chopped mushrooms
- 1 ½ tsps dried thyme
- 1 ½ tsps dried rosemary
- 2 tsps salt
- 1 ½ tsps pepper
- 6 cups cubed whole wheat bread
- 2 large Rome beauty apples - peeled, cored, and chopped
- 1 cup raisins
- 1 (14.5 ounce) can chicken broth

Directions

1. Boil water in a medium pot and mix in wild rice. Reduce the temperature. Cover and cook for 45 minutes, or until the water is absorbed and the rice is soft.
2. Preheat the oven to 350 ° Fahrenheit (175 ° C).
3. In a big, heavy skillet, melt butter over medium heat. Combine the sausage, onions, and celery in a mixing bowl. Cook for 10 to 12 minutes, or until sausage is evenly browned. Drain and add mushrooms, thyme, and rosemary to the pan. Cook for another 2 minutes, or until the mushrooms are gently browned. Season with salt and pepper after removing from the fire.
4. Combine the sausage mixture, cooked rice, whole wheat bread, apples, and raisins in a large mixing bowl. Blend in the chicken broth in small increments until the mixture is moistened.
5. Fill a large baking dish halfway with the mixture. Bake for 30 minutes, or until lightly browned in a preheated oven.

Nutrition Facts

Per Serving:

453 calories; protein 11.4g; carbohydrates 50.3g; fat 24.4g; cholesterol 46.1mg; sodium 845.7mg.

58. EASY AND YUMMIEST KULFI RECIPE

Prep: 10 mins

Additional: 8 hrs

Total: 8 hrs 10 mins

Servings: 12

Ingredients

- 2 (5 ounce) cans evaporated milk
- 2 (7.6 ounce) cans canned table cream (media crema)
- 1 (14 ounce) can sweetened condensed milk
- 2 slices white bread
- ¼ tsp ground cardamom
- 12 blanched almonds

Directions

1. In a blender, combine evaporated milk, canned cream, and sweetened condensed milk; shred bread into small pieces and add to blender. Blend in the cardamom and almonds for 3 to 4 minutes, or until liquified. Freeze for 8 hours or overnight in a 9x13-inch glass dish before cutting into squares and serving.

Nutrition Facts

Per Serving:

256 calories; protein 4.8g; carbohydrates 22.5g; fat 15.6g; cholesterol 21.7mg; sodium 120.1mg.

59. APPLE PIE SPICE RECIPE

Prep: 5 mins

Total: 5 mins

Servings: 4

Ingredients

- 1 tbsp ground cinnamon
- 1 ½ tsps ground nutmeg
- ¾ tsp ground allspice
- ¾ tsp ground cardamom

Directions

2. In an airtight jar, combine cinnamon, nutmeg, allspice, and cardamom.

Nutrition Facts

Per Serving:

12 calories; protein 0.2g; carbohydrates 2.5g; fat 0.5g; sodium 0.7mg.

60. ORANGED CRANBERRY SAUCE

Prep: 10 mins

Cook: 1 hr 15 mins

Total: 1 hr 25 mins

Servings: 24

Ingredients

- 2 (12 ounce) packages fresh cranberries
- 1 orange, zested
- 3 cinnamon sticks
- 2 cups orange juice
- 2 cups packed brown sugar

Directions

1. Combine the cranberries, orange zest, cinnamon, orange juice, and brown sugar in a medium saucepan. Bring to a boil over high heat with enough water to cover. Reduce heat to low and

continue to cook for about 1 hour, or until the sauce has thickened. If necessary, taste for sweetness and add more sugar if necessary. You can't overcook it, so keep cooking until it's a nice thick consistency. Allow to cool before refrigerating in an airtight container.

Nutrition Facts

Per Serving:

93 calories; protein 0.3g; carbohydrates 23.9g; fat 0.1g; sodium 5.9mg.

61. ELEGANT MUSHROOM PIE RECIPE

Prep: 25 mins

Cook: 40 mins

Total: 1 hr 5 mins

Servings: 8

Ingredients

- 6 tbsps butter, divided
- 1 ½ pounds baby bella (crimini) mushrooms, sliced
- ¼ cup chopped sweet onion
- ½ lemon, juiced
- ½ tsp dried thyme
- 5 tbsps all-purpose flour
- 1 ¼ cups Swanson® Chicken Broth
- 1/3 cup Marsala wine
- 2 tbsps half-and-half
- salt and pepper to taste
- 1 (17.3 ounce) package frozen puff pastry, thawed
- 1 egg, beaten

Directions

1. Preheat the oven to 375 ° Fahrenheit (190 ° C). Using non-fat cooking spray, coat a 9-inch pie plate.
2. In a large skillet, melt 3 tbsps butter over medium heat. Stir in the mushrooms and onions until the liquid from the mushrooms has evaporated, about 10 minutes. Cook for 2 minutes after adding the lemon juice and thyme.
3. In a separate pot, melt 3 tbsps butter. In a separate bowl, whisk together the flour and stir continually for about 1 minute. Whisk in the Swanson® Chicken Broth, Marsala, and half-and-

half in a slow, steady stream until the sauce is smooth and thickened, about 3 minutes. The sauce should be rich and creamy. Season with salt and pepper to taste.

4. Stir the mushroom mixture into the sauce broth/Marsala combination until everything is completely combined.

5. To fit the pie plate, roll out one layer of puff pastry. Trim the excess pastry and press evenly into the bottom and edges of the pie plate. Fill the pastry shell with the mushroom mixture.

6. Place the second piece of puff pastry on top of the first. Trim the excess and secure the edge with a crimp. Make a few slits in the top to let steam out. Brush the beaten egg over the top of the pie.

7. Cook for about 40 minutes in a preheated oven until golden brown and the mushroom mixture is bubbling. Before serving, allow the pie to cool somewhat.

Cook's Note:

White button mushrooms can be used instead of baby bellas, and whole milk can be used instead of half-and-half. Start making your roux/sauce while you're sautéing the mushrooms. You will save some time as a result of this.

Allstars are members of the Allrecipes community who have been chosen as brand ambassadors based on their onsite activity, enthusiasm, and dedication. Allrecipes Allstars may be compensated for their involvement in the program.

Nutrition Facts

Per Serving:

496 calories; protein 10g; carbohydrates 37.2g; fat 33.2g; cholesterol 48.3mg; sodium 428mg.

62. HOMEMADE BAKING POWDER RECIPE

Prep: 5 mins

Total: 5 mins

Servings: 6

Ingredients

- 2 tsps cream of tartar
- 1 tsp baking soda
- 1 tsp cornstarch (Optional)

Directions

1. In a separate bowl, combine the cream of tartar and baking soda. To keep the mixture fresh, whisk cornstarch into it and store it in an airtight container.

Nutrition Facts

Per Serving:

4 calories; carbohydrates 1g; sodium 210.3mg.

63. ROASTED TOMATILLO AND GARLIC SALSA

Prep: 10 mins

Cook: 30 mins

Total: 40 mins

Servings: 20

Ingredients

- 1 pound fresh tomatillos, husks removed
- 1 head garlic cloves, separated and peeled
- 3 fresh jalapeno peppers
- 1 bunch fresh cilantro
- ½ cup water, or as needed
- salt and pepper to taste

Directions

1. Preheat the broiler in the oven. On a baking sheet, arrange the whole garlic cloves, tomatillos, and jalapenos. Place under the broiler for a few minutes to cook. To avoid developing a bitter flavor, remove garlic cloves as soon as they are toasted. Continue to roast the jalapenos and tomatillos, tossing them regularly, until they are evenly browned. Allow to cool before serving. The charred parts of the tomatillos and peppers should not be removed. They give the dish a wonderful flavor.
2. In a blender, combine the peppers, tomatillos, garlic, and cilantro. If required, add a little water to the mixture to make it easier to blend. To taste, season with salt and pepper. Refrigerate until ready to serve.

Nutrition Facts

Per Serving:

13 calories; protein 0.5g; carbohydrates 2.5g; fat 0.3g; sodium 2mg.

64. CREOLE CHICKEN RECIPE

Prep: 10 mins

Cook: 45 mins

Total: 55 mins

Servings: 4

Ingredients

- 4 skinless chicken thighs, or more to taste
- 1 pinch Creole seasoning, or more to taste
- 2 tbsps butter
- 1 (15 ounce) can diced tomatoes with green chile peppers
- 1 cup water
- 1 (8 ounce) can tomato sauce
- 1 (6.8 ounce) package Spanish-style rice mix

Directions

1. Chicken thighs should be seasoned with Creole seasoning.
2. Cook chicken in melted butter in a pan over medium heat until browned, 3 to 4 minutes per side. Place the chicken on a plate. In the same skillet, combine the tomatoes, green chile peppers, water, tomato sauce, and Spanish-style rice mix; stir well. Bring the chicken back to a boil in the rice mixture. Reduce heat to low, cover skillet, and cook for 40 minutes, or until chicken is no longer pink in the center and rice is soft. Serve the rice on a dish with the chicken on top.

Nutrition Facts

Per Serving:

400 calories; protein 27.3g; carbohydrates 41.9g; fat 14.2g; cholesterol 93mg; sodium 1750.6mg.

65. EASIEST ASPARAGUS RECIPE

Prep: 5 mins

Cook: 10 mins

Total: 15 mins

Servings: 5

Ingredients

- 2 tbsps butter, or more as needed
- 1 bunch asparagus, trimmed
- 1 tsp honey
- 1/8 tsp garlic powder
- 1/8 tsp cayenne pepper

Directions

1. In a pan over medium-low heat, melt 2 tbsps butter. Cook asparagus in heated butter for 6 to 8 minutes, stirring occasionally.
2. Season with garlic powder and cayenne pepper after drizzling honey over the asparagus.

Cook's Notes:

If the asparagus starts to stick to the pan, add up to 1 tbsp extra butter while cooking.

Use 2 tbsps extra-virgin olive oil instead of butter for a healthier alternative.

Nutrition Facts

Per Serving:

64 calories; protein 2.1g; carbohydrates 4.8g; fat 4.7g; cholesterol 12.2mg; sodium 34.6mg.

66. THE WORLD'S GREATEST CRAB RECIPE

Prep: 10 mins

Cook: 6 mins

Total: 16 mins

Servings: 4

Ingredients

- ½ cup olive oil
- ½ cup butter
- ½ cup minced garlic
- 4 pounds Snow Crab clusters, thawed if necessary

Directions

1. Heat an outside barbecue to high temperatures. When the grate is hot, lightly oil it.
2. Brush the crab with a good amount of the olive oil, butter, and garlic mixture.
3. Cook crab over a hot grill, flipping once, for about 6 minutes, or until the shell begins to brown.

Nutrition Facts

Per Serving:

957 calories; protein 68.9g; carbohydrates 5.8g; fat 72.7g; cholesterol 394.5mg; sodium 1292.9mg.

67. DELICIOUS PIZZA SAUCE RECIPE

Prep: 10 mins

Cook: 10 mins

Total: 20 mins

Servings: 4

Ingredients

- 2 tbsps olive oil
- 1 (28 ounce) can crushed tomatoes
- 2 leaves basil, chopped
- 3 cloves garlic, chopped
- 1 pinch salt and ground black pepper to taste
- 1 pinch grated Parmesan cheese

Directions

1. In a saucepan, heat the olive oil. Place the smashed tomatoes in a saucepan over low heat. Bring the tomatoes to a simmer with the basil, garlic, salt, and black pepper. To serve, stir in the Parmesan cheese.

Nutrition Facts

Per Serving:

127 calories; protein 3.5g; carbohydrates 15g; fat 7.4g; cholesterol 0.2mg; sodium 263.1mg.

68. ORANGED CRANBERRY SAUCE

Prep: 10 mins

Cook: 1 hr 15 mins

Total: 1 hr 25 mins

Servings: 24

Ingredients

- 2 (12 ounce) packages fresh cranberries
- 1 orange, zested
- 3 cinnamon sticks
- 2 cups orange juice
- 2 cups packed brown sugar

Directions

1. Combine the cranberries, orange zest, cinnamon, orange juice, and brown sugar in a medium saucepan. Bring to a boil over high heat with enough water to cover. Reduce heat to low and continue to cook for about 1 hour, or until the sauce has thickened. If necessary, taste for sweetness and add more sugar if necessary. You can't overcook it, so keep cooking until it's a nice thick consistency. Allow to cool before refrigerating in an airtight container.

Nutrition Facts

Per Serving:

93 calories; protein 0.3g; carbohydrates 23.9g; fat 0.1g; sodium 5.9mg.

69. PATE RECIPE

Prep: 15 mins

Cook: 25 mins

Additional: 4 hrs

Total: 4 hrs 40 mins

Servings: 24

Ingredients

- 1 pound bacon strips, diced
- 3 medium onions, chopped
- 3 cloves garlic
- 1 pound chicken livers, trimmed and chopped
- 1 pound veal, trimmed and cubed
- 1 cup heavy cream
- ½ cup milk
- ¾ cup butter
- 1 pinch salt and pepper to taste

Directions

1. In a large skillet over medium-high heat, cook the bacon. Add the onion and whole garlic cloves when the spinach has wilted. Cook until the onion is tender, stirring regularly. Cook until the chicken livers and veal cubes are no longer pink in the skillet. Allow to cool before serving.
2. Set aside a 9x5 inch loaf pan or mold lined with waxed paper or sprayed with cooking spray. Place the meat mixture in a food processor container and pulse until finely minced. Do not purée the ingredients. In a large skillet over medium heat, melt the butter. Stir in the beef mixture, heavy cream, and milk. Cook until well heated. Season to taste with salt and pepper before pouring into the loaf pan or shape. Before serving, chill for at least 4 hours.

Nutrition Facts

Per Serving:

178 calories; protein 10.1g; carbohydrates 2.2g; fat 14.2g; cholesterol 155.3mg; sodium 214mg.

70. GRANDMOTHER'S LAMB RECIPE

Prep: 25 mins

Cook: 1 hr 50 mins

Additional: 1 hr

Total: 3 hrs 15 mins

Servings: 6

Ingredients
Grandmother's Chile Paste:

- 1 tsp cumin seeds
- 6 dried red chile peppers (preferably Kashmiri)
- ¼ cup apple cider vinegar
- 1 clove garlic, coarsely chopped - or more to taste
- 3 tbsps vegetable oil
- 2 onions, finely chopped
- 2 tsps ginger garlic paste
- 5 tbsps tomato paste
- 1 tsp ground red pepper (cayenne) or to taste
- ¼ tsp ground turmeric
- ¼ tsp ground cinnamon
- ¼ tsp ground cloves
- 2 pounds lamb shanks, cut into 1 1/2-inch pieces
- ½ tsp salt
- 3 cups water
- 1 tbsp chopped fresh cilantro

Directions

1. In a dry skillet over medium heat, toast the cumin seeds, turning regularly, until they emit a roasted aroma and turn a deeper brown, about 1 minute. Place the seeds in a basin and set aside to cool. Grind them with a mortar and pestle or a clean spice grinder once they've cooled. Set aside the ground seed.
2. Remove the stems from the chiles if required, and soak the pods in apple cider vinegar for at least 1 hour. In a blender or food processor, combine the softened chiles, vinegar, cumin, and garlic, and pulse until a paste forms, 30 seconds to 1 minute or as needed.
3. In a large pot over medium heat, heat the vegetable oil and sauté and stir the onions until gently browned, about 10 minutes. Add 1 tsp of the Grandmother's Chile Paste mixture, or as desired, to the ginger garlic paste. Reduce the heat to medium-low and cook the onions and spice pastes together for 5 minutes to mix the flavors. Bring to a simmer with the tomato paste,

ground red pepper, turmeric, cinnamon, and cloves. Cook for 20 minutes to allow flavors to combine.

4. Stir in the lamb shank pieces and season with salt and pepper; cook for 20 minutes, then add the water. Bring the lamb and sauce to a boil, then reduce to a low heat and continue to cook for 45 minutes, or until the lamb is very soft and the sauce has thickened. To serve, garnish with chopped cilantro.

Nutrition Facts

Per Serving:

262 calories; protein 19.1g; carbohydrates 10.8g; fat 15.4g; cholesterol 59.4mg; sodium 409.2mg.

71. RABBIT GREEK RECIPE

Prep: 10 mins

Cook: 45 mins

Total: 55 mins

Servings: 4

Ingredients

- ¼ cup olive oil
- 1 (3 pound) rabbit, cut into pieces
- 2 bay leaves
- 1 tsp salt
- 4 whole allspice berries
- ½ tsp oregano
- 1 lemon, juiced
- ½ cup white wine
- warm water, to cover

Directions

1. In a large saucepan, heat 1/4 cup olive oil over medium heat. Fry rabbit pieces until they are evenly browned in heated oil. To the pot, add bay leaves, salt, allspice berries, oregano, and lemon juice. Over the rabbit, pour white wine. Cook for 4 to 5 minutes after bringing the mixture to a simmer. Fill the pot with enough water to completely cover the rabbit.
2. Cook, stirring occasionally, until the rabbit is cooked through and the liquid has evaporated, about 40 minutes.

Nutrition Facts

Per Serving:

567 calories; protein 62g; carbohydrates 1.3g; fat 30.7g; cholesterol 174.7mg; sodium 694.4mg.

72. ORANGED CRANBERRY SAUCE

Prep: 10 mins

Cook: 1 hr 15 mins

Total: 1 hr 25 mins

Servings: 24

Ingredients

- 2 (12 ounce) packages fresh cranberries
- 1 orange, zested
- 3 cinnamon sticks
- 2 cups orange juice
- 2 cups packed brown sugar

Directions

1. Combine the cranberries, orange zest, cinnamon, orange juice, and brown sugar in a medium saucepan. Bring to a boil over high heat with enough water to cover. Reduce heat to low and continue to cook for about 1 hour, or until the sauce has thickened. If necessary, taste for sweetness and add more sugar if necessary. You can't overcook it, so keep cooking until it's a nice thick consistency. Allow to cool before refrigerating in an airtight container.

Nutrition Facts

Per Serving:

93 calories; protein 0.3g; carbohydrates 23.9g; fat 0.1g; sodium 5.9mg.

73. LEMON CRUMB MUFFINS RECIPE

Prep: 20 mins

Cook: 40 mins

Additional: 5 mins

Total: 1 hr 5 mins

Servings: 40

Ingredients

- 6 cups all-purpose flour
- 4 cups white sugar
- ¾ tsp baking soda
- ¾ tsp salt
- 8 eggs
- 2 cups sour cream
- 2 cups butter, melted
- 3 tbsps lemon zest
- 0 tbsps lemon juice
- ¾ cup all-purpose flour
- ¾ cup white sugar
- ¼ cup cubed cold butter

Directions

1. Preheat the oven to 350 ° Fahrenheit (175 ° C). 40 muffin cups should be greased or lined with paper liners.
2. In a large mixing basin, combine 6 cups flour, 4 cups sugar, baking soda, and salt. In a separate bowl, whisk together eggs, sour cream, melted butter, lemon zest, and lemon juice until smooth; pour egg mixture into flour mixture. Stir until everything is well blended. Fill the muffin cups 3/4 full with batter after they've been prepared.
3. In a mixing dish, combine 3/4 cup flour and 3/4 cup sugar; chop cold butter cubes into flour mixture until coarse crumbs form. Top each muffin with a sprinkling of the crumb mixture.
4. Bake for 20 to 25 minutes, or until a knife inserted in the center of a muffin comes out clean. Cool in the pans for 5 minutes before transferring to wire racks to cool fully.

Nutrition Facts

Per Serving:

300 calories; protein 3.9g; carbohydrates 40.6g; fat 14g; cholesterol 69.7mg; sodium 161.3mg.

74. CANDIED PUMPKIN RECIPE

Prep: 15 mins

Cook: 25 mins

Total: 40 mins

Servings: 12

Ingredients

- ¼ cup unsalted butter
- 3 cups fresh pumpkin, cut into 1/2-inch cubes
- 1/3 cup white sugar
- ¾ cup maple syrup
- 1 tbsp minced fresh ginger
- ½ tsp ground cinnamon

Directions

1. In a large skillet over medium-low heat, melt the butter. Cook the pumpkin in the butter for about 20 minutes, or until it is soft. Stir in the sugar until it is completely dissolved. Remove from the heat and stir in the syrup, ginger, and cinnamon; set aside to cool. Cover and transfer to a bowl. Before serving, chill for at least 2 hours.

Nutrition Facts

Per Serving:

115 calories; protein 0.3g; carbohydrates 20.8g; fat 3.9g; cholesterol 10.2mg; sodium 2.7mg.

75. TUDOR RECIPE FOR GINGER BEER

Prep: 10 mins

Cook: 20 mins

Additional: 2 weeks

Total: 2 weeks

Servings: 16

Ingredients

- 1 (0.6 ounce) cake compressed fresh yeast
- 2 tsps castor sugar or superfine sugar
- 2 tsps ground ginger
- 2 cups cold water
- 7 tsps castor sugar or superfine sugar, divided
- 7 tsps ground ginger, divided
- 3 ¾ cups white sugar
- 5 cups boiling water
- 12 ½ cups cold water
- ½ cup strained fresh lemon juice

Directions

1. Combine the yeast, 2 tsps castor sugar, and 2 tsps ground ginger in a sterilized 2 quart container. Stir in the cold water until everything is fully combined. Cover with a clean cheesecloth and set aside in a convenient corner of the kitchen for the next seven days at room temperature.
2. Feed the yeast mixture with 1 tsp castor sugar and 1 tsp ground ginger every morning for the next seven days.
3. Give the mixture a thorough stir on the eighth day, then drain it into a large fresh plastic bucket, bin, or glass carbuoy via a clean tea towel. Set the cloth aside after wringing out all of the liquid. This is something you'll have to deal with later.
4. Stir rapidly to dissolve the white sugar in 5 cups boiling water. Fill the bucket with cold water and ginger juice, then add the sugar syrup and lemon juice.
5. Fill sterilized screw-top bottles to within 2 inches of the top with the mixture. It'll enough if you use old soda bottles that have been cleaned empty. Screw the tops on firmly. Store the ginger beer bottles in a cool, dark place where they will not be disturbed for at least 7 days. The beer is extremely bubbly when first opened, so proceed with caution.

6. Return to the cloth at this point. The residue appears to be revolting! Lay the towel flat, with the nasty side facing up. Scrape the contents to the middle with a knife, then divide in half and place each half into its own sterilized jar. After that, fill each jar with 2 cups of cold water and you're good to go. Twice! For following batches, start with step 2. Unless you're extremely thirsty, I recommend giving one of them away.

Nutrition Facts

Per Serving:

197 calories; protein 0.2g; carbohydrates 50.8g; fat 0.1g; sodium 0.7mg.

76. SHRIMPS SAGANAKI (GREEK RECIPE)

Prep: 5 mins

Cook: 35 mins

Total: 40 mins

Servings: 4

Ingredients

- 1 pound medium shrimp, with shells
- 1 onion, chopped
- 2 tbsps chopped fresh parsley
- 1 cup white wine
- 1 (14.5 ounce) can diced tomatoes, drained
- ¼ tsp garlic powder (Optional)
- ¼ cup olive oil
- 1 (8 ounce) package feta cheese, cubed
- 1 pinch salt and pepper to taste

Directions

1. In a large saucepan, bring 2 inches of water to a boil. Add the shrimp and just cover them with water. Boil for 5 minutes, then drain and set aside, saving the liquid.
2. In a saucepan, heat about 2 tsps of oil. Cook, stirring constantly, until the onions are tender. Combine the parsley, wine, tomatoes, garlic powder, and the remaining olive oil in a large mixing bowl. Simmer for about 30 minutes, stirring regularly, or until the sauce has thickened.
3. The shrimps should be cold enough to handle while the sauce is boiling. Remove the legs first by pinching them, then the shells, leaving the head and tail on.

4. Stir in the shrimp stock and shrimp after the sauce has thickened. Bring to a low boil, then reduce to a low heat and cook for about 5 minutes. Remove the pan from the heat and add the feta cheese. Allow to sit until the cheese begins to melt. Warm the dish before serving.

Nutrition Facts

Per Serving:

441 calories; protein 27.8g; carbohydrates 10.1g; fat 26.6g; cholesterol 223.1mg; sodium 1035.3mg.

77. MOST AMAZING SANGRIA RECIPE EVER!

Prep: 10 mins

Total: 10 mins

Servings: 6

Ingredients

- 4 ½ cups red wine
- ¾ cup ginger ale
- ½ cup orange juice
- 2 fluid ounces brandy
- 1 fluid ounce triple sec (orange-flavored liqueur)
- 1 tsp white sugar
- 1 pinch ground cinnamon
- 2 cups crushed ice
- ½ Granny Smith apple, diced

Directions

1. In a big pitcher, combine red wine, ginger ale, orange juice, brandy, triple sec, sugar, cinnamon, and apple.
2. In six large wine glasses, evenly distribute crushed ice.
3. Pour the red wine mixture into each wine glass, being careful to include a few apple slices in each serving.

Nutrition Facts

Per Serving:

223 calories; protein 0.3g; carbohydrates 13.9g; fat 0.1g; sodium 11.5mg.

78. CELYNE'S GREEN JUICE - JUICER RECIPE

Prep: 10 mins

Total: 10 mins

Servings: 2

Ingredients

- 2 oranges, peeled
- 1 lemon, peeled
- 1 green apple, quartered
- 1 cup fresh spinach
- 1 leaf kale

Directions

1. Juice oranges, lemons, green apples, spinach, and kale according to the manufacturer's instructions.

Nutrition Facts

Per Serving:

44 calories; protein 0.9g; carbohydrates 11.1g; fat 0.2g; sodium 16.8mg.

79. BIG RAY'S RHUBARB RELISH RECIPE

Prep: 15 mins

Cook: 30 mins

Total: 45 mins

Servings: 8

Ingredients

- 2 ¼ cups packed brown sugar
- 2 cups finely chopped rhubarb
- 2 cups chopped strawberries
- ½ cup white vinegar
- ½ tsp ground cinnamon
- ½ tsp ground allspice

- ¼ tsp ground cloves
- ¼ tsp ground nutmeg

Directions

1. In a medium saucepan, combine brown sugar, rhubarb, strawberries, vinegar, cinnamon, allspice, cloves, and nutmeg. Cook and stir for 30 minutes, or until relish thickens. Allow to cool completely before transferring to a sealable container and storing in the refrigerator.

Cook's Note:

1/4 tsp cornstarch can be used to thicken the relish more rapidly.

Nutrition Facts

Per Serving:

257 calories; protein 0.6g; carbohydrates 65.6g; fat 0.2g; sodium 19.2mg.

80. DELICIOUS SWEET POTATO PIE RECIPE

Prep: 15 mins

Cook: 1 hr 25 mins

Additional: 20 mins

Total: 2 hrs

Servings: 8

Ingredients

- 2 sweet potatoes, peeled and cut into chunks
- 1 (9 inch) refrigerated pie crust
- 1 cup white sugar
- 2 eggs, beaten
- 2 tbsps butter
- 1 tsp vanilla extract
- 1 tbsp all-purpose flour
- 1 tsp pumpkin pie spice
- ½ tsp salt
- ½ cup buttermilk
- ¼ tsp baking soda

Directions

1. Fill a big pot halfway with water and bring to a boil with sweet potatoes. Reduce heat to medium-low and cook for 10 to 15 minutes, or until vegetables are soft. Drain well and set aside to cool.
2. Preheat the oven to 350 ° Fahrenheit (175 ° C). Pie crust should be used to line the bottom of a pie plate.
3. Use a potato masher or a fork to mash sweet potatoes. 2 cups mashed potatoes in a large mixing basin Combine the sugar eggs, butter, and vanilla essence in a mixing bowl.
4. In a separate basin, combine the flour, pumpkin pie spice, and salt. Toss it up with the sweet potato mixture.
5. In a small basin, combine buttermilk and baking soda. Combine the sweet potato and flour in a mixing bowl. Stir the batter thoroughly before pouring it into the prepared crust.
6. Bake for 1 hour and 10 minutes in a preheated oven until set. Allow to cool for at least 20 minutes on a wire rack.

Nutrition Facts

Per Serving:

327 calories; protein 4.7g; carbohydrates 51.3g; fat 11.8g; cholesterol 54.7mg; sodium 394.8mg.

81. HOMEMADE HAIR GROWTH CONDITIONER RECIPE

Prep: 5 mins

Cook: 5 mins

Additional: 5 mins

Total: 15 mins

Servings: 3

Ingredients

- ¼ cup shea butter
- 3 tbsps coconut oil
- 1 tbsp argan oil
- 2 tbsps aloe vera juice
- 7 drops rosemary essential oil
- 3 to 4 capsules vitamin E oil

Directions

1. In the top of a double boiler, melt shea butter, coconut oil, and argan oil over low heat. 5 minutes, stirring occasionally until melted Remove from heat and set aside for 5 minutes to cool somewhat but not harden.
2. Fill a food processor or blender halfway with the shea butter mixture and process on high until smooth. Slowly drizzle in the aloe vera juice, mixing until smooth, 3 to 5 minutes. Blend in the essential oil and vitamin E oil until completely combined.

Nutrition Facts

Per Serving:

117 calories; fat 13.6g.

82. MY CHICKEN PHO RECIPE

Prep: 10 mins

Cook: 30 mins

Total: 40 mins

Servings: 2

Ingredients

- 4 ounces dry Chinese egg noodles
- 6 cups chicken stock
- 5 tbsps fish sauce
- 4 cloves garlic, minced
- 2 tsps minced fresh ginger root
- 1 tbsp minced lemon grass
- 5 green onions, chopped
- 2 cups cubed cooked chicken
- 1 cup bean sprouts
- 1 cup chopped bok choy

Directions

1. Over high heat, bring a large pot of water to a boil. Return the water to a boil with the noodles. Boil for about 8 minutes, or until the potatoes are tender. Drain the noodles and set them aside.
2. In a big pot, bring chicken stock, fish sauce, garlic, ginger, lemongrass, and green onions to a boil. Reduce the heat to a low heat and cook for 10 minutes. Combine the chicken, bean sprouts, and bok choy in a mixing bowl. Cook for about 5 minutes, or until the pho is well heated.
3. Using 2 big dishes, divide the cooked noodles. Pour the pho over the noodles and serve right away.

Nutrition Facts

Per Serving:

521 calories; protein 49.8g; carbohydrates 54.4g; fat 13.7g; cholesterol 107.2mg; sodium 3270.2mg.

83. CHOCOLATE PIE RECIPE

Prep: 15 mins

Additional: 1 hr 10 mins

Total: 1 hr 25 mins

Servings: 6

Ingredients

First Layer:

- 1 (8 ounce) package cream cheese (such as Philadelphia®), softened
- 1 cup frozen whipped topping (such as Cool Whip®), thawed
- 1 cup confectioners' sugar
- 1 (9 inch) prepared graham cracker crust

Second Layer:

- 2 (3.9 ounce) packages instant chocolate pudding mix
- 3 cups milk

Third Layer:

- 1 cup frozen whipped topping (such as Cool Whip®), thawed - or to taste

Directions

1. In a mixing bowl, combine cream cheese, 1 cup whipped topping, and confectioners' sugar; spread into the prepared graham cracker crust.
2. In a mixing bowl, combine the chocolate pudding mix and milk; pour over the cream cheese layer before it sets. Refrigerate for 10 minutes or until pudding has set.
3. 1 cup whipped topping on top; chill for at least 1 hour more before serving.

Nutrition Facts

Per Serving:

687 calories; protein 9.7g; carbohydrates 91.2g; fat 32.4g; cholesterol 50.8mg; sodium 914.6mg.

84. BEARNAISE GRAMMA'S RECIPE

Prep: 10 mins

Cook: 10 mins

Total: 20 mins

Servings: 16

Ingredients

- ¼ cup dry white wine
- ¼ cup rice vinegar
- 2 tbsps chopped shallot
- 1 tsp chopped fresh tarragon
- 1 tsp ground black pepper
- 6 large egg yolks
- 4 tsps hot water
- 1 tsp salt
- 1 dash hot sauce
- 1 cup melted butter

Directions

1. In a saucepan, combine white wine, vinegar, shallot, tarragon, and black pepper; bring to a boil. Reduce heat to low and cook for 5 to 10 minutes, or until the mixture has been reduced to approximately 1/4 cup.
2. In a mixing basin, whisk together the egg yolks, boiling water, salt, and spicy sauce until thoroughly combined, about 2 minutes.
3. Over simmering water, pour the white wine mixture into the top of a double boiler. Whisk the egg yolk mixture into the wine mixture until it is thoroughly combined. Pour in the butter and whisk for 5 minutes, or until the sauce is smooth and thickened.

Cook's Notes:

Rice vinegar can be replaced with white wine vinegar. Shallots can be replaced with green onions.

Instead of whisking, you can puree the egg yolk mixture for 1 minute in a blender.

Nutrition Facts

Per Serving:

126 calories; protein 1.2g; carbohydrates 0.6g; fat 13.2g; cholesterol 107.3mg; sodium 232.1mg.

85. HOT PEPPER SHRIMP

Total: 30 mins

Yield: 4 to 6

Ingredients

- ¼ cup vegetable oil
- ½ cup finely chopped onion
- 4 garlic cloves, minced
- 8 scallions, 2 minced and 6 cut into 1-inch lengths
- one 2-inch piece of fresh ginger, peeled and minced
- 6 tbsps thyme leaves
- 2 tbsps sweet paprika
- 2 tsps ground allspice
- ½ Scotch bonnet or habanero chile, stemmed and minced
- Koshar salt
- Pepper
- 20 extra-large shell-on shrimp, deveined (see Note)
- 2 tbsps white wine vinegar

Directions

1. 2 tbsps oil, heated in a large nonstick skillet Season with salt and pepper and sauté over high heat until the onions, garlic, minced scallions, ginger, thyme, paprika, allspice, and chile are softened and beginning to brown, about 5 minutes. Scrape the mixture into a basin.
2. Heat the remaining 2 tbsps of oil in the same skillet. Season the shrimp with salt and pepper and cook, rotating once, over high heat until curled, about 4 minutes. Add the remaining scallions and the vinegar to the skillet with the sautéed aromatics. Cook for 3 minutes, stirring occasionally, until the shrimp are evenly coated and the scallions are softened. Place the shrimp on a serving plate and serve.

Notes

Remove the intestinal vein from shell-on shrimp by slitting them down the back with kitchen shears and rinsing well.

86. JAMAICAN RUB

Ingredients

- ¼ cup plus 2 tbsps Scotch bonnet or habanero hot sauce
- 3 scallions (minced)
- 2 tbsps vegetable oil
- 2 tsps ground allspice
- 2 tsps kosher salt
- 1 tsp ground cinnamon

Directions

1. To make a paste, combine all of the ingredients.
2. Salad of tomato and shredded cabbage with garlic vinaigrette to serve.

87. JAMAICAN BOK CHOY

Ingredients

- 1 tbsp olive oil
- 16 heads of baby bok choy, trimmed, or 4 pounds large bok choy, leaves and upper stems only, cut into 2-inch pieces
- 2 garlic cloves, minced
- 1 to 2 tsps seeded minced Scotch bonnet chile
- 1 tbsp unsalted butter
- salt and freshly ground pepper

Directions

1. In a large enameled casserole or a large wok, heat the oil. Stir-fry the bok choy for 3 minutes over moderately high heat, or until it begins to wilt. Stir in the garlic and chile and simmer for 1 minute, or until the garlic is fragrant. Add the butter and mix well. Serve immediately after seasoning with salt and pepper.

88. TERIYAKI CHICKEN BOK CHOY

Total: 15 mins

Yield: 2 to 4

Ingredients

- 1 pound baby bok choy
- 2 tbsps grapeseed or canola oil (or other high flashpoint oil)
- ¾ pound ground chicken
- ½ medium onion, diced
- 2 tbsps soy sauce
- 2 tbsps sake or dry vermouth
- 2 tbsps brown sugar
- 2 tsps rice vinegar

Directions

1. Trim the bok choy stems and ends. Set aside after washing and drying with paper towels.
2. Over medium-high heat, heat a large skillet or wok. After that, add the onion and the oil. Add the ground chicken after cooking for 1-2 minutes or until tender. Cook for about 5 minutes, stirring regularly to break up and turn the chicken, or until the chicken is evenly browned and cooked through.
3. Cook for 1 minute after adding the soy sauce, sake (or vermouth), brown sugar, and rice vinegar. Cook for 1 minute, or until the bok choy is cooked and the sauce is thoroughly heated. Warm the dish before serving.

89. SPICY PORK BOK CHOY

Total: 15 mins

Yield: 2 to 4

Ingredients

- 1 pound baby bok choy
- 1 tbsp grapeseed or canola oil (or other high flashpoint oil)
- 3 cloves garlic (minced)
- ¾ pound ground pork
- 1 tbsp soy sauce
- 1 tbsp chili garlic sauce
- ½ tsp sesame seed oil

Directions

1. Trim the bok choy stems and ends. Set aside after washing and drying with paper towels.
2. Over medium-high heat, heat a large skillet or wok. Stir in the garlic after adding the oil. Add the pork and cook for about 1 minute, or until tender. Cook for 3-5 minutes, stirring occasionally to break up and turn the pork, or until it is lightly browned and cooked through.
3. Combine the soy sauce, chili garlic sauce, and sesame seed oil in a large mixing bowl. Stir in the bok choy after 1 minute of cooking. Cook for 1 minute, or until the bok choy is slightly wilted and soft. Warm the dish before serving.

90. PORK DUMPLINGS WITH CHILE-SESAME SAUCE

Total: 1 hr 30 mins

Yield: about 5 dozen dumplings

Ingredients
Dumplings

- 3 tbsps vegetable oil
- ½ pound shiitake mushrooms, stems discarded and caps thinly sliced
- 6 large scallions, light green parts, finely chopped
- ¾ pound baby bok choy, finely chopped
- 1 medium carrot, coarsely shredded
- 4 large garlic cloves, finely chopped
- 2 tbsps minced fresh ginger
- ¼ cup low-sodium soy sauce
- 2 tsps mirin or sweet sherry
- 1 tsp Asian chile-garlic sauce
- koshar salt
- 1 pound ground pork
- 2 packages wonton wrappers
- 2 tbsps cornstarch mixed with 1 cup of water

Sauce

- 1 cup low-sodium soy sauce
- ¼ cup Chinese black bean sauce
- ¼ cup toasted sesame oil
- 4 tsps minced fresh ginger
- 4 tsps Asian chile-garlic sauce
- 4 tsps mirin or sweet sherry

Directions
Make the Dumplings

1. Heat the oil in a skillet until it shimmers. Stir-fry the shiitake, scallions, bok choy, and carrot for 5 minutes over high heat, or until tender. Cook for 3 minutes, or until the liquid has evaporated, adding the garlic, ginger, soy sauce, mirin, and chile-garlic sauce. Season with salt and pepper. Refrigerate for 15 minutes after transferring to a bowl.
2. Wax paper should be used to line a big baking sheet. Mix in the pork to the filling. Brush 3 wonton wrappers with the cornstarch solution on a work surface, then scoop a scant tbsp of the filling into the center. Seal the edges, squeezing out any trapped air. Fold the wrappers over to make triangles. Trim the wrappers with scissors, leaving a 1/4-inch rim around the

filling. Place the dumplings seam side up on the baking pan. Cover the dumplings with a damp paper towel to keep them warm. Replace the wonton wrappers and filling with the remaining wonton wrappers and filling.

Make the Sauce

1. In a medium mixing bowl, combine all of the ingredients.
2. Bring a wok or a large skillet to a boil with 2 inches of water. Arrange the dumplings in a double-tiered bamboo steamer lined with oiled wax paper, working in batches, and place the steamer over boiling water. Cover and steam the dumplings for 6 minutes, or until the filling is cooked through and firm.
3. 1 cup of the sauce should be used to toss the dumplings in. Transfer the dumplings to a dish using a slotted spoon. Along with the leftover chile-sesame sauce, serve.
4. Prepare ahead of time
5. The sauce can be stored in the refrigerator for up to three days. Uncooked dumplings can be frozen in a single layer on a parchment-lined baking sheet for up to a month after being moved to an airtight container.

91. BOK CHOY CHOW MEIN

Total: 30 mins

Yield: 2 to 3

Ingredients

- 8 ounces yellow Chinese egg noodles
- 2 tbsps soy sauce
- 2 tbsps oyster sauce
- 1 tbsp hoisin
- 1 tbsp rice vinegar
- 1 tsp brown sugar
- 2 tbsps water
- 2 tbsps vegetable oil
- 4 cloves garlic, minced
- ½ medium onion, chopped
- 1 tbsp minced fresh ginger
- ½ pound baby bok choy
- ½ medium bell pepper, seeded and sliced

Directions

1. Follow the package directions for cooking the noodles. Drain and set aside after rinsing under cold water.
2. Combine soy sauce, oyster sauce, hoisin, rice vinegar, brown sugar, and water in a medium mixing basin. Set aside the sauce mixture.
3. Over medium-high heat, heat a large pan or wok. Stir in the garlic, onion, and ginger with the oil. Cook, stirring occasionally, until the garlic and onions are tender and fragrant, about 2 to 3 minutes.
4. Add the bok choy and bell peppers and mix well. Cook until the vegetables are soft, about 2 to 3 minutes.
5. Toss in the noodles with the sauce mixture in the pan. Stir until everything is well combined, about 2 minutes. Serve immediately.

92. BOK CHOY WITH SHIITAKE MUSHROOMS

Total: 15 mins

Yield: 2 to 4

Ingredients

- 1 pound baby bok choy
- 1 tbsp grapeseed or canola oil (or other high flashpoint oil)
- 2 tbsps sliced shallots
- 3 cloves garlic (minced)
- ½ pound shiitake mushrooms (sliced)
- 1 tbsp fish sauce
- 1 tsp rice vinegar
- ½ tsp sugar
- Fresh cracked black pepper (to taste)

Directions

1. Trim the bok choy stems and ends. Set aside after washing and drying with paper towels.
2. Over medium-high heat, heat a large skillet or wok. Stir in the garlic and shallots after adding the oil. Stir in the shiitake mushrooms after cooking for 1-2 minutes, or until soft. Cook the mushrooms for 2-3 minutes, stirring periodically, or until they are browned and have released some of their liquid.
3. Add the bok choy and mix well. Cook for 1-2 minutes, or until bok choy has wilted slightly.
4. Cook for about 1 minute, or until cooked through, stirring in the fish sauce, rice vinegar, sugar, and black pepper. Warm the dish before serving.

93. JAMAICAN CHICKEN STIR-FRY

Ingredients

- 2 large egg whites
- 2 tsps cornstarch
- 2 tbsps plus 2 tsps soy sauce
- 1 pound skinless, boneless chicken breast halves, cut crosswise into 1/2-inch-thick slices
- Salt and freshly ground pepper
- Mixture of Jamaican Jardinière Pickles—2 garlic cloves, 2 ginger slices, 1 to 2 Scotch bonnet chile halves, 8 cauliflower florets, 2 carrot sticks, 2 bell pepper strips
- 1 tbsp vegetable oil
- 2 small tomatoes, coarsely chopped
- ½ tsp Asian sesame oil
- ¼ cup pickling liquid from the jar of the Jamaican Jardinière Pickles
- Steamed rice, for serving

Directions

1. Combine the egg whites, cornstarch, and 2 tbsps soy sauce in a shallow bowl. Turn in the chicken and season with a touch of salt and pepper. Refrigerate for 30 minutes before serving.
2. Slivers of pickled garlic and ginger should be used. Seed and finely slice the Scotch bonnet chile pickle. Cut the rest of the pickles into small pieces.
3. Preheat a wok to high heat. Heat the vegetable oil until it begins to smoke. Stir in the pickled garlic and ginger for 10 seconds. Stir in the chicken and simmer for 3 minutes, or until almost done. Stir in the tomatoes and cook for 1 minute. Stir-fry for 10 seconds to combine the pickled veggies and chiles, pickling liquid, and the remaining 2 tbsps of soy sauce. Stir in the sesame oil after seasoning with salt and pepper. Serve with steaming rice right away.

94. GREENS-STUFFED PATTIES

Active: 1 hr

Total: 2 hrs

Yield: Makes 2 dozen

Ingredients

- ½ each green, red and yellow bell pepper, chopped
- 5 scallions, coarsely chopped
- 4 garlic cloves, crushed
- 1 medium onion, coarsely chopped
- 1 Scotch bonnet or habanero chile, stemmed and halved
- ¼ cup extra-virgin olive oil
- Kosher salt
- Pepper
- Pepper pounds Swiss chard, stems removed and leaves coarsely chopped (21 lightly packed cups)
- 4 ounces cream cheese, softened
- 30 sheets phyllo dough, from 2 packages (see Note)
- 1 stick unsalted butter, melted
- 1 large egg, beaten with 1 tbsp water

Directions

1. Combine the bell peppers, chopped scallions, garlic, onion, and Scotch bonnet in a food processor. Pulse until the mixture is very finely chopped.
2. Heat the olive oil in a big, deep skillet until it shimmers. Add a good tsp of salt and pepper to the chopped vegetable combination. Cook, turning occasionally, until the veggies are softened and just beginning to brown, about 8 minutes over moderately high heat. Cook, stirring in one-third of the Swiss chard at a time, until the greens are soft and any liquid has evaporated, about 5 minutes per batch. Remove the pan from the heat and mix in the cream cheese until completely combined. Using salt and pepper, season the filling. Scrape the filling into a bowl and set aside to cool completely before chilling for 30 minutes.
3. Preheat the oven to 350 ° Fahrenheit. Preheat oven to 350°F. Line two baking pans with parchment paper. 1 sheet of phyllo should be placed on a work surface with the long side facing you. Brush the phyllo with melted butter and top with another sheet. Brush and stack the sheets until you have a stack of 5 buttered sheets. Cut the phyllo crosswise into four 4-by-12-inch strips with a sharp knife. Using a moist cloth, cover the leftover phyllo.
4. 2 tbsps filling, 1/2 inch from the top of 1 phyllo strip; fold the other corner over the filling to form a triangle. Continue folding the triangle down and over until the strip reaches the end.

Brush the patties with melted butter and place on a preheated baking sheet. Steps 3 and 4 should be repeated with the leftover phyllo dough and filling.

5. Brush the egg wash on the patties. Make slits 1/2 inch apart over the top of each patty with a paring knife, being careful not to cut through to the filling. Bake for 25 minutes, or until golden brown, turning the pans halfway through. Allow 5 minutes to cool before serving.

Notes

Stack and trim your phyllo sheets to 12 by 16 inches if required.

95. CHICKEN STEW

Active: 30 mins

Total: 1 hr 30 mins

Yield: 6

Ingredients

- 3 pounds chicken thighs
- Kosher salt
- Freshly ground black pepper
- 2 tbsps vegetable oil
- 1 medium onion, chopped
- 4 garlic cloves, finely chopped
- 2 tbsps finely chopped fresh ginger
- 1 pound carrots, sliced
- 1 pound potatoes, peeled and cut into cubes
- ½ head cabbage, cut into chunks
- 2 bay leaves
- 1 whole Scotch bonnet pepper
- 3 sprigs fresh thyme
- 3 cups water
- 1 tbsp Worcestershire sauce
- Cooked white rice for serving

Directions

1. 2 1/2 tsps salt and 1 tsp pepper to season the chicken. Brown the chicken in batches, about 6 minutes per batch, in a large heavy saucepan over medium high heat until hot. As soon as they've browned, transfer them to a dish.
2. Cook, stirring periodically, until the onion, garlic, and ginger are golden, about 5 to 7 minutes. Carrots, potatoes, cabbage, bay leaves, Scotch bonnet pepper, thyme, water, and

Worcestershire sauce are added to the stew. Return the chicken to the pot, along with any accumulated juices, and cover. Cook the stew for 1 hour, or until the chicken is extremely soft. To taste, season with salt and pepper. Serve with rice that has been prepared.

96. CHICKEN AND POTATO CURRY

Active: 20 mins

Total: 50 mins

Yield: 4 to 6

Ingredients

- 2 tbsps vegetable oil
- 1 yellow onion, chopped
- 2 garlic cloves, minced
- One 1-inch piece fresh ginger, peeled and minced
- 1 Scotch bonnet or habanero chile, minced
- 3 tbsps Jamaican curry powder
- 1 cup chicken stock
- One 13 1/2-ounce can coconut milk, well shaken
- 1 tsp salt
- 1 1/2 pounds potatoes, peeled and cut into 3/4-inch cubes
- 1 pound boneless, skinless chicken breasts, thinly sliced
- 2 tsps white vinegar
- Coarsely chopped cilantro leaves, for garnish

Directions

1. In a large saucepan over moderately high heat, heat the vegetable oil. Cook, turning occasionally, until the onion, garlic, and ginger are cooked, about 5 to 8 minutes.
2. Cook for 2 minutes, stirring occasionally, with the Scotch bonnet pepper and curry powder. Bring to a boil the chicken stock, coconut milk, and salt. Reduce the heat to low and simmer, turning occasionally, for 15 minutes, or until the potatoes are soft when pierced with a fork.
3. Cook for 5 to 8 minutes, or until the chicken is cooked through. After that, add the vinegar and serve the chicken curry in bowls with chopped cilantro on top.

97. JAMAICAN COCO BREAD

Active: 25 mins

Total: 2 hrs 5 mins

Yield: 8

Ingredients

- 6 tbsps unrefined coconut oil, plus more melted oil for greasing and brushing
- 1 cup full-fat well-shaken and stirred coconut milk (from a 13.5-ounce can)
- ¼ cup granulated sugar
- 1 tsp kosher salt
- 1 (1/4-ounce) envelope active dry yeast (2 1/4 tsps)
- 1 large egg, lightly beaten
- 3 1/2 cups (about 14 7/8 ounces) all-purpose flour, plus more for dusting and rolling

Directions

1. Line a large rimmed baking sheet with parchment paper and lightly coat a big bowl with melted coconut oil. In a medium microwaveable bowl, combine the coconut oil, coconut milk, sugar, and salt; microwave on HIGH for 1 minute, or until the sugar has dissolved and the oil has melted. (Alternatively, 1 minute on low heat in a small saucepan.) To blend everything, whisk it together. Combine the yeast and the egg in a large mixing bowl. To make a soft dough, combine the flour and coconut milk mixture.

2. Gently knead the dough on a lightly floured surface for about 2 minutes, or until smooth and thoroughly mixed. Avoid adding extra flour; the softer the dough, the lighter and more tender the coco bread will be. Place dough in a greased mixing basin and cover with a clean kitchen towel. Allow dough to rise for 1 hour in a warm (75°F) location.

3. Preheat the oven to 350 ° Fahrenheit and set the rack in the middle. Using a lightly floured surface, punch down the dough. Cut the dough in half with a bread knife or a bench scraper, then into four equal sections. Roll each part into a 6- to 7-inch oval the size of your hand. A quarter-inch thick oval should be used. To make a semicircle, brush the surface of each oval with melted coconut oil and fold in half crosswise. More melted coconut oil should be brushed on top. Place the folded dough 1 to 2 inches apart on the prepared baking sheet and set it to rest for 15 minutes at room temperature. Preheat oven to 350°F and bake for 17 minutes, or until golden brown. Before serving, let aside for 5 minutes to cool. Warm food is best.

98. JAMAICAN JARDINIÈRE PICKLES

Ingredients

- 1 1/2 pounds cauliflower, separated into small florets
- 4 medium carrots, cut into 3-by-1/2-inch sticks
- 1 large red bell pepper, cut into 1/2-inch-thick strips
- 12 Scotch bonnet or habanero chiles, 6 halved
- 6 large garlic cloves, peeled
- 6 large thyme sprigs
- One 2-inch piece of ginger, peeled and sliced 1/4 inch thick
- 1 quart white vinegar, plus more if needed
- 1/3 cup whole allspice berries, 1 tbsp crushed
- 1 cup sugar
- ¼ cup kosher salt
- 1 tbsp whole black peppercorns, coarsely crushed

Directions

1. Blanch the cauliflower for 1 minute in a medium saucepan of boiling water. Drain and set aside to cool.
2. Pack the cauliflower, carrots, bell pepper, chiles, garlic cloves, thyme sprigs, and ginger slices in a beautiful design in one 2 1/2-quart heatproof jar or a few smaller jars.
3. Bring the vinegar, allspice, sugar, salt, and peppercorns to a boil in a saucepan. Simmer, stirring occasionally, until the sugar has dissolved. Fill the jar halfway with pickling liquid. Add extra vinegar if necessary to cover the vegetables. Allow the pickles to cool completely before covering with a lid and storing in the refrigerator for at least 10 days.

99. CORNBREAD FRITTERS

Ingredients

- 1 cup all-purpose flour
- ½ cup cornmeal
- 1 ½ tbsps sugar
- ¾ tsp salt
- ¼ tsp baking powder
- 1/8 tsp baking soda
- ¾ cup water
- 2 tsps vegetable oil, plus more for frying

Directions

1. Combine the flour, cornmeal, sugar, salt, baking powder, and baking soda in a mixing dish. Stir in the water and 2 tsps of oil with a wooden spoon until thoroughly combined. Cover with plastic wrap and set aside for 1 hour at room temperature.
2. 1 inch of oil, heated to 350° in a medium saucepan Roll tbsp-size pieces of dough about 3 inches long using well-oiled hands, then flatten slightly and drop into the heated oil. Peel the dough off your hands if it sticks to them; don't bother about the shape. Fry 3 or 4 fritters at a time, about 2 minutes per side, until golden brown. Transfer the fritters to a rack positioned over a baking sheet to drain using a slotted spoon. If required, adjust the heat to keep the temperature at 350°. Serve right away.

100. JAMAICAN GIN AND GINGERS

Ingredients

- ½ cup sugar
- ¼ cup chopped candied ginger
- Honey
- 2 ½ cups gin
- 6 ⅔ cups cold Jamaican ginger beer

Directions

1. Combine the sugar and candied ginger in a mini-processor and grind to a coarse powder. Fill a small basin halfway with water. Honey the rims of ten red wine glasses or water goblets lightly. Dip the glasses in the ginger sugar and then freeze until ready to use, if desired; do not freeze your best crystal.
2. 1/4 cup gin in each glass, half-filled with ice cubes Fill each glass with 2/3 cup ginger beer and serve.

101. JERK HOT WINGS

Active: 15 mins

Total: 1 hr

Yield: 2 to 4

Ingredients

- 2 tbsps all-purpose flour
- 1 tsp salt
- ½ tsp dried garlic
- ½ tsp dried onion
- ½ tsp dried thyme
- 2 pounds chicken wingettes and drumettes (see Note)
- 2 ½ tbsps red hot sauce, preferably Frank's Red Hot
- 2 tbsps unsalted butter, melted
- 1 tsp jerk paste
- Fresh thyme leaves, for sprinkling

Directions

1. Preheat the oven to 500 ° Fahrenheit. Spray a large baking sheet with vegetable oil after lining it with foil. Combine the flour, salt, garlic, onion, and thyme in a mixing basin. Toss in the chicken to coat it. Spray the chicken with vegetable oil and spread it out on the baking pan in a single layer. Roast for 45 minutes, turning once or twice, until the chicken is browned and crispy.
2. Whisk together the hot sauce, butter, and jerk paste in a mixing bowl. Toss the chicken wings with the sauce. Serve with a sprinkling of fresh thyme leaves.

Notes

Wingettes and drumettes are frequently sold in different packages.

102. BLACK CAKE

Active: 1 hr

Total: 5 hrs

Yield: Makes two 9-inch cakes

Ingredients

- ¾ cup pitted prunes (about 14-16 prunes depending on size)
- ¾ cup raisins (8 ounces)
- ¾ cup dried currants (3 1/2 ounces)
- ¾ cup dried unsweetened cherries (3 1/2 ounces)
- 2 ½ cups white rum, divided
- 1 ½ cups Manischewitz wine
- 1 cup (2 sticks) unsalted butter, softened, plus more for pans
- 2 ½ cups dark brown sugar (1 pound)
- 4 large eggs
- 2 tsps finely grated lime zest (from 1 lime)
- 2 tsps pure vanilla extract
- 1 tbsp pure almond extract
- 1 ½ cups unbleached all-purpose flour, plus more for cake pans (7 ounces)
- 2 tsps baking powder
- 1 tbsp ground allspice
- 2 tsps ground nutmeg
- ¼ plus 1 tbsp dark unsulfured molasses
- ¼ cup raw sliced almonds (1 ounce)

Directions

1. Combine the prunes, raisins, currants, dried cherries, 1 1/2 cup rum, and Manischewitz wine in a big container with a tight-fitting lid. Combine all ingredients in a mixing bowl, cover, and leave aside for at least two days (and up to 6 months).
2. Preheat the oven to 250°F when you're ready to bake. Butter two 9-inch round cake pans lightly and line the bottoms with parchment paper. Lightly grease the parchment, then flour the insides of the cake pans and tap out any excess flour.
3. In a food processor, combine the soaked dry fruit and soaking liquid. Pulse until a rough paste develops, leaving a few pieces of fruit intact. Remove from the equation.
4. In a stand mixer fitted with the paddle attachment, beat the butter and brown sugar on medium speed until frothy and aerated, about 8 minutes. One at a time, add the eggs to the mixture, beating after each addition. Combine the lime zest, vanilla essence, and almond extract in a mixing bowl.

5. In a small mixing bowl, combine the dry ingredients flour, baking powder, allspice, and nutmeg. Gently fold the dry ingredients into the butter mixture in two batches on the lowest speed, just until combined. Combine the crushed dried-fruit combination and the molasses in a mixing bowl. Remove the bowl from the stand mixer and use a rubber spatula to fold in the almonds.

6. Smooth the tops of the cakes with a rubber spatula after dividing the batter amongst the prepared cake pans. Bake for 1 hour, then decrease to 225°F and bake for another 2 1/2 to 3 hours, or until a cake tester inserted in the center comes out clean. Allow 10 minutes for the cakes to cool on a wire rack before brushing the tops with the reserved 1 cup rum. Allow another 10 minutes for the cakes to rest before brushing and chilling them again until all of the rum has been absorbed.

7. Wrap the cakes in wax paper and then foil after inverting them onto big plates. Keep the black cake at room temperature for at least one day and up to one month. To serve, cut into wedges.

103. STEW PEAS AND SPINNERS

Active: 30 mins

Total: 1 hr 25 mins

Servings: 6

Ingredients
For the red peas:

- 2 cups (14 ounces) dried red kidney beans
- 10 large garlic cloves (5 whole, 5 minced), divided
- 1 (13.5-ounce) can full-fat coconut milk
- 1 small Yellow onion, choped
- 1 cup chopped scallions, plus more for garnish (about 8 scallions)
- 1 large or 2 small carrots (3 ounces total), diced
- ¼ cup fresh thyme leaves, chopped
- ½ Scotch bonnet (or habanero) pepper, seeds and veins removed, finely chopped

For the spinners:

- ¾ cup all-purpose flour
- 1 ½ tsps kosher salt
- 1/3 cup water

For finishing the stew:

- 2 tbsps coconut oil
- 1 tbsp kosher salt

- 1 tsp coarsely ground black pepper
- 1 tsp ground allspice
- 1/3 cup finely chopped red bell pepper
- 1/3 cup finely chopped green bell pepper
- 1/3 cup cup finely chopped yellow bell pepper
- Cooked white parboiled rice, for serving

Directions

1. Make the red peas: Sort and rinse the red kidney beans the night before you plan to cook them. Place the 5 entire garlic cloves in a medium bowl with 6 cups of water. Allow to sit at room temperature overnight.
2. Transfer the beans, whole garlic cloves, and soaking liquid to a big pot the next day. Bring the coconut milk to a boil in a large pot over high heat; reduce the heat to low, cover, and cook for 20 minutes.
3. Combine the minced garlic, onion, scallions, carrots, thyme, and Scotch Bonnet peppers in a large mixing bowl. Stir to incorporate, then reduce to a low heat and continue to cook for 20 to 25 minutes, or until the red beans are soft and "break" when squeezed with the back of a spoon.
4. Make the spinners while the beans are simmering: Whisk together the flour, salt, and water in a mixing basin; add the water and mix the ingredients together with your hands to produce a dough that is just slightly wet enough to stick to your hands without leaving any residue. Knead the dough for approximately 2 minutes on a floured work surface.
5. Form the dough into a disc and score it into quarters, then into thirds for each quarter. Cut the dough along the scoring lines with a sharp knife or bench scraper. Roll each piece of dough between your palms to form a long, thick dumpling that measures 3 to 3 1/2 inches in length and 1/4 to 1/2 inch in thickness.
6. Finish the stew by adding 1/4 cup water and the coconut oil when the beans are soft. Place each dumpling in the pot with care. Cook, covered, for another 15 to 20 minutes, or until the dumplings are firm. Combine the salt, black pepper, and allspice in a mixing bowl. Remove the pot from the heat and add the bell peppers, stirring to combine. Season to taste and serve with extra chopped scallions on top of freshly cooked rice.

104. JAMAICAN BRAISED OXTAILS WITH CARROTS AND CHILES

Active: 1 hr 20 mins

Total: 3 hrs 20 mins

Servings: 4

Ingredients

- 2 pounds oxtails, cut into 2-inch pieces
- 2 small yellow onions, finely chopped
- 1 cup thinly sliced scallions (white and light green parts), plus sliced dark green tops, for garnish
- 1/3 cup packed light brown sugar
- 2 tbsps soy sauce
- 2 tbsps ground allspice
- 1 tbsp black pepper
- 1 tbsp Worcestershire sauce
- 2 ½ tsps kosher salt, or to taste
- 4 medium garlic cloves, smashed
- 2 fresh Scotch bonnet chiles, stemmed and chopped
- 1 ¼ cups dried butter beans
- 2 tbsps vegetable oil
- 4 cups water, divided
- 2 tsps fresh thyme leaves
- 3 medium carrots, chopped into 1 ½-inch pieces

Directions

1. In a large mixing bowl, whisk together the oxtails, onions, white and light green scallion pieces, brown sugar, soy sauce, allspice, black pepper, Worcestershire sauce, salt, garlic, and chilies. Wrap the dish in plastic wrap. Fill a separate big basin with cold water to cover the beans by about 3 inches. Wrap the dish in plastic wrap. Refrigerate both bowls for at least 8 hours or up to 12 hours.
2. Drain the beans and lay them aside until you're ready to use them. In a large Dutch oven, heat the oil over medium-high heat until it shimmers. Add the oxtails using a slotted spoon or tongs, reserving the marinade in the bowl. Cook oxtails for 15 minutes, flipping occasionally, until uniformly browned on all sides. Remove the pan from the heat.
3. Take the oxtails out of the Dutch oven and set them aside. Return the oxtails to the Dutch oven after discarding the drippings. Add the beans, oxtail marinade, 3 cups water, and thyme to the pot.

4. Cook, covered, over low heat, stirring mixture and rotating oxtails every 30 minutes and adjusting heat as required to maintain a very low simmer, until flesh is cooked but not falling apart when pierced with a paring knife, about 2 hours.

5. Cover and cook over low, undisturbed heat, increasing heat as needed to maintain a very low simmer, until carrots are soft and sauce begins to thicken, about 45 minutes, scraping fat from surface as needed. Stir in the remaining 1 cup water a little at a time until the sauce achieves a gravy consistency.

6. Remove oxtails from pot if desired; shred meat and discard bones. Return the shredded meat to the pot. Divide the mixture evenly among the bowls and top with the dark green scallion segments that were set aside.

7. Prepare ahead of time

8. Oxtails can be prepared up to three days ahead of time.

105. PAN-SEARED CHICKEN BREASTS WITH JAMAICAN CURRY

Total: 45 mins

Yield: 4

Ingredients

- 2 tsps vegetable oil
- 1 scallion, minced
- 2 tsps curry powder
- 2 tsps minced fresh ginger
- ½ tsp ground allspice
- ½ tsp Scotch bonnet hot sauce (see Note)
- Four 6-ounce boneless chicken breast halves, with skin
- Curry
- Salt and freshly ground pepper
- 2 tbsps vegetable oil
- 1 medium onion, thinly sliced
- 1 scallion, thinly sliced
- 1 tsp curry powder
- 2 tsps minced fresh ginger
- ¼ tsp ground allspice
- ½ tsp Scotch bonnet hot sauce
- 1 ½ cups water
- 1 tbsp unsalted butter
- Sliced Salad, for serving

Directions

1. Combine the oil, scallion, curry powder, ginger, allspice, and hot sauce in a shallow dish. Turn the chicken breasts to cover them with the sauce. Refrigerate overnight, covered.
2. Season the chicken with salt and pepper after removing it from the marinade. Heat the oil in a big skillet. Place the chicken skin side down in the pan. Cook for 2 minutes over moderately high heat, or until the skin browns. Reduce the heat to medium and cook for another 4 minutes, or until the skin is crisp. Reduce the heat to low, turn the chicken, and cook for another 7 minutes, or until it is completely white. Place the chicken on a serving plate.
3. Add the onion to the skillet and simmer, turning regularly, for 6 minutes, or until softened. Cook, stirring constantly, for 5 minutes, until the scallion, curry, ginger, allspice, and spicy sauce are fragrant. Bring the water to a boil over high heat, scraping off any browned bits from the pan's bottom. Cook for 5 minutes, or until the sauce has reduced to about 1 cup.
4. Return the chicken to the skillet, skin side up, and cook for 2 minutes, or until heated through. Place the chicken on serving platters. Season the curry sauce with salt and pepper after mixing in the butter. Serve the breasts with the sauce and the Sliced Salad on the side.

106. DOUGH ORNAMENT RECIPE

Servings: 1

Yield: 15 ornaments

Ingredients

- 4 cups all-purpose flour
- 1 cup salt
- 1 ½ cups warm water

Directions

1. Preheat the oven to 325°F (165 ° C).
2. Combine flour and salt in a large mixing bowl. Gradually pour in the water, stirring constantly with a large spoon. Complete the mixing process by using your hands. Knead until the dough is soft and malleable.
3. Roll out 1/8 inch thick on a floured surface. Cookie cutters are used to make the shapes. Place the cookies on cookie sheets. Make a hole in the top of the ornament using a toothpick for stringing. Bake for 1 hour at 325 ° F (165 ° C) until firm. To keep the look, use paint and varnish.

Nutrition Facts

Per Serving:

1820 calories; protein 51.6g; carbohydrates 381.5g; fat 4.9g; cholesterol 0mg; sodium 93427.4mg.

107. HAITIAN BEEF PATTIES

Prep: 45 mins

Cook: 1 hr 5 mins

Additional: 8 hrs 35 mins

Total: 10 hrs 25 mins

Servings: 12

Ingredients

- 3 cups all-purpose flour
- 1 cup cold water
- 1 tsp salt
- 1 cup vegetable shortening
- ¼ cup butter
- 2 shallots, chopped
- 2 tsps chopped fresh parsley
- 1 clove garlic, chopped
- 1 pinch chile powder, or to taste
- 1 pound ground beef
- 1 onion, diced
- 1 tbsp beef broth
- 1 egg yolk, beaten

Directions

1. In a large mixing bowl, sift the flour. In the center, dig a well and fill it with water and salt. With a wooden spoon, lightly combine the ingredients until a dough forms. Refrigerate for 30 minutes after wrapping in plastic wrap.
2. In a small mixing dish, combine shortening and butter.
3. Transfer dough to a flat work surface and roll into a 1/4-inch-thick rectangle. 1/2 of the shortening mixture should be spread on top. Fold one side of the rectangle into the middle and top with the remaining shortening. Like a letter, fold the other side of the rectangle over the first. Make a 1/4-inch-thick rectangle and fold it in thirds. Once more, repeat the rolling and folding operation.
4. Wrap dough in plastic wrap and chill for 8 to 12 hours.
5. Fill a baking pan halfway with water and place it on the oven's bottom rack. Preheat the oven to 375 ° Fahrenheit (190 ° C).

6. Using a mortar and pestle, pound shallots, parsley, garlic, and chili powder into a paste.

7. Cook and stir the beef in a large skillet over medium heat until it is browned, about 5 minutes. Combine the shallot paste, onion, and beef broth in a mixing bowl. Cover and cook, stirring regularly, for about 10 minutes, or until juices are absorbed. Allow 5 minutes for cooling.
8. Roll cooled dough into a 1/2-inch thick rectangle. 2 1/2-inch circles should be cut out. 1 1/3 tbsp of the beef mixture should be placed on one edge of each circle. To seal the edges, fold them over and lightly press them together.
9. Fill the patties with the filling and place them on a baking pan. Egg yolk should be brushed on the tops and edges.
10. Bake for 30 minutes in a preheated oven until fluffy. Reduce the oven temperature to 300 ° F (150 ° C) and bake for another 20 minutes, or until golden brown.

Cook's Note:

These can also be filled with chicken that has been seasoned.

Nutrition Facts

Per Serving:

386 calories; protein 10.3g; carbohydrates 27.2g; fat 26.2g; cholesterol 50.9mg; sodium 250.7mg.

108. EASY CHICKEN MADRAS RECIPE

Prep: 20 mins

Cook: 1 hr 5 mins

Total: 1 hr 25 mins

Servings: 4

Ingredients

- 2 onions, coarsely chopped
- 2 red chile peppers, stemmed and seeded
- 1 (2 inch) piece fresh ginger, grated
- 2 cloves garlic
- 1 splash water, or as needed
- salt and ground black pepper to taste
- 1 tbsp vegetable oil
- ¼ cup Madras curry powder
- 4 skinless, boneless chicken breasts, cut into large chunks
- 1 (14 ounce) can chopped tomatoes
- ½ cup chopped cilantro, or to taste

Directions

1. In a blender, combine the onions, chile peppers, ginger, and garlic with a splash of water. Season with salt and pepper after blending into a smooth paste.
2. In a big, high-sided pan, heat the oil over medium heat. Cook for 5 minutes, or until the paste is slightly browned.
3. Over medium-low heat, heat a small skillet. Cook and stir for 2 to 3 minutes, until the Madras curry powder is aromatic. Incorporate into the paste.
4. 5 to 10 minutes, cook and toss the chicken in the spice paste mixture until it is browned. Toss in the tomatoes. Fill the tomato can halfway with water and add it to the mix as well. Simmer for 50 minutes over medium-low heat until liquid is reduced. Salt & pepper to taste. Garnish with cilantro.

Cook's Note:

If you like, you can replace the chicken with 1 pound of veggies or fish.

Nutrition Facts

Per Serving:

246 calories; protein 25.6g; carbohydrates 20.7g; fat 6.8g; cholesterol 58.5mg; sodium 255.7mg.

109. EASIEST FOCACCIA RECIPE

Prep: 30 mins

Cook: 20 mins

Total: 50 mins

Servings: 4

Ingredients

- 1 tsp white sugar
- 1 (.25 ounce) package active dry yeast
- 1/3 cup warm water (110 ° F/45 ° C)
- 2 cups all-purpose flour
- 2 tbsps olive oil
- ¼ tsp salt

Directions

1. Sugar and yeast should be dissolved in warm water in a small bowl. Allow 10 minutes for the mixture to become creamy.
2. Incorporate the yeast mixture and flour in a large mixing basin and stir well to combine. 1 tbsp at a time, stir in more water until all of the flour is absorbed. Turn the dough out onto a lightly floured surface and knead for about 1 minute after it has pulled together.
3. Lightly grease a large mixing bowl, then set the dough in it and turn to coat it in oil. Cover with a moist towel and set aside in a warm place to rise for 30 minutes or until doubled in volume.
4. Preheat the oven to 475 ° Fahrenheit (245 ° C).
5. Deflate the dough and place it on a lightly floured board to knead for a few minutes. Place the dough on a lightly greased baking sheet and pat or roll it into a sheet. Drizzle some oil on the dough and season it with salt.
6. Bake focaccia for 10 to 20 minutes in a preheated oven, depending on crispiness desired. If you like it moist and fluffy, then you'll have to wait only about 10 minutes. You may have to wait 20 minutes if you prefer it crunchier and darker on the outside.

Nutrition Facts

Per Serving:

296 calories; protein 7.1g; carbohydrates 49.4g; fat 7.4g; sodium 147.6mg.

110. SEAFOOD SEASONING RECIPE

Prep: 15 mins

Total: 15 mins

Servings: 180

Ingredients

- 6 ⅓ tbsps salt
- 3 ⅔ tbsps ground celery seed
- 2 ½ tsps dry mustard powder
- 2 ½ tsps red pepper flakes, ground
- 1 ½ tsps ground black pepper
- 1 ½ tsps ground bay leaves
- 1 ½ tsps paprika
- 1 tsp ground cloves
- 1 tsp ground allspice
- 1 tsp ground ginger
- ¾ tsp ground cardamom
- ½ tsp ground cinnamon

Directions

1. In a mixing bowl, combine the salt, celery seed, dry mustard powder, red pepper, black pepper, bay leaves, paprika, cloves, allspice, ginger, cardamom, and cinnamon. Keep the container sealed.

Nutrition Facts

Per Serving:

1 calories; carbohydrates 0.1g; fat 0.1g; sodium 245.7mg.

111. OYSTER STUFFING RECIPE

Prep: 20 mins

Cook: 5 mins

Total: 25 mins

Servings: 8

Ingredients

- 1 tbsp olive oil
- 1 onion, minced
- 2 stalks celery, minced
- 2 (6 ounce) packages bread stuffing mix
- 1 pint shucked oysters
- ½ cup butter, melted
- 1 tsp poultry seasoning, or to taste
- 2 ½ cups hot water or as needed

Directions

1. In a large skillet, heat the olive oil over medium heat and sauté the onion and celery, stirring occasionally, until the onion is translucent, about 5 minutes. Place the vegetables in a large mixing bowl. Combine the stuffing mix, oysters, melted butter, and seasonings in a mixing bowl; add boiling water until desired moistness is achieved. Stuffing will require less moisture if used to stuff a turkey.

Nutrition Facts

Per Serving:

385 calories; protein 15.8g; carbohydrates 41g; fat 17.3g; cholesterol 86.8mg; sodium 887.4mg.

112. OYSTER STEW CHRISTMAS EVE RECIPE

Prep: 10 mins

Cook: 20 mins

Additional: 5 mins

Total: 35 mins

Servings: 6

Ingredients

- ¼ cup butter
- 1 cup finely chopped celery
- ½ cup chopped green onion
- ½ cup chopped red bell pepper
- 2 pints half-and-half
- 1 tsp dried parsley
- salt and ground black pepper to taste
- 1 (12 ounce) can oysters
- 2 dashes Louisiana-style hot sauce

Directions

1. In a large saucepan, melt the butter over medium heat until it foams.
2. In the hot butter, cook and toss the celery, onion, and red bell pepper until tender, about 10 minutes.
3. Season with salt and black pepper and stir in the half-and-half and parsley into the vegetable mixture.
4. Cook until the mixture just begins to boil, then add the oysters and any liquid from the can, as well as the Louisiana-style spicy sauce to the stew. Bring the mixture to a low simmer and cook for another 10 to 15 minutes, or until the oysters begin to curl.
5. Remove the stew from the heat and let it aside for 5 minutes before serving.

Nutrition Facts

Per Serving:

352 calories; protein 9.2g; carbohydrates 11.8g; fat 30.3g; cholesterol 114.2mg; sodium 209.2mg.

113. SWEET POTATO AND FRUITY FRITTER

Prep: 15 mins

Cook: 15 mins

Total: 30 mins

Servings: 16

Ingredients

- 1 cup all-purpose flour
- 1 tsp baking powder
- ½ tsp salt
- ½ tsp ground nutmeg
- 1 tsp ground cinnamon
- 2 tbsps dark rum
- 2 cups cooked, mashed sweet potatoes
- 1 cup mashed banana
- 1 cup crushed pineapple, drained
- ¼ cup butter, melted
- vegetable oil, for deep-fat frying
- powdered sugar for dusting

Directions

1. Set aside a bowl containing the flour, baking powder, salt, nutmeg, and cinnamon. Combine the rum, sweet potatoes, banana, pineapple, and butter in a large mixing bowl and stir well. Toss the flour into the sweet potato mixture until it is evenly distributed.
2. Preheat the deep-fryer oil to 375 ° F. (190 ° C).
3. Drop tbsp-sized batter pieces into the hot oil and cook until golden brown. Using paper towels, absorb excess liquid and sprinkle with powdered sugar.

Nutrition Facts

Per Serving:

177 calories; protein 1.7g; carbohydrates 20.2g; fat 9.9g; cholesterol 7.6mg; sodium 148mg. F

114. RICOTTA PIE

Prep: 45 mins

Cook: 45 mins

Additional: 1 hr 30 mins

Total: 3 hrs

Servings: 24

Ingredients
Pie Filling:

- 12 large eggs eggs
- 2 cups white sugar
- 2 tsps vanilla extract
- 3 pounds ricotta cheese
- ¼ cup miniature semisweet chocolate chips, or to taste

Sweet Crust:

- 4 cups all-purpose flour
- 5 tsps baking powder
- 4 cup white sugar
- ½ cup shortening, chilled
- 1 tbsp shortening, chilled
- 4 large eggs eggs, lightly beaten
- 1 tsp vanilla extract
- 1 tbsp milk

Directions

1. In a large mixing bowl, whisk together the 12 eggs, 2 cups sugar, and vanilla extract. If used, stir in the ricotta cheese and chocolate chips (see Cook's Note). Remove from the equation.
2. Mix together the flour, baking powder, and 1 cup sugar. 1/2 cup + 1 tbsp shortening, chopped until mixture resembles coarse crumbs Combine 4 beaten eggs and 1 tsp vanilla essence in a mixing bowl. Chill dough for at least 30 minutes after dividing it into four balls and wrapping it in plastic.
3. Preheat the oven to 325°F (165 ° C). 2 deep-dish pie pans, greased
4. 2 of the balls should be rolled out to fit into the pie pans. Because the crust will expand during cooking, don't make it too thick. Do not flute the dough's edges. For the top of the crust, roll out the remaining two balls of dough and cut each into eight narrow strips. (Alternatively, you can cut out shapes with cookie cutters and set them on top of the pies.)

5. Fill the pie crusts evenly with the ricotta filling. 8 small strips of dough or cookie cut-outs should be placed on top of each pie. If desired, brush the top of the pie with milk to make it shine. Wrap foil around the crust's edge.
6. Remove foil and bake for 20 to 30 minutes in a preheated oven. Rotate the pies on the rack to ensure equal baking. Continue baking for another 25 to 30 minutes, or until a knife inserted in the center of each pie comes out clean. On wire racks, cool entirely. Refrigerate until ready to serve.

Cook's Note:

1 tbsp fresh lemon zest can be substituted for the chocolate chips.

Nutrition Facts

Per Serving:

352 calories; protein 12.9g; carbohydrates 45.6g; fat 13.4g; cholesterol 141.6mg; sodium 220.1mg.

115. LENTIL AND CACTUS SOUP

Prep: 20 mins

Cook: 1 hr 30 mins

Total: 1 hr 50 mins

Servings: 10

Ingredients

- 14 cups water
- 3 cloves garlic, cut into thirds
- 1 pound lentils, picked over and rinsed
- 1 ½ tbsps chicken bouillon (such as Knorr®)
- 1 tsp extra-virgin olive oil
- ½ small onion, chopped
- 2 cloves garlic, chopped
- 1 tomato, chopped
- ¼ tsp ground cumin, or to taste
- 2 tsps chicken bouillon (such as Knorr®), or to taste
- 1 cup cooked nopales (cactus), drained
- 3 small potatoes, peeled and chopped

Directions

1. In a soup pot, bring the water to a boil with 3 garlic cloves. Combine the lentils and 1 1/2 tbsps chicken bouillon in a mixing bowl. Simmer for 1 hour over medium-low heat, or until lentils are practically tender.
2. In a skillet, heat extra-virgin olive oil and saute and toss the onion and 2 chopped garlic cloves until the onion is transparent, about 5 minutes. Cook, stirring constantly, for another 5 minutes, or until the tomato loses its juice. Add the tomato mixture, cumin, and 2 tbsps of chicken bouillon, or to taste, to the lentil soup. Bring the soup to a low simmer, then add the nopales and potatoes and boil for 20 minutes, or until the potatoes are cooked.

Nutrition Facts

Per Serving:

187 calories; protein 11.9g; carbohydrates 33.7g; fat 1.2g; cholesterol 0.2mg; sodium 261.4mg.

116. SPICED ORANGE CRANBERRY SAUCE

Servings: 64

Yield: 4 cups

Ingredients

- 2 pounds cranberries
- 2 tbsps orange zest
- 3 cinnamon sticks
- 1 pint orange juice
- 2 cups packed brown sugar
- 2 cups water

Directions

1. In a saucepan, combine the cranberries, grated orange peel, cinnamon, orange juice, brown sugar, and enough water to completely cover the cranberries. Over high heat, bring the mixture to a boil. Reduce the heat to low and continue to cook for about 1 hour, or until the sauce has thickened. If necessary, taste for sweetness and add more sugar if necessary. You can't overcook it, so keep cooking until it's a nice thick consistency. Allow to cool slightly before refrigerating in an airtight container.

Nutrition Facts

Per Serving:

37 calories; protein 0.1g; carbohydrates 9.4g; sodium 2.5mg.

117. CANADIAN VEGAN PEANUT BUTTER GRANOLA RECIPE

Prep: 5 mins

Cook: 20 mins

Total: 25 mins

Servings: 16

Ingredients

- ½ cup natural, salted peanut butter
- ¼ cup maple syrup
- 1 tbsp flaxseed meal
- 2 tsps vanilla extract
- 2 tsps ground cinnamon
- 4 cups rolled oats
- ½ cup shredded coconut, or to taste
- ¼ cup pumpkin seeds, or to taste
- ¼ cup raisins, or to taste

Directions

1. Preheat the oven to 350°F (180°C) (175 ° C). Use parchment paper to line 1 big or 2 smaller baking pans.
2. In a large mixing bowl, combine peanut butter, maple syrup, flaxseed meal, vanilla essence, and cinnamon. Mix in the oats and coconut until everything is well mixed. Place the mixture on the baking sheets that have been prepared.
3. Bake for 10 minutes in a preheated oven until toasted and aromatic. Stir in the pumpkin seeds and granola. Continue baking for another 9 minutes, or until evenly browned and dry to the touch.
4. Allow granola to cool slightly before serving. Toss in the raisins. Granola should be kept in an airtight container.

Cook's Note:

If desired, dried cranberries can be used instead of raisins.

Nutrition Facts

Per Serving:

180 calories; protein 5.6g; carbohydrates 22.1g; fat 8.5g; sodium 40.6mg.

118. FRENCH APPLE CAKE

Prep: 20 mins

Cook: 50 mins

Total: 1 hr 10 mins

Servings: 8

Ingredients

- ¾ cup white sugar
- 2 eggs
- ¾ tbsp vanilla extract
- 3 tbsps rum
- ¾ stick butter, softened, divided
- ¾ cup all-purpose flour
- ¾ tsp baking powder
- 1 pinch salt
- 4 cups chopped peeled apples, or more taste

Directions

1. Preheat the oven to 350°F (180°C) (175 ° C). Using butter, grease a 9-inch springform pan.
2. In a mixing bowl, combine the sugar, eggs, and vanilla extract; beat with an electric mixer until smooth. Pour in the rum. 1/2 of the butter should be added now.
3. In a separate basin, combine flour, baking powder, and salt. 1/2 of the flour mixture should be added to the egg mixture and mixed thoroughly. Combine the remaining butter and flour in a mixing bowl. Apples should be folded in.
4. Scrape the batter into the pan that has been prepared. Gently smooth the top.
5. Bake for 50 to 60 minutes, or until golden brown on top and a toothpick inserted in the center comes out clean.

Cook's Note:

You can use any combination of apples. You may need additional sugar if you use Granny Smith apples because they are sour.

Nutrition Facts

Per Serving:

258 calories; protein 3g; carbohydrates 36.7g; fat 10.1g; cholesterol 69.4mg; sodium 144.9mg.

119. GRANOLA RECIPE BARS

Servings: 12

Yield: 1 -9 inch square pan

Ingredients

- 1 ¼ cups all-purpose flour
- ½ cup butter flavored shortening
- 1/3 cup white sugar
- ¾ cup raspberry preserves
- ½ cup raisins
- ½ cup milk chocolate chips
- ¼ cup honey
- 2 tbsps butter
- ¾ cup quick cooking oats
- 1/3 cup shredded coconut
- 1/3 cup sliced almonds
- 2 tbsps sesame seeds

Directions

1. Preheat the oven to 350 ° Fahrenheit (175 ° C). One 9x9 inch square pan should be greased.
2. Combine the flour, 1/2 cup shortening, and sugar in a mixing basin. Reduce to a low speed and continue to beat until the mixture is crumbly. In the prepared pan, press the mixture into the bottom.
3. Preheat oven to 350 ° Fahrenheit (175 ° Celsius) and bake for 15 to 20 minutes.
4. Stir together the preserves, raisins, and chocolate pieces until well combined. Remove from the equation.
5. Combine the honey and butter or margarine in a saucepan. Cook, stirring constantly, until the cheese has melted. Blend in the oats, coconuts, almonds, and sesame seeds until everything is well combined.
6. Spread the raspberry preserves over the hot crust, then spoon the oat mixture on top and spread evenly to the pan's edges. Bake for 15 to 20 minutes more, or until lightly browned. To serve, cut the cake into bars.

Nutrition Facts

Per Serving:

346 calories; protein 3.6g; carbohydrates 49.7g; fat 16g; cholesterol 6.6mg; sodium 21.2mg.

120. BASIC FRUIT BREAD RECIPE

Prep: 10 mins

Cook: 40 mins

Total: 50 mins

Servings: 10

Ingredients

- 3 cups all-purpose flour
- 2 tsps baking powder
- 1 tsp baking soda
- ½ tsp salt
- 1 cup white sugar
- ½ cup vegetable oil
- 2 eggs
- 1 cup shredded apple
- ¾ cup chopped walnuts
- ½ tsp vanilla extract

Directions

1. Preheat the oven to 350 ° Fahrenheit (175 ° C). Grease a four-and-a-half-inch-by-eight-and-a-half-inch-by-eight-and
2. Only stir together the flour, baking powder, soda, salt, sugar, oil, eggs, apple, walnuts, and vanilla until the dry components are moistened.
3. Bake for 35 to 40 minutes in a greased 4 1/2 x 8 1/2 inch loaf pan at 350 ° F (175 ° C).

Note

This recipe can be made with one cup of any shredded fruit or vegetable. You may need to add some water to the mixture depending on what you use. We recommend adding 1 tbsp at a time until all of the ingredients are evenly moist.

Nutrition Facts

Per Serving:

391 calories; protein 6.5g; carbohydrates 52.1g; fat 18.1g; cholesterol 37.2mg; sodium 357.1mg.

121. THE LAST CAESAR SALAD RECIPE

Prep: 20 mins

Additional: 1 hr

Total: 1 hr 20 mins

Servings: 32

Ingredients

- 2 anchovy fillets
- 2 cloves garlic, chopped, or to taste
- 1 cup mayonnaise
- 1/3 cup grated Parmesan cheese
- ¼ cup half-and-half
- 2 tbsps fresh lemon juice
- 1 tbsp Dijon mustard
- 2 tsps Worcestershire sauce

Directions

1. In a food processor, combine anchovy fillets and garlic and pulse several times to produce a paste. To make the dressing, whisk together mayonnaise, Parmesan cheese, half-and-half, lemon juice, Dijon mustard, and Worcestershire sauce with the anchovy mixture until smooth. Before serving, chill for at least 1 hour.

Cook's Note:

For a lowfat version, substitute light mayo and lowfat milk for regular mayo and half-and-half.

Nutrition Facts

Per Serving:

57 calories; protein 0.5g; carbohydrates 0.6g; fat 5.9g; cholesterol 4.3mg; sodium 77mg.

122. SWEET HAM

Prep: 10 mins

Cook: 8 hrs

Total: 8 hrs 10 mins

Servings: 24

Ingredients

- 1 (7 pound) canned ham
- 2 cups orange juice
- ½ cup water
- 1 (20 ounce) can crushed pineapple
- 3 tbsps brown sugar

Directions

1. In a slow cooker, place the ham. Over the ham, pour the orange juice, water, and pineapple. Brown sugar should be sprinkled on the top and sides of the cake. Cook on Low for 8 hours, covered.

Nutrition Facts

Per Serving:

220 calories; protein 24g; carbohydrates 7.5g; fat 9.9g; cholesterol 50.3mg; sodium 1690.6mg.

123. SALAD RECIPE WITH PIECES OF FRUIT

Prep: 15 mins

Cook: 5 mins

Total: 20 mins

Servings: 8

Ingredients

- 1 cup slivered almonds
- ½ cup white sugar
- ½ cup olive oil
- ¼ cup distilled white vinegar
- 2 tbsps white sugar
- salt and pepper to taste
- ½ head iceberg lettuce - rinsed, dried, and chopped
- ½ head leaf lettuce - rinsed, dried, and chopped
- 1 cup chopped celery
- ¼ cup chopped fresh chives
- ½ cup dried, sweetened cranberries
- ½ cup mandarin orange segments, drained
- ½ cup sliced fresh peaches

- ½ cup diced mango
- ½ cup chopped fresh strawberries

Directions

1. Cook and stir the almonds and 1/2 cup sugar in a pan over medium heat for 5 minutes, or until the almonds are well-coated and gently browned.
2. Combine the olive oil, vinegar, 2 tbsps sugar, salt, and pepper in a mixing bowl. Remove from the equation.
3. Gently toss the almonds, iceberg lettuce, leaf lettuce, celery, chives, cranberries, mandarin orange, peaches, mango, and strawberries together in a large mixing dish. Serve with as much oil and vinegar dressing as you like.

Nutrition Facts

Per Serving:

317 calories; protein 3.8g; carbohydrates 31.7g; fat 20.6g; sodium 24mg.

124. REFRIED BEAN ROLL

Prep: 10 mins

Additional: 5 mins

Total: 15 mins

Servings: 4

Ingredients

- 1 (16 ounce) can Old El Paso® fat-free refried beans
- ½ cup Old El Paso® Thick 'n Chunky salsa
- ½ tsp chili powder
- 8 fat free flour tortillas (8 to10 inch)
- 1 cup shredded lettuce
- ½ cup shredded Monterey Jack cheese

Directions

1. Warm the beans, salsa, and chili powder in a 1-quart saucepan over medium heat for 5 minutes, stirring periodically.
2. Fill each tortilla with about 1/4 cup bean mixture and spread it out slightly. Serve with lettuce and cheese on top. Tortillas should be rolled up. If preferred, serve with more salsa.

Tips

Health Tip: Each serving of this lighter version of refried bean roll-ups contains 70 calories and 7 grams of fat less than the original recipe.

Purchasing: Refried beans are made in the same way that their name suggests. Traditionally, cooked beans are mashed and fried in fat. Look in your grocery store for fat-free refried beans that are just as wonderful.

If you prefer your tacos "laden," then do the same with them! Add chopped or sliced jalapeos, sliced ripe or green olives, diced tomato, or chopped bell pepper to add color and flavor.

With relatively little hands-on time, a slow cooker can produce a tasty, authentic food.

Nutrition Facts

Per Serving:

547 calories; protein 19.5g; carbohydrates 86.8g; fat 4.4g; cholesterol 12.6mg; sodium 1413.7mg.

125. BEST GREEN JUICE RECIPE

Prep: 10 mins

Total: 10 mins

Servings: 4

Ingredients

- 1 Gala apple - peeled, cored, and chopped
- 4 leaves kale, chopped
- 1 cup fresh coconut meat
- ½ cucumber, chopped
- 1 stalk celery, chopped
- ½ cup spinach
- 1 cup coconut water
- ½ cup almond milk
- ½ cup water
- 1 lemon, juiced

Directions

1. In a blender, combine the apple, kale, coconut meat, cucumber, celery, and spinach; add the coconut water, almond milk, water, and lemon juice and blend until smooth. Blend for 30 seconds to 1 minute on high.

Cook's Note:

Depending on your blender's capabilities, blend until smooth. It's possible that you'll need to strain your combination to get a drinkable consistency.

Nutrition Facts

Per Serving:

126 calories; protein 2.4g; carbohydrates 14.8g; fat 7.4g; sodium 108.5mg.

126. BEST BUTTERBEER RECIPE

Prep: 5 mins

Total: 5 mins

Servings: 4

Ingredients

- ½ cup butterscotch schnapps
- 3 ½ cups chilled cream soda

Directions

1. In a small pitcher, pour the butterscotch schnapps. Pour in the cream soda slowly to avoid losing the carbonation. To serve, gently stir and pour into goblets.

Nutrition Facts

Per Serving:

229 calories; protein 0g; carbohydrates 44.3g; fat 0.1g; cholesterol 0mg; sodium 29.4mg.

127. GREEN JUICE RECIPE

Prep: 10 mins

Total: 10 mins

Servings: 4

Ingredients

- 1 Gala apple - peeled, cored, and chopped
- 4 leaves kale, chopped
- 1 cup fresh coconut meat
- ½ cucumber, chopped
- 1 stalk celery, chopped
- ½ cup spinach
- 1 cup coconut water
- ½ cup almond milk
- ½ cup water
- 1 lemon, juiced

Directions

1. In a blender, combine the apple, kale, coconut meat, cucumber, celery, and spinach; add the coconut water, almond milk, water, and lemon juice and blend until smooth. Blend for 30 seconds to 1 minute on high.

Cook's Note:

Depending on your blender's capabilities, blend until smooth. It's possible that you'll need to strain your combination to get a drinkable consistency.

Nutrition Facts

Per Serving:

126 calories; protein 2.4g; carbohydrates 14.8g; fat 7.4g; sodium 108.5mg.

128. NUTELLA BRIOCHE STAR RECIPE

Prep: 45 mins

Cook: 20 mins

Additional: 1 hr 20 mins

Total: 2 hrs 25 mins

Servings: 8

Ingredients

- 3 ⅓ cups bread flour
- 1/3 cup white sugar
- 2 tsps active dry yeast
- 1 pinch salt
- ¾ cup milk, warmed
- 2 large eggs, separated
- 2 tbsps unsalted butter, melted
- 1 tsp vegetable oil, or as needed
- 1 cup chocolate-hazelnut spread (such as Nutella)

Directions

1. In the bowl of a stand mixer, combine bread flour, sugar, yeast, and salt. Using a fork, combine the ingredients. Combine the milk, egg yolks, and butter in a mixing bowl. Attach the dough hook and knead for about 10 minutes, or until the dough forms a ball and feels smooth and elastic.

2. In a large mixing bowl, pour the vegetable oil. Roll the dough in the oil to coat it. Allow to rise in a warm location for 1 to 2 hours, covered with a moist cloth.

3. Place the dough on a flat surface. Knead lightly to release the air. Make a flat oblong form with the dough, then roll it into a log. Divide the dough into four equal halves. While working with 1 piece at a time, keep the dough covered with a damp cloth.

4. Dust the work surface with flour. Roll out the first piece of dough with a rolling pin. Invert a round 8-inch pan or plate on top; cut dough into an 8-inch circle by tracing the rim with a sharp knife.

5. Place the circle on a baking sheet lined with parchment paper. To make it easier to spread, warm the chocolate-hazelnut spread in the microwave for a few seconds. A third should be spread over the dough circle.

6. Repeat with the remaining chocolate-hazelnut spread and two additional dough pieces. Place the final piece of dough on top, rolled out and cut into an 8-inch round. To form a complete circle, invert the pan or plate over the stack and cut through all of the layers.

7. In the center of the circle, place a small drinking class. From the base of the drinking glass to the outside edge, cut the dough into quarters using a sharp knife. Quarters should be cut into eighths, then sixteenths.

8. Take two slices and twist them in opposing directions twice. Rep all of the previous steps all the way around the circle. All of the ends should be pinch and sealed. Allow for a 20-minute rise by covering with a moist cloth.

9. Preheat the oven to 350°F (180°C) (175 ° C). Lightly beat the egg whites and brush them over the dough.

10. Cook for 20 minutes in a preheated oven until golden brown. Allow it cool for a few minutes before serving.

Cook's Note:

One of my 'Carla in the Kitchen' fans specifically requested this one! As a result, this one is for her.

Nutrition Facts

Per Serving:

436 calories; protein 10.7g; carbohydrates 65.2g; fat 15g; cholesterol 56mg; sodium 78.2mg.

129. HAM AND SPLIT PEA SOUP RECIPE - A GREAT SOUP

Prep: 20 mins

Cook: 1 hr 30 mins

Total: 1 hr 50 mins

Servings: 8

Ingredients

- 2 tbsps butter
- ½ onion, diced
- 2 ribs celery, diced
- 3 cloves garlic, sliced
- 1 pound ham, diced
- 1 bay leaf
- 1 pound dried split peas
- 1 quart chicken stock
- 2 ½ cups water
- salt and ground black pepper to taste

Directions

1. In a large soup pot over medium-low heat, melt the butter. Combine the onion, celery, and sliced garlic in a mixing bowl. Cook for 5 to 8 minutes, or until the onions are transparent but not brown.
2. Combine the ham, bay leaf, and split peas in a mixing bowl. Combine chicken stock and water in a large mixing bowl. Stir to incorporate, then reduce to a low heat and cook for 1 hour and 15 minutes, or until the peas are soft and the soup is thick. Stir once in a while. To serve, season with salt and black pepper.

Nutrition Facts

Per Serving:

374 calories; protein 25.1g; carbohydrates 37g; fat 14.4g; cholesterol 39.8mg; sodium 1186.7mg.

130. DEVILED EGGS WITH ZIP

Prep: 15 mins

Cook: 30 mins

Total: 45 mins

Servings: 12

Ingredients

- 12 eggs
- 2 tbsps mayonnaise
- 1 tsp Chinese hot prepared mustard
- 2 tsps yellow mustard
- salt and pepper to taste
- paprika, for garnish

Directions

1. In a large saucepan, crack the eggs and cover them with cold water. Bring the water to a boil and then remove it from the heat. Allow eggs to sit in hot water for 10 to 12 minutes, covered. Remove from the boiling water, allow to cool, then peel.
2. Remove the yolks from the eggs by slicing them in half lengthwise. In a medium mixing bowl, combine the yolks with the mayonnaise, Chinese spicy prepared mustard, yellow mustard, salt, and pepper.
3. Fill the egg yolk mixture into the hollowed-out egg whites. Paprika can be added as a garnish. Keep refrigerated until ready to serve.

Nutrition Facts

Per Serving:

88 calories; protein 6.3g; carbohydrates 0.5g; fat 6.8g; cholesterol 186.9mg; sodium 88.5mg.

131. LOADED BBQ CHICKEN NACHOS RECIPE

Prep: 15 mins

Cook: 20 mins

Total: 35 mins

Servings: 6

Ingredients

- cooking spray
- 1 (10 ounce) bag tortilla chips, or to taste
- 1 cup barbeque sauce, or to taste
- 4 cups shredded roasted chicken breasts
- 1 tbsp fresh lime juice
- ¼ tsp ground cumin
- ¼ tsp chili powder
- 2 ½ cups shredded Cheddar cheese

Directions

1. Preheat the oven to 350 ° Fahrenheit (175 ° C). Coat a rimmed baking sheet with cooking spray and line with aluminum foil.
2. In a medium saucepan, combine the chicken, barbecue sauce, lime juice, cumin, and chili powder. Reduce heat to low and cook, stirring periodically, for about 10 minutes, or until chicken is thoroughly cooked. Remove the pan from the heat.
3. On the prepared baking sheet, spread a single layer of tortilla chips. 1 1/4 cup Cheddar cheese and half of the chicken mixture on top. Over the cheese, put another layer of tortilla chips, then top with the remaining chicken mixture and cheese.
4. Bake for 10 minutes in a preheated oven until the Cheddar cheese is melted and golden brown.

Nutrition Facts

Per Serving:

623 calories; protein 41.3g; carbohydrates 47.1g; fat 29.8g; cholesterol 120.3mg; sodium 1020.9mg.

132. DEEP DARK OLD RECIPE BRAN MUFFINS

Prep: 10 mins

Cook: 20 mins

Additional: 1 hr

Total: 1 hr 30 mins

Servings: 18

Ingredients

- 2 ½ cups wheat bran
- 1 ½ cups sifted all-purpose flour
- 1 tsp salt
- 1 ½ tsps baking soda
- 2 eggs
- 1 ½ cups buttermilk
- ½ cup white sugar
- ¼ cup molasses
- 2 ½ tbsps vegetable shortening, melted
- ½ cup chopped raisins

Directions

1. Preheat the oven to 350 ° Fahrenheit (175 ° C). Grease or line 18 muffin cups with paper liners. In a mixing basin, combine the bran, flour, salt, and baking soda; set aside.
2. In a mixing dish, whisk together the eggs. Combine the buttermilk, sugar, molasses, and melted shortening in a mixing bowl and whisk until smooth. Stir in the raisins and bran mixture until no dry lumps remain. Fill the prepared muffin tins little more than 2/3 full.
3. Bake for 20 minutes in a preheated oven, or until a toothpick inserted in the center comes out clean. Cool for 10 minutes in the pans before removing to a wire rack to cool fully.

Nutrition Facts

Per Serving:

136 calories; protein 3.8g; carbohydrates 26.8g; fat 3g; cholesterol 21.5mg; sodium 265.8mg.

133. COCOA TEA MIX RECIPE

Prep: 10 mins

Total: 10 mins

Servings: 1

Ingredients

- 1 ½ cups boiling water
- 1 Earl Grey tea bag
- 3 tbsps milk
- 1 ½ tbsps hot cocoa mix
- 2 tsps white sugar

Directions

1. Fill a mug halfway with boiling water and steep the tea bag for 2 minutes. Remove the tea bag and combine the milk, hot cocoa mix, and sugar in a mixing bowl. Stir for about 20 seconds, or until everything is fully incorporated.

Cook's Note:

Use 2 tea bags if you prefer stronger tea.

Nutrition Facts

Per Serving:

103 calories; protein 2.3g; carbohydrates 20.5g; fat 1.4g; cholesterol 3.7mg; sodium 89.9mg.

134. WHOLE WHEAT PIZZA DOUGH SECRET FAMILY RECIPE

Prep: 10 mins

Additional: 25 mins

Total: 35 mins

Servings: 8

Ingredients

- 1 tbsp dry yeast
- 1 tsp white sugar
- 1 cup warm water
- ¼ cup olive oil
- 3 cups hard white whole wheat flour, or more as needed
- 1 ½ tsps salt

Directions

1. In a large mixing basin, combine yeast and sugar with warm water; leave aside for 5 to 10 minutes, or until the liquid begins to bubble and foam. Pour in the oil. Stir in the flour and salt until the dough is smooth; add additional flour as needed.
2. Knead the dough for 5 minutes on a lightly floured surface before placing it in a large mixing bowl and covering it with a moist towel. Allow 20 to 30 minutes for the dough to rise. Roll out the dough using a rolling pin on a pizza stone.

Nutrition Facts

Per Serving:

231 calories; protein 6.6g; carbohydrates 37.1g; fat 7.6g; sodium 437.8mg.

135. DIJON-BACON DIP FOR PRETZELS

Prep: 10 mins

Additional: 30 mins

Total: 40 mins

Servings: 16

Ingredients

- 1 cup mayonnaise
- ½ cup Dijon mustard
- ½ cup real bacon bits, divided
- 1 tsp prepared horseradish, or more to taste

Directions

1. In a mixing bowl, combine mayonnaise, mustard, half of the bacon bits, and horseradish. Refrigerate for at least 30 minutes after wrapping the bowl with plastic wrap. Before serving, scatter the leftover bacon bits over the dip.

Nutrition Facts

Per Serving:

119 calories; protein 1.6g; carbohydrates 2g; fat 11.7g; cholesterol 7.7mg; sodium 376.6mg.

136. PERFECT FRIED CHICKEN RECIPE

Prep: 20 mins

Cook: 50 mins

Additional: 3 hrs

Total: 4 hrs 10 mins

Servings: 6

Ingredients

- 6 chicken leg quarters, cut into thighs and drumsticks
- 3 cups buttermilk
- 1 cup all-purpose flour
- 2 tsps onion powder
- 2 tsps garlic powder
- 2 tsps seasoned salt
- 1 ½ tsps chicken bouillon granules
- ¾ tsp crumbled dried sage
- ½ tsp ground black pepper
- ¼ tsp ground thyme
- 1 pinch dried marjoram
- 2 eggs
- ½ cup milk
- 1 cup vegetable oil for frying, or as needed

Directions

1. Pour buttermilk over the chicken thighs and drumsticks in a mixing dish. Toss to coat. Refrigerate for 3 hours after covering and marinating (or up to overnight).
2. Preheat the oven to 425 ° Fahrenheit (220 ° C).
3. In a 1-gallon resealable plastic bag, combine flour, onion powder, garlic powder, seasoned salt, chicken bouillon granules, sage, black pepper, thyme, and marjoram. To incorporate the flour and seasonings, close the bag and shake it. In a large mixing basin, whisk together the eggs and milk.
4. In a cast-iron skillet or an oven-safe glass or metal pan, pour vegetable oil. In a hot oven, heat a skillet with oil for 10 minutes.
5. Drain the buttermilk from the chicken pieces and set them in a plastic bag with seasoned flour while the oil heats up. Shake the bag to coat each chicken piece in seasoned flour. Each coated piece should be dipped in the egg mixture, then returned to the flour mixture bag and shaken to coat a second time. Place the coated chicken pieces on a platter and set aside for 5 minutes to allow the coating to harden.

6. Place the covered chicken in a skillet with heated oil and bake for 30 minutes. Turn the chicken over and bake for another 20 minutes, or until the inside is no longer pink and the coating is golden brown. Before serving, drain the oil from the chicken pieces on a rack.

Cook's Notes:

If desired, 3 cups water + 1 tbsp salt can be used instead of buttermilk. Bake boneless chicken breasts for 30 minutes total (15 minutes on each side).

Nutrition Facts

Per Serving:

491 calories; protein 50.5g; carbohydrates 24.8g; fat 20g; cholesterol 211.5mg; sodium 698.7mg.

137. BAKED FRESH LOBSTER

Prep: 20 mins

Cook: 35 mins

Total: 55 mins

Servings: 2

Ingredients

- 1 (1 1/2 pound) fresh lobster
- ½ cup butter, melted and divided
- 1 cup crushed buttery round crackers

Directions

1. Preheat oven to 400 ° Fahrenheit (200 ° C). To properly kill the lobster, plunge the tip of a sharp knife straight down directly behind the animal's eyes.
2. Place the lobster on its back and cut open the cavity with a sharp knife. Remove and discard the stomach and intestines. In a separate bowl, set aside the tomalley. Combine the cracker crumbs and tomalley in a bowl and spoon into the body cavity. 2 tbsps butter drizzled over the top Place the lobster in a baking dish with a depth of 2 inches.
3. Cover and bake the lobster for 30 minutes. Preheat the oven to Broil and toast the crackers for 3 to 5 minutes before serving. With the remaining melted butter, serve.

Nutrition Facts

Per Serving:

1366 calories; protein 77.3g; carbohydrates 74.4g; fat 82.5g; cholesterol 361mg; sodium 1955.5mg.

138. LOADED VEGETARIAN QUICHE

Prep: 20 mins

Cook: 55 mins

Additional: 5 mins

Total: 1 hr 20 mins

Servings: 8

Ingredients

- 1 (9 inch) unbaked deep dish pie crust
- 1 tbsp olive oil
- ½ cup sliced onion
- ½ cup chopped green bell pepper
- ½ cup mushrooms, sliced
- ½ cup chopped zucchini
- 1 large tomato, sliced
- 2 tbsps all-purpose flour
- 2 tsps dried basil
- 3 eggs, beaten
- ½ cup milk
- ½ tsp salt
- ¼ tsp ground black pepper
- 1 ½ cups shredded Colby-Monterey Jack cheese, divided

Directions

1. Preheat the oven to 400 ° Fahrenheit (200 ° C).
2. In a preheated oven, bake the pie crust for about 8 minutes, or until firm. Take the crust out of the oven and set it aside. Preheat the oven to 350 ° F. (175 ° C).
3. In a large skillet, heat the olive oil over medium heat. 5 to 7 minutes, cook and stir onion, green bell pepper, mushrooms, and zucchini in high oil until tender. Take the vegetables out of the skillet and set them aside.
4. Toss tomato slices with flour and basil and fry for 1 minute per side in a skillet.
5. In a small bowl, whisk together the eggs, milk, salt, and pepper.
6. In the bottom of the pie crust, spread 1 cup Colby-Monterey Jack cheese. Over the cheese, layer the vegetable mixture, then top with the tomatoes. Fill the pie crust halfway with the egg mixture. Top the quiche with the remaining 1/2 cup of cheese.
7. Bake for 40 to 45 minutes in a preheated oven, or until a knife inserted near the center comes out clean. Allow to cool for 5 minutes before serving.

Nutrition Facts

Per Serving:

284 calories; protein 10.5g; carbohydrates 17.2g; fat 19.6g; cholesterol 95.5mg; sodium 524mg.

139. BOLOGNESE

Prep: 20 mins

Cook: 50 mins

Total: 1 hr 10 mins

Servings: 4

Ingredients

- 1 tbsp olive oil
- 1 onion, diced
- 2 carrots, diced, or more to taste
- 2 stalks celery, diced
- 8 cloves garlic, diced
- 1 pound lean ground turkey
- 1 pinch salt to taste
- 1 pinch garlic powder, or to taste
- 1 pinch onion powder, or to taste
- 1 pinch dried oregano, or to taste
- 1 pinch red pepper flakes, or to taste
- 1 ½ cups white wine
- 1 (28 ounce) can diced tomatoes
- 2 cups hot water, or more to taste
- 2 tbsps ketchup, or more to taste

Directions

1. In a large pot, heat the olive oil over medium heat. Cook, stirring occasionally, until the onion, carrots, and celery begin to brown, about 10 minutes. Stir in the garlic and simmer for 1 to 2 minutes, or until fragrant. Season with salt, garlic powder, onion powder, oregano, and red pepper flakes before adding the turkey. Cook, stirring occasionally, until the turkey begins to brown, about 5 to 8 minutes.
2. Pour white wine into the pot and use a wooden spoon to remove any browned bits from the bottom. Combine tomatoes, hot water, and ketchup in a mixing bowl. Simmer for about 30 minutes, or until the flavors have melded.

Cook's Note:

This keeps well in the freezer. Cook on the burner to defrost, seasoning as needed.

Nutrition Facts

Per Serving:

374 calories; protein 25.9g; carbohydrates 22.8g; fat 12.2g; cholesterol 83.9mg; sodium 547mg.

140. CARIBBEAN BARLEY SALAD

Prep: 20 mins

Cook: 25 mins

Additional: 20 mins

Total: 1 hr 5 mins

Servings: 4

Ingredients

- 3 cups water
- ½ tsp salt
- ½ cup barley
- 1 large mango, peeled and diced, divided
- 3 tbsps lime juice
- 2 tbsps olive oil
- ½ tsp ground cumin
- ½ tsp salt
- 1 ½ cups cooked black beans
- 1 cup grape tomatoes, halved
- ½ cup diced red onion
- ¼ cup chopped fresh cilantro
- 1 tbsp minced jalapeno pepper

Directions

1. In a saucepan, bring water and 1/2 tsp salt to a boil. Cover and cook for 20 minutes, or until barley is soft but firm to the bite. Allow 20 to 30 minutes to cool completely after draining any extra cooking liquid.

2. Using a fork or a potato masher, mash 1/4 of the mango against the edge of a big bowl. Lime juice, olive oil, cumin, and 1/2 tsp salt are whisked in. Toss together the barley, leftover mango, black beans, grape tomatoes, red onion, cilantro, and jalapeño.

Cook's Notes:

If you prefer, use one 15-ounce can of black beans, drained.

If you want, mint can be used instead of cilantro.

Nutrition Facts

Per Serving:

294 calories; protein 9.4g; carbohydrates 49.8g; fat 8g; sodium 942.9mg.

CARIBBEAN RECIPES

1. DREAM CHILI

Prep: 10 mins

Cook: 1 hr 15 mins

Total: 1 hr 25 mins

Servings: 8

Ingredients

- 2 tbsps vegetable oil
- 1 small onion, chopped
- 2 tbsps bottled minced garlic
- 1 pound ground pork
- 1 pound ground sirloin
- 1 (28 ounce) can whole peeled tomatoes
- 2 cups low-sodium beef broth
- 1 (15 ounce) can black beans, rinsed and drained
- ½ cup golden raisins
- 2 tbsps chili powder
- 1 tsp ground cumin
- 1 tsp ground cinnamon
- 1 tsp salt

- ½ tsp ground allspice
- ¼ tsp ground cloves
- ¼ cup halved green olives
- ¼ cup slivered almonds

Directions

1. In a big pot over medium heat, heat the oil. Cook, stirring frequently, until the onion and garlic are tender, about 2 minutes. Cook and stir until the pork and sirloin are browned, about 8 to 10 minutes. Using a strainer, remove any excess fat from the pot.
2. Hand-crush the tomatoes and add them to the pot, along with their liquids. Add the beef broth. Combine the black beans, raisins, chili powder, cumin, cinnamon, salt, allspice, and cloves in a large mixing bowl. Bring to a boil, then reduce to a low heat and cover and cook for 30 minutes, or until raisins are tender.
3. Green olives and almonds should be added to the pot. Simmer for about 30 minutes, or until the flavors have melded.

Nutrition Facts

Per Serving:

392 calories; protein 26.3g; carbohydrates 24.1g; fat 21.7g; cholesterol 71.2mg; sodium 864.8mg.

2. CALYPSO HOT SAUCE

Prep: 15 mins

Cook: 5 mins

Total: 20 mins

Servings: 8

Ingredients

- 5 habanero peppers
- 1 tbsp olive oil
- 1 onion, chopped
- 2 cloves garlic, chopped
- 2 tbsps lime juice
- 2 tbsps brown sugar
- 2 tbsps apple cider vinegar
- 1 tbsp tequila
- 2 tsps salt

- 2 tsps mustard powder
- 1 tsp ground allspice

Directions

1. Wearing gloves, stem and seed habanero peppers.
2. In a skillet, heat the olive oil over medium heat. Cook and stir onion and garlic for 5 minutes, or until onion is translucent.
3. In a blender, purée the habanero peppers, onion, garlic, lime juice, brown sugar, apple cider vinegar, tequila, salt, mustard powder, and allspice.

Tips

If you prefer, rum can be used instead of tequila.

Nutrition Facts

Per Serving:

46 calories; protein 0.5g; carbohydrates 5.8g; fat 2g; sodium 583.9mg.

3. CARIBBEAN SLAW

Prep: 20 mins

Additional: 1 hr

Total: 1 hr 20 mins

Servings: 8

Ingredients

- ½ head green cabbage, shredded
- 1 red bell pepper, thinly sliced
- ½ red onion, thinly sliced
- 2 carrots, peeled and shredded
- 1 mango - peeled, seeded, and diced
- ½ cup fresh cilantro, chopped
- 1/3 cup nonfat plain yogurt
- 2 tbsps reduced-fat mayonnaise
- 1 tbsp prepared yellow mustard
- 1 tbsp apple cider vinegar
- 1 tsp agave nectar
- salt and black pepper to taste

- 1 dash habanero hot sauce, or more to taste

Directions

1. In a large mixing bowl, combine the cabbage, red bell pepper, red onion, carrots, mango, and cilantro.
2. In a small mixing bowl, combine the yogurt, mayonnaise, mustard, cider vinegar, agave nectar, salt, pepper, and spicy sauce; pour over the cabbage mixture and toss to coat. Allow the slaw to marinade for at least 1 hour in the refrigerator to allow the flavors to meld.

Nutrition Facts

Per Serving:

61 calories; protein 2.1g; carbohydrates 13.1g; fat 0.6g; cholesterol 0.2mg; sodium 94.5mg.

4. FRUITY SALSA

Prep: 25 mins

Total: 25 mins

Servings: 8

Ingredients

- 1 cup diced fresh mango
- ½ cup diced fresh pineapple
- ½ cup diced papaya
- 1 fresh jalapeno pepper, seeded and minced
- ½ medium red onion, finely diced
- 3 tbsps lime juice
- 1 tbsp olive oil
- 1 tsp salt, or to taste
- 1 tbsp chopped fresh mint

Directions

1. In a mixing dish, combine the mango, pineapple, papaya, jalapeño pepper, and red onion. Combine the lime juice and olive oil in a mixing bowl. Season with salt and pepper to taste, then whisk to blend. Before serving, garnish with chopped mint leaves.

Nutrition Facts

Per Serving:

47 calories; protein 0.4g; carbohydrates 8.4g; fat 1.8g; sodium 292.1mg.

5. RUM PUNCH

Prep: 10 mins

Total: 10 mins

Servings: 20

Ingredients

- 1 cup fresh lime juice
- 2 cups simple syrup
- 3 cups amber rum
- 4 cups orange juice
- 4 dashes bitters
- freshly grated nutmeg

Directions

1. Lime juice, simple syrup, rum, and orange juice should be combined in a pitcher. To taste, add a splash of bitters and a pinch of grated nutmeg. Pour over ice and serve chilled.

Nutrition Facts

Per Serving:

166 calories; protein 0.4g; carbohydrates 21.4g; fat 0.1g; cholesterol 0mg; sodium 1.8mg.

6. ZUCCHINI BREAD

Prep: 20 mins

Cook: 40 mins

Additional: 25 mins

Total: 1 hr 25 mins

Servings: 24

Ingredients

- 2 cups all-purpose flour
- 1 cup whole wheat flour
- 1 tsp salt
- 1 tsp baking soda
- 1 ½ tsps baking powder
- 1 tbsp ground cinnamon
- ½ tsp nutmeg
- 2 ripe bananas, mashed
- 3 eggs
- ½ cup vegetable oil
- ½ cup unsweetened applesauce
- 1 cup packed brown sugar
- 1 cup white sugar
- 2 tsps vanilla extract
- 2 ½ cups grated zucchini
- 1 cup chopped walnuts
- ½ cup shredded coconut

Directions

1. Preheat the oven to 325 ° Fahrenheit (165 ° C). 2 9x5-inch loaf pans, greased and floured
2. In a mixing bowl, combine the all-purpose flour, whole wheat flour, salt, baking soda, baking powder, cinnamon, and nutmeg. In a separate big mixing bowl, combine the bananas, eggs, vegetable oil, applesauce, brown sugar, white sugar, and vanilla. In a separate bowl, whisk together the flour, baking soda, and salt. In a large mixing bowl, blend the zucchini, walnuts, and coconut until well incorporated. Pour into the pans that have been prepared.
3. Cook for 40 to 50 minutes in a preheated oven, or until a toothpick inserted in the center comes out clean. Cool for 25 minutes in the pans before removing to a wire rack to cool fully.

Nutrition Facts

Per Serving:

226 calories; protein 3.6g; carbohydrates 34.1g; fat 9.1g; cholesterol 23.3mg; sodium 197.6mg.

7. CARIBBEAN CHICKEN

Prep: 15 mins

Cook: 30 mins

Total: 45 mins

Servings: 4

Ingredients

- 1 tsp paprika
- 1 tsp onion powder
- 1 tsp garlic powder
- 1 tsp dried parsley
- ½ tsp dried oregano
- 1 tsp salt
- 1 tsp pepper
- 4 boneless, skinless chicken breast halves
- ¼ b cup duck sauce
- ¼ cup marinara sauce
- 1 tsp mango hot sauce
- ¾ cup fresh pink grapefruit juice, divided
- 1 cup Italian seasoned bread crumbs
- 1 ripe nectarine, pitted and sliced

Directions

1. Preheat the oven to 375 ° Fahrenheit (190 ° C). Using parchment paper, line a baking dish.
2. Combine paprika, onion powder, garlic powder, parsley, oregano, salt, and pepper in a large mixing basin. Toss the chicken breasts in the dressing until they are well coated. Combine the duck sauce, marinara sauce, mango spicy sauce, and 1/4 cup grapefruit juice in a mixing bowl. Coat the chicken in the sauce mixture evenly. In a shallow dish, coat the chicken in bread crumbs until it is evenly breaded. In a baking dish, place the chicken. Arrange nectarine slices along the baking dish's edge.
3. Bake for 15 minutes in a preheated oven. Cook for another 15 minutes or until done, turning the chicken and pouring 1/2 cup grapefruit juice over it.

Nutrition Facts

Per Serving:

319 calories; protein 32.9g; carbohydrates 37.8g; fat 3.7g; cholesterol 68.4mg; sodium 1239.5mg.

8. CARIBBEAN-STYLE CHICKEN SALAD

Prep: 30 mins

Cook: 12 mins

Additional: 1 hr

Total: 1 hr 42 mins

Servings: 4

Ingredients

- ¼ cup lime juice
- 1 tbsp red wine vinegar
- 1 clove garlic, minced
- 2 tbsps honey
- ¼ tsp salt
- ¼ tsp black pepper
- ¼ cup olive oil
- 1 pound skinless, boneless chicken breast halves
- 1 ripe mango, peeled, pitted and diced
- 1 (15.5 ounce) can black beans, drained and rinsed
- 1 red bell pepper, seeded and cut into thin strips
- ½ jicama, sliced into matchsticks
- ½ head green leaf lettuce, rinsed and torn

Directions

1. Lime juice, red wine vinegar, garlic, honey, salt, and pepper are whisked together until smooth. Slowly drizzle in the olive oil until it is fully incorporated. Refrigerate for 1 hour after mixing half of the dressing with the chicken breasts. Keep the remaining dressing refrigerated for later use.
2. Pre-heat an outside grill to medium-high.
3. 6 minutes per side on the grill until chicken breasts are no longer pink. Set aside to chill while you continue with the process. In a large mixing bowl, combine mango, black beans, bell pepper, and jicama with the leftover dressing. Toss with salad after slicing the chicken into bite-size pieces.
4. To serve, place the green leaf lettuce in the bottom of a serving bowl and top with the chicken salad.

Nutrition Facts

Per Serving:

462 calories; protein 34.6g; carbohydrates 47.6g; fat 15.6g; cholesterol 65.9mg; sodium 657.1m

9. CARIBBEAN JERK STIR-FRY

Prep: 15 mins

Cook: 20 mins

Total: 35 mins

Servings: 2

Ingredients

- 1 tbsp vegetable oil
- 1 green bell pepper, seeded and cubed
- 1 red bell pepper, seeded and cubed
- ¼ cup sliced sweet onions
- ¾ pound skinless, boneless chicken breast, cut into strips
- 2 ½ tsps Caribbean jerk seasoning
- ½ cup plum sauce
- 1 tbsp soy sauce
- ¼ cup chopped roasted peanuts

Directions

1. In a large skillet, heat the oil over medium-high heat. 5 to 7 minutes, cook and toss the bell pepper and onion in the oil until slightly soft. Set aside the pepper and onion from the skillet. Add the chicken to the skillet, season with jerk seasoning, and cook, stirring occasionally, until the chicken is no longer pink on the inside. Pour the plum sauce over the chicken, then toss in the bell peppers and onions. Cook for 3 to 5 minutes, or until the peppers and onions are completely heated. To serve, top with soy sauce and chopped peanuts.

Nutrition Facts

Per Serving:

549 calories; protein 44.3g; carbohydrates 41g; fat 21.4g; cholesterol 103.7mg; sodium 1620.6mg.

10. CARIBBEAN HOLIDAY SHRIMP

Prep: 10 mins

Additional: 1 hr

Total: 1 hr 10 mins

Servings: 8

Ingredients

- 1 tbsp vegetable oil
- 2 tbsps minced fresh ginger root
- 2 limes, juiced
- 2 cloves garlic, minced
- 1 tbsp soy sauce
- ½ tsp white sugar
- ½ tsp crushed red pepper flakes
- 2 pounds large cooked shrimp, peeled, tails on
- ½ cup chopped fresh cilantro

Directions

1. Mix together the oil, ginger, lime juice, garlic, soy sauce, sugar, and red pepper in a large mixing bowl. Combine the shrimp and cilantro in a mixing bowl. Before serving, cover and chill for 1 to 4 hours. While cooling, give it a stir every now and again.

Note

The full amount of marinade ingredients is included in the nutrition facts for this dish. The amount of marinade used varies depending on marinating duration, ingredients, cooking style, and other factors.

Nutrition Facts

Per Serving:

138 calories; protein 24.1g; carbohydrates 2.9g; fat 3.1g; cholesterol 221.3mg; sodium 369mg.

11. COCONUT BREAD

Prep: 15 mins

Cook: 1 hr

Additional: 15 mins

Total: 1 hr 30 mins

Servings: 8

Ingredients

- 1 tsp butter, softened
- 1 ¾ cups all-purpose flour
- 1 ½ cups white sugar
- 1 cup shredded coconut
- 1 tsp baking powder
- ¾ tsp salt
- 2 eggs
- 1/3 cup low-fat milk
- ¼ cup water
- ¼ cup canola oil
- 1 ¼ tsps coconut extract (Optional)
- 1 tsp vanilla extract
- ½ tsp ground cinnamon

Directions

1. Preheat the oven to 350 ° Fahrenheit (175 ° C). Butter a loaf pan and set aside.
2. In a large mixing basin, combine flour, sugar, coconut, baking powder, and salt; stir once or twice with a wooden spoon. Combine the eggs, milk, water, oil, coconut extract, vanilla extract, and cinnamon in a large mixing bowl. Mix thoroughly until the batter is evenly distributed.
3. Pour the batter into the loaf pan that has been oiled.
4. Bake for 1 hour in a preheated oven, or until a toothpick inserted in the center comes out clean. Allow 15 minutes to cool in the pan. To cool entirely, invert onto a wire rack.

Cook's Notes:

Brown sugar can be substituted for white sugar, or a combination of the two might be used.

If desired, coconut milk can be substituted for the milk. Unless you absolutely want a strong coconut flavor, leave out the coconut essence.

Nutrition Facts

Per Serving:

415 calories; protein 5.5g; carbohydrates 62g; fat 16.7g; cholesterol 48.7mg; sodium 309.4mg.

12. FISH WITH MANGO SALSA

Prep: 45 mins

Cook: 10 mins

Additional: 30 mins

Total: 1 hr 25 mins

Servings: 5

Ingredients
Fish Spice:

- 1 tbsp paprika
- 2 tsps curry powder
- 2 tsps ground cumin
- 1 ½ tsps ground allspice
- 1 tsp ground ginger
- 1 tsp ground coriander
- ¾ tsp salt
- ½ tsp freshly ground black pepper
- ¼ tsp ground fennel seed (Optional)
- 1/8 tsp cayenne pepper (Optional)

Mango Salsa:

- 1 mango - peeled, seeded and diced
- 1 cup chopped fresh pineapple
- ½ red bell pepper, chopped
- ½ cup black beans, rinsed and drained (Optional)
- ½ red onion, finely chopped
- 3 tbsps chopped fresh cilantro
- 3 tbsps fresh lime juice
- 1 egg
- 1/3 cup milk
- 1 cup panko bread crumbs
- 1 tbsp dried unsweetened coconut, or to taste (Optional)

- 1 tbsp olive oil, or as needed
- 5 (4 ounce) fillets tilapia

Directions

1. In a large mixing bowl, combine the paprika, curry powder, cumin, allspice, ginger, coriander, salt, black pepper, fennel, and cayenne pepper; set aside.
2. Toss the mango, pineapple, red bell pepper, black beans, red onion, and cilantro in a bowl with a light toss; drizzle the lime juice over the mango mixture and toss again. Refrigerate the bowl for at least 30 minutes after covering it.
3. In a mixing dish, whisk together the egg and milk. Combine the panko crumbs and coconut in a small bowl. 1 tbsp of the spice combination, or to taste, should be stirred into the panko crumb mixture.
4. In a skillet, heat the olive oil over medium heat. Dip the tilapia fillets in the egg mixture, then gently push them into the panko crumb mixture to coat both sides. Brush any crumbs off the fillets before placing them in the heated oil. 3 to 5 minutes per side or as needed, pan-fry until the salmon is opaque inside and golden brown outside. Serve with mango salsa on the side.

Cook's Notes

The spice blend can be used as needed and will last for a long time.

Cook the scallops for 2 minutes on each side. The fish/scallops should be cooked lightly, especially the scallops; if they're overcooked, they'll be tough.

Nutrition Facts

Per Serving:

312 calories; protein 29.9g; carbohydrates 36.7g; fat 7.9g; cholesterol 79.9mg; sodium 645.6mg.

13. SPICED ROAST CHICKEN

Prep: 15 mins

Cook: 1 hr 30 mins

Total: 1 hr 45 mins

Servings: 4

Ingredients

- 1 ½ tbsps fresh lime juice
- 2 fluid ounces rum
- 1 tbsp brown sugar
- ¼ tsp cayenne pepper
- ¼ tsp ground clove
- ½ tsp ground cinnamon
- ½ tsp ground ginger
- 1 tsp black pepper
- ½ tsp salt
- ½ tsp dried thyme leaves
- 1 (3 pound) whole chicken
- 1 tbsp vegetable oil

Directions

1. Preheat the oven to 325°F (165 ° C).
2. Combine the lime juice, rum, and brown sugar in a small bowl; set aside.
3. Combine the cayenne pepper, clove, cinnamon, ginger, pepper, salt, and thyme leaves in a large mixing bowl. Brush the chicken with oil before sprinkling the spice mixture on top.
4. Bake for 90 minutes, or until the juices run clear and a meat thermometer inserted in the thickest portion of the thigh reads 180 ° F. During the cooking process, baste the chicken with the saved sauce every 20 minutes. Allow 10 minutes for the chicken to rest before carving.

Nutrition Facts

Per Serving:

508 calories; protein 46.1g; carbohydrates 4.8g; fat 29.1g; cholesterol 145.5mg; sodium 432.5mg.

14. GRILLED CARIBBEAN CHICKEN

Servings: 6

Yield: 6 servings

Ingredients

- 3 skinless, boneless chicken breasts
- ¼ cup orange juice
- 2 tbsps fresh lime juice
- 2 tbsps mango chutney
- 2 tsps grated fresh ginger
- 1 tbsp olive oil
- ½ tsp hot pepper sauce
- 1 tsp minced fresh oregano
- 2 cloves garlic, minced

Directions

1. Combine the orange juice, lime juice, chutney, ginger, oil, pepper sauce, oregano, and cloves in a nonporous glass dish or bowl. Combine all of the ingredients and add the chicken. Toss to coat, then cover and chill the dish. Marinate for at least 24 hours.
2. Preheat the grill to high or the oven to broil.
3. Remove the chicken from the dish (discard the marinade) and grill or broil it 6 inches away from the heat source.

Note

The full amount of marinade ingredients is included in the nutrition facts for this dish. The amount of marinade used varies depending on marinating duration, ingredients, cooking style, and other factors.

Nutrition Facts

Per Serving:

111 calories; protein 13.5g; carbohydrates 4.4g; fat 4.2g; cholesterol 36mg; sodium 43.1mg.

15. CARIBBEAN COCONUT CHICKEN BITES

Prep: 30 mins

Cook: 20 mins

Additional: 45 mins

Total: 1 hr 35 mins

Servings: 8

Ingredients

- 4 thin slices prosciutto
- 4 skinless, boneless chicken breast halves - pounded to 1/4-inch thickness
- 1 ripe mango - peeled and cut into eight 1-inch wide strips
- 1 cup all-purpose flour
- ½ tsp salt
- ½ tsp curry powder
- 1/8 tsp ground black pepper
- 1/8 tsp finely crumbled dried thyme
- 2 eggs, beaten
- 2 cups unsweetened shredded coconut
- vegetable oil for deep frying, or as needed
- 1 lime, juiced
- 1 lime, cut into wedges

Directions

1. On each chicken breast, place a slice of prosciutto. Prosciutto should be trimmed to fit inside the chicken breast with a 1/2-inch chicken border.
2. In the center of each prosciutto slice, place two slices of mango.
3. To completely wrap the mango and prosciutto, roll the chicken breast lengthwise. To securely seal rolls, tuck and pinch the ends.
4. Place the chicken rolls on a baking sheet and chill for 30 minutes, or until extremely firm.
5. In a mixing bowl, combine flour, salt, curry powder, black pepper, and thyme. Place the mixture on a platter.
6. On a separate plate, pour the beaten eggs.
7. On a third plate, strew coconut.
8. Using a sharp knife, cut the chicken rolls into 1 to 1 1/2-inch pieces.
9. Shake off any excess flour after rolling the chicken in the flour mixture.
10. Allow excess egg to drop off the chicken after coating it in the beaten egg.
11. Roll the chicken in shredded coconut.

12. Arrange the coated chicken rolls in a single layer on a platter. Cover and chill for 15 minutes to allow the coating to harden.
13. Preheat the oven to 325°F (165 ° C).
14. In a deep, heavy skillet, heat enough vegetable oil to completely submerge the chicken rolls. Reduce the heat to medium.
15. Fry half of the chicken rolls in the heated oil for about 4 minutes, or until golden brown.
16. Using a slotted spoon, remove the chicken rolls and drain on several layers of paper towels. Rep with the rest of the chicken rolls.
17. On a baking sheet, arrange the chicken rolls.
18. Cook for 10 minutes in a preheated oven until the chicken is no longer pink in the center and the juices run clear.
19. Serve lime wedges beside chicken rolls that have been sprayed with lime juice.

Nutrition Facts

Per Serving:

420 calories; protein 17.9g; carbohydrates 22.1g; fat 30g; cholesterol 83.2mg; sodium 270.3mg.

16. CARIBBEAN COOK UP

Prep: 50 mins

Total: 50 mins

Servings: 5

Ingredients

- ½ pound chicken wings
- 2 onions, chopped
- ¼ cup chopped celery
- 1 tsp browning sauce
- 4 cups water
- 2 cups white rice
- 1 cup pigeon peas
- ½ pound cod
- 3 tomatoes, cubed
- 1 cup grated carrots
- 1 tsp salt

Directions

1. Rinse the chicken, pat it dry, and season with salt & pepper to taste. In a large skillet, heat the oil over medium-high heat. Brown the chicken, then add the onion, celery, and gravy browning and cook until the celery and onion are tender. After that, combine the water, rice, peas, fish, tomatoes, carrots, and salt in a large mixing bowl. Cover skillet and cook for 25 to 35 minutes, or until rice and peas are cooked but gritty, on medium low heat.

Nutrition Facts

Per Serving:

491 calories; protein 25.3g; carbohydrates 75.8g; fat 8.8g; cholesterol 54.5mg; sodium 553.6mg.

17. CABBAGE IN WINE SAUCE

Prep: 5 mins

Cook: 20 mins

Total: 25 mins

Servings: 4

Ingredients

- ½ cup water
- ½ medium head cabbage, cored and cut into wedges
- 1 ear corn
- ½ cup butter, melted
- 1/8 cup dry vermouth or white wine
- ½ tsp minced shallots
- 2 large cloves garlic, minced
- salt and black pepper to taste
- crushed red pepper flakes to taste

Directions

1. Fill a big saucepan halfway with water. Remove the leaves from the cabbage and set them in a steamer basket. Place the basket in the water-filled pot. Bring to a boil over medium heat, then remove the ear of corn and lay it on top of the cabbage. Steam for 15 to 20 minutes, or until corn is soft, covered. Remove the basket from the saucepan and set aside to cool.
2. Cut the ear of corn into four pieces and combine with the cabbage in a serving bowl. Combine the butter, vermouth, shallots, garlic, salt, pepper, and red pepper flakes in a mixing bowl; pour over the cabbage and toss to evenly coat. Divide the salad among four dishes and top with a piece of corn on each.

Nutrition Facts

Per Serving:

279 calories; protein 3g; carbohydrates 15.3g; fat 23.6g; cholesterol 61mg; sodium 190.4mg.

18. CARIBBEAN FISH SOUP

Prep: 35 mins

Cook: 1 hr

Additional: 30 mins

Total: 2 hrs 5 mins

Servings: 8

Ingredients

- 2 whole fish, scaled and cleaned, or more to taste
- 1 lemon, juiced
- 8 cups water
- 4 green bananas, chopped
- 1 pound pumpkin, cut into 1-inch pieces, or more to taste
- 2 potatoes, chopped
- 2 ears corn, cut into 1-inch pieces
- 4 ounces carrots, cut into 1/2-inch pieces
- ½ cup chopped okra
- 4 scallions, chopped
- 1 hot chile pepper
- 2 cloves garlic, chopped
- 1 tsp salt
- 1 tsp ground black pepper
- 4 sprigs fresh thyme, leaves stripped

Directions

1. Drain the fish after rinsing it with lemon juice.
2. In a large mixing bowl, bring water to a boil. Add the salmon and cook for about 30 minutes, or until it is soft. Remove the fish from the soup and set aside. Allow the fish to cool. Remove bones while attempting to preserve huge portions of fish.
3. To make the broth, bring it to a boil. Green bananas, pumpkin, potatoes, maize, carrots, okra, scallions, chile pepper, garlic, salt, pepper, and thyme should all be added to the saucepan.

Bring the water back to a boil. Reduce heat to low and cook for about 10 minutes, or until potatoes are almost tender. Add the fish and mix well. Cook for another 5 minutes, or until the flavors have melded.

4. Remove the soup from the heat and let it aside for 30 minutes before serving. Remove the chile pepper and toss it out.

Cook's Notes:

If you don't want a lot of heat, don't slit the chile pepper.

When reheating leftovers, do not boil; this will cause the fish to break down.

Nutrition Facts

Per Serving:

203 calories; protein 11.6g; carbohydrates 35g; fat 3.3g; cholesterol 25.5mg; sodium 338mg.

19. CARIBBEAN BBQ SAUCE

Prep: 10 mins

Cook: 10 mins

Total: 20 mins

Servings: 12

Ingredients

- 1 tsp vegetable oil
- 3 slices bacon, diced
- 1 medium onion, finely chopped
- 1 cup tomato sauce
- ½ cup black rum
- 1 lemon, juiced
- 1/3 cup brown sugar
- 1 dash chili sauce

Directions

1. In a medium skillet over medium high heat, combine the vegetable oil, bacon, and onion. Cook until the bacon is evenly browned and the onions are soft.
2. Reduce the heat to low and stir in the tomato sauce and rum with the bacon and onion in the skillet. Cook for roughly 2 minutes on low heat. Combine the lemon juice, brown sugar, and chili sauce in a mixing bowl. Continue to cook for another 8 minutes.

Nutrition Facts

Per Serving:

92 calories; protein 1.3g; carbohydrates 9g; fat 3.6g; cholesterol 4.8mg; sodium 168.9mg.

20. CARIBBEAN-INSPIRED GRILLED CHICKEN KABOBS

Prep: 15 mins

Cook: 15 mins

Additional: 4 hrs

Total: 4 hrs 30 mins

Servings: 4

Ingredients

- 1 cup cream of coconut
- 1 cup lemon juice
- 1 tbsp chicken bouillon granules
- 2 tsps dried marjoram
- 1 tsp garlic powder
- 1 tsp red pepper flakes
- 1 pound skinless, boneless chicken breast halves, cut into chunks
- 1 red bell pepper, cut into chunks, or to taste
- 1 sweet onion, cut into chunks, or to taste
- 1 cup fresh pineapple chunks, or to taste (Optional)
- skewers

Directions

1. In a bowl, whisk together the coconut cream, lemon juice, bouillon, marjoram, garlic powder, and red pepper flakes until the marinade is smooth.
2. In a shallow dish, combine the chicken, red bell pepper, onion, and pineapple and cover with 1/2 of the marinade. Refrigerate for 4 to 6 hours, covered in plastic wrap.
3. Preheat an outside grill to medium-high heat and brush the grate liberally with oil.
4. Shake off any extra marinade from the chicken, veggies, and pineapple. Remove and discard any remaining marinade. Using skewers, thread chicken, veggies, and pineapple.
5. 5 to 10 minutes per side on a hot grill, basting with the leftover marinade regularly until chicken is no longer pink in the center and vegetables are cooked.

Nutrition Facts

Per Serving:

409 calories; protein 25.9g; carbohydrates 49.3g; fat 13g; cholesterol 64.8mg; sodium 363.3mg.

21. CARIBBEAN HEALTH DRINK

Prep: 10 mins

Total: 10 mins

Servings: 2

Ingredients

- 1 cup chopped carrot
- 1 banana
- 1 kiwi, peeled
- 1 apple - peeled, cored, and sliced
- 1 cup chopped pineapple
- 1 cup ice cubes

Directions

1. In a blender, combine the carrot, banana, kiwi, apple, pineapple, and ice cubes until smooth.

Nutrition Facts

Per Serving:

178 calories; protein 2.3g; carbohydrates 45.4g; fat 0.8g; sodium 47.4mg.

22. GRILLED CARIBBEAN-SPICED PORK TENDERLOIN WITH PEACH SALSA

Prep: 15 mins

Cook: 20 mins

Additional: 5 mins

Total: 40 mins

Servings: 4

Ingredients

- ¾ cup fresh peaches, peeled and diced
- 1 small red bell pepper, chopped
- 2 tbsps finely chopped red onion
- 2 tbsps minced fresh cilantro
- 1 tbsp lime juice
- 1 clove garlic, minced
- 1/8 tsp salt
- 1/8 tsp ground black pepper
- 2 tbsps olive oil
- 1 tbsp brown sugar
- 1 tbsp Caribbean jerk seasoning
- 1 tsp dried thyme
- 1 tsp dried rosemary
- ½ tsp seasoned salt
- 1 pork tenderloin

Directions

1. In a large mixing bowl, combine peaches, bell pepper, red onion, cilantro, lime juice, garlic, salt, and pepper. Set aside the peach salsa.
2. In a second small bowl, combine olive oil, brown sugar, Caribbean jerk seasoning, thyme, rosemary, and seasoned salt. Rub the spice mixture all over the tenderloin.
3. Preheat an outside grill to medium heat and brush the grate gently with oil.
4. Place the tenderloin on a hot grill and cook for 9 to 11 minutes, covered. Turn and cook for another 9 to 11 minutes, or until tenderloin is slightly pink in the center. At least 145 ° F should be read on an instant-read thermometer put into the center (63 ° C). Before slicing, remove from heat, cover, and let aside for 5 minutes. Serve with a peach salsa on the side.

Cook's Note:

You can use pineapple instead of peaches and fresh parsley instead of cilantro.

Nutrition Facts

Per Serving:

233 calories; protein 23.9g; carbohydrates 8.6g; fat 11g; cholesterol 73.8mg; sodium 580.2mg.

23. CARIBBEAN-SPICED PORK SIDE RIBS

Prep: 20 mins

Cook: 1 hr 30 mins

Total: 1 hr 50 mins

Servings: 6

Ingredients

- 2 tbsps brown sugar
- 2 tsps fresh ginger root, grated
- ¼ tsp cayenne pepper
- ¼ tsp ground clove
- ½ tsp ground cinnamon
- 1 tsp paprika
- 1 tsp dried oregano
- 2 tsps black pepper
- 1 tsp salt
- 2 limes, zested and juiced
- 1 cup orange juice
- 1 rack pork spareribs, cut in half

Directions

1. Preheat the oven to 350 ° Fahrenheit (175 ° C).
2. Set aside the brown sugar, ginger, cayenne, clove, cinnamon, paprika, oregano, pepper, salt, and lime zest that have been mixed together. Add the lime juice to the orange juice after squeezing the limes. Rub the spice mixture all over the ribs. Pour the juice into a glass baking dish and mix well.
3. Bake for 90 minutes, covered, in a preheated oven. Uncover and cook for another 20 to 30 minutes, or until attractively colored. While the ribs are cooking, brush them with the pan juices a few times.

Nutrition Facts

Per Serving:

574 calories; protein 39.2g; carbohydrates 12.3g; fat 40.4g; cholesterol 160.4mg;

24. CARIBBEAN CHICKEN WITH PINEAPPLE-CILANTRO RICE

Prep: 20 mins

Cook: 30 mins

Total: 50 mins

Servings: 4

Ingredients

- 1 tbsp light brown sugar
- 1 tsp ground black pepper
- 1 tsp dried thyme
- 1 tsp ground cumin
- 1 tsp garlic salt
- 1 tsp paprika
- ½ tsp chili powder
- ½ tsp ground nutmeg
- 4 skinless, boneless chicken breast halves
- 1 cup uncooked white rice
- 1 ½ cups water
- 1 (8 ounce) can sliced pineapple in juice, drained - divided
- 2 tbsps chopped fresh cilantro
- 1 tsp olive oil
- 1 pinch garlic salt
- 1 pinch ground black pepper

Directions

1. Preheat the oven to 350 ° Fahrenheit (175 ° C).
2. In a large mixing bowl, add the light brown sugar, 1 tsp black pepper, thyme, cumin, 1 tsp garlic salt, paprika, chili powder, and nutmeg. Place the chicken breasts in a 9x9-inch baking dish and rub both sides with the spice mixture. If desired, top the chicken with any remaining spice mix.
3. Bake for 30 minutes in a preheated oven until the chicken is lightly browned on the outside, no longer pink on the inside, and the juices flow clear. In the thickest section of a chicken breast, an instant-read meat thermometer should read at least 160 ° F. (70 ° C).

4. In a saucepan over high heat, bring the rice and water to a boil while the chicken is roasting. Reduce heat to medium-low, cover, and cook for 20 to 25 minutes, or until the rice is soft and the liquid has been absorbed.
5. Half of the pineapple pieces should be chopped. Toss the cooked rice with the chopped pineapple, cilantro, and olive oil, and season with a pinch of garlic salt and black pepper to taste. Transfer the rice to a serving tray and fluff it up with a fork. Serve with the leftover pineapple pieces on top of the cooked chicken.

Nutrition Facts

Per Serving:

367 calories; protein 28.5g; carbohydrates 51g; fat 4.8g; cholesterol 67.2mg;

25. RICK'S CARIBBEAN ROPA VIEJA

Prep: 15 mins

Cook: 45 mins

Total: 1 hr

Servings: 8

Ingredients

- ¼ cup butter
- 1 red onion, chopped
- 8 ounces fresh mushrooms, chopped
- 2 pounds flank steak
- 1 ½ cups red wine
- 1 (13.5 ounce) can coconut milk
- ½ cup sour cream
- 8 ounces flaked coconut (Optional)
- ¼ cup brown sugar
- 1 tbsp ground allspice
- 1 tsp salt
- ½ tsp black pepper

Directions

1. In a skillet over medium heat, melt the butter and sauté the onion and mushrooms until nicely browned. In a skillet, brown the flank steak on all sides. Pour the wine in. Reduce to low heat and simmer for another 30 minutes, or until the meat is very soft. Remove the meat, shred it, and put it back in the skillet.

2. Fill the skillet with coconut milk. Combine the sour cream, coconut flakes, brown sugar, allspice, salt, and pepper in a large mixing bowl. Cook for another 10 minutes, or until well heated.

Nutrition Facts

Per Serving:

571 calories; protein 17.9g; carbohydrates 19.4g; fat 45.6g; cholesterol 57.3mg; sodium 396.9mg.

26. BEEF LOIN STEAKS

Prep: 10 mins

Cook: 6 mins

Additional: 2 hrs 30 mins

Total: 2 hrs 46 mins

Servings: 6

Ingredients

- 1 fluid ounce coconut-flavored rum
- ¼ tsp salt
- ¼ tsp ground black pepper
- 1/8 tsp ground cinnamon
- ½ tsp garlic powder
- ½ tsp dried oregano
- ¼ tsp dried sage
- ½ tsp white vinegar
- 1 tbsp fresh lemon juice
- 4 slices onion
- 6 (8 ounce) beef top sirloin steaks
- 1 tbsp olive oil

Directions

1. In a mixing bowl, combine the rum, salt, pepper, cinnamon, powder, oregano, sage, vinegar, and lemon juice; transfer to a gallon-size, resealable plastic bag. Toss the steaks and onions into the marinade. Squeeze out as much air as possible before closing the bag. Allow 2 1/2 hours in the refrigerator to marinate.
2. In a large skillet, heat the olive oil over medium heat. Cook the steaks in a covered skillet until done to your liking, about 3 minutes per side for medium rare.

Per Serving:

381 calories; protein 37.3g; carbohydrates 2.3g; fat 23.1g; cholesterol 122.4mg; sodium 183.9mg.

27. GOURMET GELLY SHOTS: MALIBU GOODNESS

Prep: 10 mins

Additional: 8 hrs

Total: 8 hrs 10 mins

Servings: 12

Ingredients

- 1 cup boiling water
- 1 (6 ounce) box strawberry-banana-flavored Jell-O mix
- 1 cup coconut-flavored rum (such as Malibu)

Directions

1. On a baking sheet, arrange 12 2-ounce plastic cups.
2. While whisking, slowly pour hot water over gelatin mix in a bowl. While whisking, slowly pour the rum into the gelatin mixture. Fill plastic cups halfway with the mixture.
3. Refrigerate for 8 hours to overnight until set.

Nutrition Facts

Per Serving:

104 calories; protein 2.2g; carbohydrates 15.8g; fat 1.6g; cholesterol 12.1mg; sodium 64mg.

28. CARIBBEAN COUSCOUS

Prep: 15 mins

Cook: 30 mins

Additional: 5 mins

Total: 50 mins

Servings: 4

Ingredients

- ½ cup chopped pecans
- 2 tbsps oil
- 1 (4 ounce) can mushrooms, drained and liquid reserved
- 1 large sweet potato, peeled and grated
- 1 ½ cups vegetable stock
- 1 orange, zested and juiced
- 2 green onions, sliced
- ¼ jalapeno pepper, seeded and chopped
- ½ tsp poultry seasoning
- ½ tsp ground cumin
- 1 pinch ground allspice
- ¾ cup couscous
- 1/3 cup chopped dried mixed fruit
- ¼ cup shredded coconut
- 1 tbsp chopped fresh cilantro

Directions

1. Preheat the oven to 400 ° Fahrenheit (200 ° C). Pecans should be spread out on a baking sheet.
2. 3 to 5 minutes in a preheated oven, until pecans are roasted and fragrant. Remove the baking sheet from the oven and set it aside to cool.
3. In a large skillet over low heat, combine the oil and mushroom liquid. Cook and stir sweet potatoes in the oil mixture for 20 minutes, or until cooked, adding a little amount of vegetable stock if needed. In a large skillet, combine the sweet potato combination, mushrooms, vegetable stock, orange zest, orange juice, green onions, jalapeño pepper, poultry seasoning, cumin, and allspice; cover and cook for 5 minutes to allow flavors to meld.
4. Remove pan from heat and combine sweet potato mixture with couscous, dried fruit, and coconut. Cover skillet and set aside for 5 minutes, or until couscous has absorbed all of the liquid. Mix in the pecans and cilantro with the couscous.

Cook's Notes:

The addition of butter and chicken broth enhances the flavor. Any kind of dried fruit will suffice: I used pre-packaged fruit chunks.

Egg pastina pasta is similar to couscous but is far less expensive.

It makes a huge difference to toast the pecans.

Nutrition Facts

Per Serving:

467 calories; protein 9g; carbohydrates 63.8g; fat 21.1g; sodium 365.6mg.

29. CARIBBEAN SANGRIA

Prep: 25 mins

Additional: 2 hrs

Total: 2 hrs 25 mins

Servings: 8

Ingredients

- 1 small orange, sliced
- 1 peach, sliced (Optional)
- 1 lemon, sliced
- 1 lime, sliced
- 3 cups dry red wine
- 1 (12 fluid ounce) can or bottle lemon-lime soda
- 1 ½ cups rum
- ¾ cup white sugar
- 3 strawberries, sliced, or more to taste

Directions

1. In the bottom of a pitcher, layer orange slices, peach slices, lemon slices, and lime slices. Stir together the red wine, lemon-lime soda, rum, and sugar until the sugar is completely dissolved.
2. Cover and chill sangria for at least 2 hours to allow flavors to blend.
3. Serve with a strawberry slice on top of each serving.

Nutrition Facts

Per Serving:

276 calories; protein 0.4g; carbohydrates 30g; fat 0.1g; sodium 10mg.

30. CARIBBEAN MEAT POCKETS

Prep: 40 mins

Cook: 1 hr 5 mins

Total: 1 hr 45 mins

Servings: 10

Ingredients
Dough:

- 3 cups all-purpose flour
- 1 tbsp curry powder
- 1 tsp salt
- 1 cup vegetable shortening
- 1 egg, beaten
- 3 tbsps water

Filling:

- ¼ cup vegetable oil
- 1 onion, chopped
- 3 green onions, chopped
- 1 clove garlic, minced
- 2 tbsps chopped pickled jalapeno peppers
- 1 pound ground beef
- 1 tsp dried thyme
- 2 tsps curry powder
- 1 tsp salt
- ½ tsp ground black pepper
- 1 ½ cups water
- ½ cup bread crumbs

Directions

1. In a mixing bowl, combine the flour, 1 tbsp curry powder, and 1 tsp of salt. Combine the vegetable shortening and the flour until it resembles cornmeal. In a separate bowl, whisk together the egg and water until the dough is no longer crumbly. Wrap in plastic wrap and chill while you make the filling.
2. In a large skillet, heat the vegetable oil over medium heat. Cook and stir the onion, green onion, garlic, and jalapeno peppers for about 5 minutes, or until the onion softens and turns translucent. Cook, stirring occasionally, until the ground beef is browned and crumbly, about 15 minutes. Remove the excess fat from the pan and add the thyme, 2 tsps curry powder, 1 tsp

salt, black pepper, and 1 1/2 cups water. Bring to a low boil, then reduce to a low heat and cook until the water has evaporated. Place the beef mixture in a food processor with the bread crumbs and pulse until the mixture forms a paste.

3. Preheat the oven to 400 ° Fahrenheit (200 ° C). Preheat oven to 350°F. Line two baking pans with parchment paper.
4. On a lightly floured surface, roll out the dough to just about 1/4-inch thickness. Cut the dough into 20 6-inch circles. Half of the circles should be filled with the beef mixture, which should be mounding in the center. Place the unfilled circles on top of the filling and seal the edges with a fork. Arrange the ingredients on the baking sheets.
5. Bake for 25 minutes in a preheated oven until golden brown and hot on the inside.

Nutrition Facts

Per Serving:

488 calories; protein 13.2g; carbohydrates 35.1g; fat 32.7g; cholesterol 47mg; sodium 581.6mg.

31. WARM MANGO SALSA

Prep: 20 mins

Cook: 15 mins

Total: 35 mins

Servings: 8

Ingredients

- 2 tbsps olive oil
- 1 small onion, chopped
- 1 jalapeno pepper, seeded and finely chopped
- 2 cloves garlic, minced
- 1 tsp lemon zest
- 1/8 tsp ground coriander
- 1 mango - peeled, seeded and diced
- 1 (8 ounce) can pineapple tidbits, drained
- ¼ cup lemon juice
- 2 tbsps butter
- salt and ground black pepper to taste

Directions

1. In a nonstick skillet, heat the olive oil over medium-high heat and sauté the onion and jalapeño pepper until soft, about 5 minutes. Stir in the garlic, lemon zest, and coriander and simmer for 1 minute, or until aromatic.
2. Push the onion and pepper combination to the pan's edges, and place the mango and pineapple in the middle. Cook, without stirring, for about 5 minutes, or until the fruit begins to caramelize. Bring the lemon juice to a boil in the pan, stirring constantly and scraping the browned bits of food off the bottom with a wooden spoon. Remove from the fire and mix in the butter until all of the ingredients are evenly combined. Season with salt and black pepper to taste and serve warm.

Nutrition Facts

Per Serving:

96 calories; protein 0.5g; carbohydrates 10.7g; fat 6.4g; cholesterol 7.6mg; sodium 21.9mg.

32. MAHI MAHI WITH COCONUT RICE AND MANGO SALSA

Prep: 30 mins

Cook: 30 mins

Additional: 1 hr

Total: 2 hrs

Servings: 4

Ingredients

- 2 tbsps olive oil
- 1 ½ tsps soy sauce
- 2 tsps lemon juice
- 1 clove garlic, crushed
- 2 tsps red pepper flakes
- 1 tsp fresh ground black pepper
- ½ tsp minced fresh ginger root
- 2 tbsps chopped green onion (Optional)
- salt to taste
- 4 (4 ounce) mahi mahi fillets
- 2 cups uncooked jasmine rice
- 2 cups water
- 1 cube chicken bouillon
- 1 tbsp butter (Optional)

- ¾ (14 ounce) can coconut milk
- 2 tbsps white sugar
- 1 ½ tsps butter (Optional)
- 1 ½ tbsps white sugar
- 1 ½ cups fresh mango, cubed

Directions

1. In a large mixing bowl, combine the olive oil, soy sauce, lemon juice, garlic, red pepper flakes, black pepper, ginger, green onion, and salt. Toss in the mahi mahi to coat evenly. Refrigerate the bowl for 1 hour after covering it with plastic wrap.
2. Set the oven rack in the centre of the oven and preheat the broiler.
3. In a saucepan over high heat, bring the rice, water, chicken bouillon, and 1 tbsp butter to a boil. Reduce the heat to medium-low, cover, and cook for about 20 minutes, or until the liquid has been absorbed. Combine the coconut milk and 2 tbsps of sugar in a mixing bowl. Stir often and continue to cook, uncovered, until the rice has absorbed the most of the coconut milk.
4. Remove the mahi mahi from the marinade and shake off any excess while the rice is cooking. Remove the remaining marinade and toss it out. Arrange the fish in a single layer in a large baking dish. Broil for 10 to 15 minutes in a preheated oven until the salmon flakes easily with a fork. Cover the baking dish with aluminum foil if the fish browns too soon.
5. In a skillet over medium-high heat, melt 1 1/2 tsps butter and 1 1/2 tbsps sugar. Stir in mango chunks when the mixture starts to bubble. Cook, stirring occasionally, until the mango is soft, about 5 minutes. Place a mahi mahi fillet on top of a scoop of heated rice and top with the mango salsa to serve.

Nutrition Facts

Per Serving:

808 calories; protein 30.9g; carbohydrates 107g; fat 28.9g; cholesterol 93.8mg; sodium 548.6mg.

33. CUCUMBER-MANGO SALAD

Prep: 20 mins

Total: 20 mins

Servings: 4

Ingredients

- 1 pound cucumbers, ends trimmed
- 1 ½ pounds mangos - peeled, pitted, and cut into 1-inch cubes
- ½ tsp rice vinegar
- 2 tsps sesame seeds
- 1 tsp agave nectar

Directions

1. Peel the cucumber lengthwise in wide stripes, alternating skinned and peel strips. Place in a salad dish and slice into 1/4-inch pieces.
2. Toss the mangos, rice vinegar, sesame seeds, and agave nectar together in a mixing dish.

Nutrition Facts

Per Serving:

141 calories; protein 1.9g; carbohydrates 34.8g; fat 1.3g; sodium 5.8mg.

34. PLANTAIN CHIPS

Prep: 15 mins

Cook: 20 mins

Total: 35 mins

Servings: 8

Ingredients

- Vegetable oil, for deep-frying
- 2 green plantains, peeled and sliced 1/8-inch thick
- salt to taste

Directions

1. Preheat the deep-fryer oil to 375 ° F. (190 ° C).
2. 3 to 4 minutes, deep fried a dozen plantain slices at a time until golden brown on both sides. While still warm, drain in a large dish lined with paper towels and season to taste.

Nutrition Facts

Per Serving:

103 calories; protein 0.6g; carbohydrates 14.3g; fat 5.7g; sodium 1.8mg.

v

35. GRILLED CARIBBEAN FREE RANGE CHICKEN

Prep: 15 mins

Cook: 15 mins

Additional: 8 hrs

Total: 8 hrs 30 mins

Servings: 8

Ingredients

- 1 cup rum
- 5 tbsps light soy sauce
- ¼ cup lime juice
- ¼ cup brown sugar
- 12 cloves garlic, minced
- 2 ½ tbsps finely minced fresh ginger root
- 2 tsps dried thyme
- 1 tsp salt
- 1 tsp ground white pepper
- 7 drops hot pepper sauce (e.g. Tabasco™) to taste
- 1 serrano pepper, finely chopped
- 4 pounds skinless, boneless chicken breast halves

Directions

1. Mix the rum, soy sauce, lime juice, brown sugar, garlic, ginger, thyme, salt, pepper, hot pepper sauce, and serrano pepper together in a mixing bowl. With a fork, pierce the chicken on both sides. Cover the chicken in the marinade in a shallow container. Refrigerate the chicken for 8 hours or overnight after sealing the container.
2. Preheat the grill to high.
3. Grease the grill grate lightly. Remove the chicken from the marinade and place it on the grill. Cook for a further 8 minutes on each side, or until juices run clear.

Nutrition Facts

Per Serving:

350 calories; protein 48.2g; carbohydrates 8.2g; fat 5.5g; cholesterol 129.4mg; sodium 743.5mg.

36. POT ROAST CARIBE

Prep: 25 mins

Cook: 8 hrs

Total: 8 hrs 25 mins

Servings: 6

Ingredients

- 2 tbsps vegetable oil
- 1 (3 pound) boneless beef chuck roast
- 2 cloves garlic, crushed
- 1 cup chopped onion
- 1 tsp salt
- 2 (8 ounce) cans tomato sauce
- 2 tbsps white sugar
- 1 tbsp all-purpose flour
- 1 tsp unsweetened cocoa powder
- 1 tsp chili powder
- 1 tsp dried oregano
- 1 tsp ground cumin
- 1 tsp ground coriander
- ¼ tsp ground cinnamon
- 1 tsp grated orange zest
- 2 large potatoes, cut into large chunks
- 3 carrots, sliced
- 1 stalk celery, chopped
- ½ cup sliced almonds

Directions

1. In a large skillet, heat the oil over medium-high heat. Place the roast in the hot oil and cook until browned on all sides, turning often. Place in a slow cooker after removing from the skillet.
2. In the meat drippings, cook the garlic and onions until soft. Combine the salt and tomato sauce in a mixing bowl. Toss the tomato sauce with the sugar, flour, cocoa powder, chili powder, oregano, cumin, coriander, cinnamon, and orange zest. In the slow cooker, pour the tomato sauce over the roast. Add the potatoes, carrots, and celery to the saucepan. Cook on Low for 6 to 8 hours, or until meat is cooked, covered. Before serving, garnish with sliced almonds.

Nutrition Facts

Per Serving:

595 calories; protein 32.9g; carbohydrates 39.8g; fat 34.2g; cholesterol 103.4mg; sodium 887.6mg.

37. BARBECUED PIG

Prep: 1 hr

Cook: 7 hrs

Additional: 12 hrs

Total: 20 hrs

Servings: 48

Ingredients

- 2 cups vegetable oil
- 1 cup achiote (annatto) seeds
- 24 cloves garlic, peeled
- 3 tbsps dried oregano
- ¾ cup salt
- ½ cup sour orange juice
- 1 whole (25 pound) suckling pig, dressed
- 16 cloves chopped garlic
- 16 peppercorns
- 12 fresh jalapeno pepper, seeded
- 2 cups extra virgin olive oil
- 1 cup distilled white vinegar
- 1 cup lime juice
- 2 tbsps salt
- cheesecloth

Directions

1. Heat the annatto oil in a small saucepan over low heat. Cook, stirring periodically, for about 5 minutes after adding the annatto seeds. Before using, let it cool and strain it to remove the seeds.
2. Crush 24 garlic cloves with oregano and 3/4 cup salt in a big mortar. Add the sour orange juice and mix well. Remove from the equation.
3. Deep cuts should be made in the pig's neck, right below the lower jaw, loin, legs, shoulders, and ribs. The seasoned orange juice should be rubbed into the cuts, as well as all over the skin and in the pig's cavities. Refrigerate the pig overnight, covered with cheesecloth.
4. Over a bed of stones, build an open charcoal fire. Adding hot coals during the long cooking period may be necessary. On either end of the fire, place a Y-shaped pole.

5. Pass a smooth, bark-free rod through the pig's body. Tightly tie the front legs to the pole. Repeat with the hind legs, stretching them out as far as you can. Place the pig over hot coals with the ends of the pole resting on the Y posts. To cook the pig evenly, rotate the pole continually and slowly, and baste it frequently with annatto oil. Roast the pig for seven hours, or until a thermometer inserted into the thickest portion of the thigh registers 145°F (63 ° C). Carve.

6. In the meantime, make the garlic sauce by crushing the remaining 16 garlic cloves, 16 peppercorns, and fresh chilies together in a mortar. Fill a small bowl halfway with the mixture. 2 tsps salt, olive oil, vinegar, and lime juice Serve with meat that has been carved.

Nutrition Facts

Per Serving:

602 calories; protein 16.1g; carbohydrates 3.5g; fat 57.9g; cholesterol 82.9mg; sodium 338.8mg.

38. GRENADIAN SPICE CAKE

Prep: 20 mins

Cook: 1 hr 30 mins

Additional: 10 mins

Total: 2 hrs

Servings: 12

Ingredients

- 2 cups sifted all-purpose flour
- ½ tsp baking powder
- 1/8 tsp salt
- 1 ½ cups white sugar
- 1 cup unsalted butter - chilled, cut into tbsp-size pieces
- 1 ½ tsps grated lime zest
- 1 tsp ground nutmeg
- ½ tsp ground cinnamon
- ¼ tsp ground allspice
- 3 eggs
- ½ cup milk

Directions

1. Preheat the oven to 350 ° Fahrenheit (175 ° C). Preheat the oven to 350°F and grease a 9x5-inch loaf pan. Combine the flour, baking powder, and salt in a sifter and set aside.
2. Cream the sugar and butter together in a medium mixing basin. One at a time, beat in the eggs, then add the lime zest, nutmeg, cinnamon, and allspice. Alternate adding the dry ingredients and the milk, stirring after each addition. Pour the batter into the pan that has been prepared.
3. In a preheated oven, bake for 75 to 90 minutes, or until a toothpick inserted in the center comes out clean. Cool for 10 minutes in the pan before putting out onto a cooling rack to cool completely.

Nutrition Facts

Per Serving:

334 calories; protein 4.2g; carbohydrates 41.8g; fat 17.2g; cholesterol 88.2mg; sodium 63.5mg.

39. BOSCOBEL BEACH GINGER CAKE

Prep: 30 mins

Cook: 45 mins

Total: 1 hr 15 mins

Servings: 12

Ingredients

- 1 cup butter
- 1 ¼ cups packed brown sugar
- 4 eggs
- ¼ cup grated fresh ginger root
- 1 tsp vanilla extract
- 1 cup milk
- 2 ½ cups all-purpose flour
- 4 tsps baking powder
- 4 tsps ground ginger
- 1 ½ tsps ground cinnamon
- ½ tsp salt
- 2 tbsps confectioners' sugar for dusting

Directions

1. Preheat the oven to 350 ° Fahrenheit (175 ° C). A 9-inch Bundt pan should be greased and floured. Combine the flour, baking powder, ginger, cinnamon, and salt in a sifter. Remove from the equation.

2. Cream the butter and brown sugar together in a large mixing mixer until light and creamy. One at a time, beat in the eggs, then toss in the shredded ginger root and vanilla extract. Alternately add the flour mixture and the milk, mixing just until combined. Pour the batter into the pan that has been prepared.

3. Bake for 45 to 50 minutes in a preheated oven, or until a toothpick inserted in the center of the cake comes out clean. Allow to cool for 10 minutes in the pan before turning out onto a serving platter. Before serving, lightly dust with confectioners' sugar.

Nutrition Facts

Per Serving:

362 calories; protein 5.7g; carbohydrates 46g; fat 17.7g; cholesterol 104.3mg; sodium 364.9mg.

40. COCONUT-LIME CHEESECAKE WITH MANGO COULIS

Prep: 35 mins

Cook: 55 mins

Additional: 8 hrs

Total: 9 hrs 30 mins

Servings: 8

Ingredients

- ¾ cup sweetened flaked coconut
- ¾ cup crushed gingersnap cookies
- 3 tbsps melted butter
- 2 (8 ounce) packages cream cheese, softened
- 1 (10 ounce) can sweetened condensed milk
- 2 eggs
- 1 tbsp lime zest
- 2 tbsps lime juice
- 1 tbsp coconut extract
- 2 cups cubed fresh mango
- 1 tsp white sugar, or more to taste

Directions

1. Preheat the oven to 325°F (165 ° C). Grease a 9-inch springform pan lightly.

2. In a mixing basin, combine the coconut, gingersnap cookies, and melted butter; stir until well combined. In the prepared pan, press the cookie mixture into the bottom and slightly up the sides.
3. In a preheated oven, bake the crust for about 10 minutes, or until golden and firm. Allow to cool before serving.
4. Preheat the oven to 300 ° F. (150 ° C).
5. In a mixer bowl, beat the softened cream cheese until smooth. Slowly pour the condensed milk into the mixing bowl, stopping to scrape the sides of the bowl as needed, with the beater set on medium-low. Add the eggs one at a time, allowing the first to fully incorporate before adding the second; scrape down the sides of the bowl as needed.
6. Half of the cream cheese batter should be placed in a separate basin. In the new bowl, whisk together the lime juice and zest; pour the batter over the springform pan's crust, smoothing it out into an equal layer.
7. Combine the remaining cream cheese batter and the coconut extract; pour over the lime-flavored batter in the springform pan, smoothing into an equal layer.
8. Bake for 45 minutes in a preheated oven, or until the top of the cheesecake springs back when lightly pressed. Turn off the oven but leave the cheesecake inside with the oven door slightly ajar until it is fully cool. Refrigerate for at least two hours, or until thoroughly cooled.
9. Puree the mango with the sugar until smooth to make mango coulis. If it's too thick, add a tsp of water at a time until it's pourable. Drizzle over the cheesecake once it's been plated.

Nutrition Facts

Per Serving:

468 calories; protein 9.4g; carbohydrates 38.4g; fat 31.6g; cholesterol 131.4mg; sodium 310.6mg.

41. BUDIN (PUERTO RICAN BREAD PUDDING)

Prep: 30 mins

Cook: 1 hr 30 mins

Additional: 3 hrs

Total: 5 hrs

Servings: 10

Ingredients

- 1 cup water
- 2 (3 inch) cinnamon sticks
- 15 whole cloves
- 1 tsp anise seed
- 2 tbsps water
- ½ cup white sugar
- 1 (1 pound) loaf day-old bread
- 4 cups evaporated milk
- 4 eggs
- 1 ½ cups white sugar
- 1 tsp vanilla extract
- ¾ tsp salt
- ¼ cup butter, melted

Directions

1. In a small saucepan over high heat, bring 1 cup of water to a boil. Combine the cinnamon sticks, cloves, and anise seeds in a mixing bowl. Cover and put aside for 15 minutes to steep.
2. In a saucepan over medium-high heat, add 2 tbsps water and 1/2 cup sugar. Stir occasionally to properly dissolve the sugar, but once the mixture reaches a boil, stop stirring. Stay close to the stove to keep an eye on the color, gently turning the pan to redistribute the caramel as the sugar darkens. Cook until the sugar turns light golden brown, about 310 ° F (160 ° C), then pour into a 9x5 inch loaf pan. Allow the caramel to thicken before serving.
3. Preheat the oven to 350 ° Fahrenheit (175 ° C).
4. Remove the crusts from the day-old bread and tear it into cubes in a large mixing dish. To remove the spices, strain the spice tea through a fine mesh strainer. Combine the bread and evaporated milk in a mixing bowl. Set aside for 10 minutes after stirring to evenly moisten. In a large mixing basin, whisk together the eggs, 1 1/2 cups sugar, vanilla extract, salt, and melted butter. In a large mixing bowl, combine the soaked bread mixture and stir until well combined. Pour over the caramel in the loaf pan.

5. Using a moist kitchen towel, line a roasting pan. Place the loaf pan into the roasting pan on the towel, and the roasting pan on the oven rack. Boil enough water in the roasting pan to come halfway up the edges of the loaf pan.

6. Bake for 1 hour and 15 minutes in a preheated oven, or until a toothpick inserted in the center comes out clean. Cool for roughly an hour in the pan before refrigerating for another 2 hours. Invert the budin onto a serving platter when it's done. The caramel will have thickened into a syrup and will coat the budin in a sauce-like coating.

Nutrition Facts

Per Serving:

488 calories; protein 13.1g; carbohydrates 74.9g; fat 15.8g; cholesterol 115.8mg; sodium 656.1mg.

42. RUM CHICKEN MARINADE

Prep: 10 mins

Total: 10 mins

Servings: 10

Ingredients

- ¼ cup lime juice
- 2 tbsps dark rum
- 2 tbsps olive oil
- 2 tbsps soy sauce
- 2 cloves garlic, minced, or more to taste
- ½ tsp ground cinnamon
- ½ tsp ground ginger
- ¼ tsp hot sauce

Directions

1. In a mixing bowl, combine lime juice, dark rum, olive oil, soy sauce, garlic, cinnamon, ginger, and spicy sauce.

Cook's Note:

To prepare the chicken, pour the marinade over it and let it sit in the refrigerator for at least 30 minutes before grilling.

Nutrition Facts

Per Serving:

36 calories; protein 0.3g; carbohydrates 1.1g; fat 2.7g; sodium 183.8mg.

43. ISLAND MANGO CHUTNEY

Prep: 15 mins

Total: 15 mins

Servings: 10

Ingredients

- 1 mango - peeled, seeded, and chopped
- 3 cloves garlic, chopped
- ½ habanero pepper, seeded and chopped, or more to taste
- 3 sprigs fresh cilantro, chopped
- 1 tbsp lime juice
- ½ tsp salt, or more to taste

Directions

1. In a blender, combine the mango, garlic, habanero pepper, cilantro, lime juice, and salt until you get the appropriate consistency.

Cook's Note:

If you want a thinner consistency, add some water to the mixture.

Nutrition Facts

Per Serving:

16 calories; protein 0.2g; carbohydrates 4g; fat 0.1g; sodium 117.2mg.

44. STUFFING RECIPE

Prep: 1 hr

Cook: 30 mins

Total: 1 hr 30 mins

Servings: 12

Ingredients

- 1 cup water
- 2 ½ cups uncooked wild rice
- ½ cup butter
- 1 pound ground pork sausage
- 2 ½ cups chopped onions
- 2 cups chopped celery
- 2 ½ cups chopped mushrooms
- 1 ½ tsps dried thyme
- 1 ½ tsps dried rosemary
- 2 tsps salt
- 1 ½ tsps pepper
- 6 cups cubed whole wheat bread
- 2 large Rome beauty apples - peeled, cored, and chopped
- 1 cup raisins
- 1 (14.5 ounce) can chicken broth

Directions

1. Boil water in a medium pot and mix in wild rice. Reduce the temperature. Cover and cook for 45 minutes, or until the water is absorbed and the rice is soft.
2. Preheat the oven to 350 ° Fahrenheit (175 ° C).
3. In a big, heavy skillet, melt butter over medium heat. Combine the sausage, onions, and celery in a mixing bowl. Cook for 10 to 12 minutes, or until sausage is evenly browned. Drain and add mushrooms, thyme, and rosemary to the pan. Cook for another 2 minutes, or until the mushrooms are gently browned. Season with salt and pepper after removing from the fire.
4. Combine the sausage mixture, cooked rice, whole wheat bread, apples, and raisins in a large mixing bowl. Blend in the chicken broth in small increments until the mixture is moistened.
5. Fill a large baking dish halfway with the mixture. Bake for 30 minutes, or until lightly browned in a preheated oven.

Nutrition Facts

Per Serving:

453 calories; protein 11.4g; carbohydrates 50.3g; fat 24.4g; cholesterol 46.1mg; sodium 845.7mg.

45. EASY AND YUMMIEST KULFI RECIPE

Prep: 10 mins

Additional: 8 hrs

Total: 8 hrs 10 mins

Servings: 12

Ingredients

- 2 (5 ounce) cans evaporated milk
- 2 (7.6 ounce) cans canned table cream (media crema)
- 1 (14 ounce) can sweetened condensed milk
- 2 slices white bread
- ¼ tsp ground cardamom
- 12 blanched almonds

Directions

1. In a blender, combine evaporated milk, canned cream, and sweetened condensed milk; shred bread into small pieces and add to blender. Blend in the cardamom and almonds for 3 to 4 minutes, or until liquified. Freeze for 8 hours or overnight in a 9x13-inch glass dish before cutting into squares and serving.

Nutrition Facts

Per Serving:

256 calories; protein 4.8g; carbohydrates 22.5g; fat 15.6g; cholesterol 21.7mg; sodium 120.1mg.

46. APPLE PIE SPICE RECIPE

Prep: 5 mins

Total: 5 mins

Servings: 4

Ingredients

- 1 tbsp ground cinnamon
- 1 ½ tsps ground nutmeg
- ¾ tsp ground allspice
- ¾ tsp ground cardamom

Directions

1. In an airtight jar, combine cinnamon, nutmeg, allspice, and cardamom.

Nutrition Facts

Per Serving:

12 calories; protein 0.2g; carbohydrates 2.5g; fat 0.5g; sodium 0.7mg.

47. BEEF GOULASH RECIPE

Prep: 20 mins

Cook: 1 hr 10 mins

Total: 1 hr 30 mins

Servings: 4

Ingredients

- 4 tbsps avocado oil
- 1 medium onion, chopped
- 4 cloves garlic, chopped
- 1 pound beef roast, diced
- 10 white button mushrooms, quartered
- 2 carrots, diced
- 1 cup bone broth
- 1 tsp ground turmeric
- 1 tbsp arrowroot powder (Optional)

- salt to taste
- 2 tbsps chopped fresh parsley

Directions

1. In a skillet, heat the oil over medium heat. Cook, stirring occasionally, until the onion and garlic are cooked, about 2 to 5 minutes. Cook and stir until the beef cubes are browned, about 5 to 7 minutes. Cook, stirring occasionally, until the mushrooms and carrots are barely cooked, 3 to 5 minutes more.
2. Reduce the heat to very low and add the bone broth and turmeric to the skillet. Cover skillet partially with lid and cook, stirring periodically, until beef is cooked, about 1 hour. If the mixture adheres to the skillet, add a splash of water.
3. If the sauce hasn't thickened enough, remove the lid and increase the heat slightly. If necessary, thicken the sauce with arrowroot. Season with salt and pepper. Serve with parsley as a garnish.

Nutrition Facts

Per Serving:

346 calories; protein 16.3g; carbohydrates 9.4g; fat 27.3g; cholesterol 51.5mg; sodium 107.2mg.

48. ISLAND SMOOTHIE

Prep: 5 mins

Total: 5 mins

Servings: 1

Ingredients

- 1 cup ice
- 2 cups pineapple juice
- ½ cup ginger ale
- 3 tbsps coconut milk
- 1 tbsp white sugar

Directions

1. In a blender, combine the ice, pineapple juice, ginger ale, coconut milk, and sugar until blended.

Nutrition Facts

Per Serving:

445 calories; protein 2.7g; carbohydrates 88.8g; fat 10.2g; sodium 30.9mg.

49. ELEGANT MUSHROOM PIE RECIPE

Prep: 25 mins

Cook: 40 mins

Total: 1 hr 5 mins

Servings: 8

Ingredients

- 6 tbsps butter, divided
- 1 ½ pounds baby bella (crimini) mushrooms, sliced
- ¼ cup chopped sweet onion
- ½ lemon, juiced
- ½ tsp dried thyme
- 5 tbsps all-purpose flour
- 1 ¼ cups Swanson® Chicken Broth
- 1/3 cup Marsala wine
- 2 tbsps half-and-half
- salt and pepper to taste
- 1 (17.3 ounce) package frozen puff pastry, thawed
- 1 egg, beaten

Directions

1. Preheat the oven to 375 ° Fahrenheit (190 ° C). Using non-fat cooking spray, coat a 9-inch pie plate.
2. In a large skillet, melt 3 tbsps butter over medium heat. Stir in the mushrooms and onions until the liquid from the mushrooms has evaporated, about 10 minutes. Cook for 2 minutes after adding the lemon juice and thyme.
3. In a separate pot, melt 3 tbsps butter. In a separate bowl, whisk together the flour and stir continually for about 1 minute. Whisk in the Swanson® Chicken Broth, Marsala, and half-and-half in a slow, steady stream until the sauce is smooth and thickened, about 3 minutes. The sauce should be rich and creamy. Season with salt and pepper to taste.
4. Stir the mushroom mixture into the sauce broth/Marsala combination until everything is completely combined.
5. To fit the pie plate, roll out one layer of puff pastry. Trim the excess pastry and press evenly into the bottom and edges of the pie plate. Fill the pastry shell with the mushroom mixture.
6. Place the second piece of puff pastry on top of the first. Trim the excess and secure the edge with a crimp. Make a few slits in the top to let steam out. Brush the beaten egg over the top of the pie.
7. Cook for about 40 minutes in a preheated oven until golden brown and the mushroom mixture is bubbling. Before serving, allow the pie to cool somewhat.

Cook's Note:

White button mushrooms can be used instead of baby bellas, and whole milk can be used instead of half-and-half. Start making your roux/sauce while you're sautéing the mushrooms. You will save some time as a result of this.

Allstars are members of the Allrecipes community who have been chosen as brand ambassadors based on their onsite activity, enthusiasm, and dedication. Allrecipes Allstars may be compensated for their involvement in the program.

Nutrition Facts

Per Serving:

496 calories; protein 10g; carbohydrates 37.2g; fat 33.2g; cholesterol 48.3mg; sodium 428mg.

50. HOMEMADE BAKING POWDER RECIPE

Prep: 5 mins

Total: 5 mins

Servings: 6

Ingredients

- 2 tsps cream of tartar
- 1 tsp baking soda
- 1 tsp cornstarch (Optional)

Directions

1. In a separate bowl, combine the cream of tartar and baking soda. To keep the mixture fresh, whisk cornstarch into it and store it in an airtight container.

Nutrition Facts

Per Serving:

4 calories; carbohydrates 1g; sodium 210.3mg.

51. BAKED MANGO-GINGER SWORDFISH

Prep: 15 mins

Cook: 30 mins

Additional: 1 hr

Total: 1 hr 45 mins

Servings: 4

Ingredients

- 2 pounds swordfish steaks
- 2 tbsps lemon juice
- ½ cup dry sherry
- 1 tbsp minced fresh ginger root
- 1 cup mango chutney

Directions

2. In a large, shallow bowl, place swordfish steaks. Combine lemon juice, dry sherry, ginger, and mango chutney in a small bowl. Pour the sauce over the swordfish steaks and turn them to coat them. Cover and marinate for 1 hour in the refrigerator.
3. Preheat the oven to 350 ° Fahrenheit (175 ° C).
4. In a medium baking dish, place swordfish steaks. Marinade should be used to cover the meat. Cook for 20 to 30 minutes in a preheated oven, basting regularly with the marinade, until the fish flakes easily with a fork.

Note

The full amount of marinade ingredients is included in the nutrition facts for this dish. The amount of marinade used varies depending on marinating duration, ingredients, cooking style, and other factors.

Nutrition Facts

Per Serving:

408 calories; protein 45.4g; carbohydrates 32.4g; fat 9.3g; cholesterol 87.5mg; sodium 374.6mg.

52. APPLE BUTTER RECIPE

Prep: 20 mins

Cook: 45 mins

Additional: 10 mins

Total: 1 hr 15 mins

Servings: 15

Ingredients

- 2 pounds Honeycrisp apples - peeled, cored, and cut into 1-inch pieces
- 2 pounds Granny Smith apples - peeled, cored, and cut into small pieces
- 1 cup apple cider
- 2 cups white sugar
- 2 tbsps lemon juice
- canning jars with lids and rings

Directions

1. In a large stainless steel or enamel-coated saucepan, combine Honeycrisp apples, Granny Smith apples, and apple cider; bring to a boil, stirring occasionally. Reduce heat to medium-low and simmer for about 20 minutes, or until the mixture has reduced by half.
2. Bring the apple mixture to a boil, stirring in the sugar and lemon juice. Reduce heat to medium-low and continue to cook at a low simmer for about 25 minutes, or until the mixture is extremely thick.
3. Boil the jars and lids for at least 5 minutes to sterilize them. Fill the heated, sterilized jars with apple butter, filling them to within 1/4 inch of the top. To eliminate any air bubbles, run a knife or a thin spatula around the insides of the jars after they've been filled. To remove any food residue, wipe the jar rims with a wet paper towel. Lids and rings are screwed on top.
4. Fill a big stockpot partly with water and place a rack in the bottom. Bring to a boil, then use a holder to lower the jars into the hot water. Make sure there's a 2-inch gap between the jars. If required, add extra boiling water to elevate the water level to at least 1 inch above the jar tops. Bring the water to a boil, then cover and set aside for 10 minutes.
5. Remove the jars from the stockpot and set them several inches apart on a cloth-covered or wood surface to cool. Once cool, squeeze the top of each lid with your finger to ensure a firm seal (lid does not move up or down at all). Keep it in a cool, dark place.

Cook's Note:

Combine 2 tsps of cinnamon, 1/2 tsp ground cloves, and 1/2 tsp allspice with the sugar to produce a spiced apple butter.

Nutrition Facts

Per Serving:

171 calories; protein 0.3g; carbohydrates 44.9g; fat 0.1g; sodium 3.1mg.

53. TURKEY-POTATO CHOWDER RECIPE

Prep: 15 mins

Cook: 20 mins

Total: 35 mins

Servings: 4

Ingredients

- 2 cups peeled and diced potatoes
- 2 cups frozen mixed vegetables
- ¼ cup chopped onion
- ¼ cup finely chopped celery
- 1 tsp chopped fresh parsley
- 2 cups Swanson® Chicken Broth
- 1 ½ cups diced cooked turkey
- ½ tsp poultry seasoning
- ¼ cup all-purpose flour
- 1 ½ cups fat free half-and-half
- ½ tsp sriracha chili garlic sauce
- 1 pinch salt and pepper to taste
- 2 slices bacon - cooked and crumbled

Directions

1. In a large saucepan, combine potatoes, mixed vegetables, onions, celery, parsley, and Swanson® Chicken Broth. Bring to a boil over medium heat; decrease heat to low, cover, and cook for 10 minutes, or until veggies are soft. Combine the turkey and poultry seasonings in a mixing bowl.
2. Combine the flour and half-and-half in a mixing bowl and whisk until smooth. Slowly pour the mixture into the pot. Stir until the mixture has thickened somewhat, or until it has a chowder-like consistency. Stir in the sriracha sauce, salt, and pepper.
3. Serve in soup bowls with crumbled bacon on top.

Cook's Note:

Serve with fresh bread or oyster crackers. This chowder has a faint sriracha flavor, but if you're worried about the heat, just leave it out—you'll still enjoy it!

Allstars are members of the Allrecipes community who have been chosen as brand ambassadors based on their onsite activity, enthusiasm, and dedication. Allrecipes Allstars may be compensated for their involvement in the program.

Nutrition Facts

Per Serving:

319 calories; protein 25.2g; carbohydrates 40.7g; fat 6.6g; cholesterol 51.9mg; sodium 869.7mg.

54. BANANA COCONUT SMOOTHIE

Prep: 5 mins

Total: 5 mins

Servings: 1

Ingredients

- 1 banana
- 1 cup milk
- 3 fluid ounces unsweetened coconut cream
- ice cubes

Directions

1. In a blender, combine the banana, milk, coconut cream, and ice cubes until smooth.

Nutrition Facts

Per Serving:

520 calories; protein 12.6g; carbohydrates 44.3g; fat 36g; cholesterol 19.5mg; sodium 108.5mg.

55. CREOLE CHICKEN RECIPE

Prep: 10 mins

Cook: 45 mins

Total: 55 mins

Servings: 4

Ingredients

- 4 skinless chicken thighs, or more to taste
- 1 pinch Creole seasoning, or more to taste
- 2 tbsps butter
- 1 (15 ounce) can diced tomatoes with green chile peppers
- 1 cup water
- 1 (8 ounce) can tomato sauce
- 1 (6.8 ounce) package Spanish-style rice mix

Directions

1. Chicken thighs should be seasoned with Creole seasoning.
2. Cook chicken in melted butter in a pan over medium heat until browned, 3 to 4 minutes per side. Place the chicken on a plate. In the same skillet, combine the tomatoes, green chile peppers, water, tomato sauce, and Spanish-style rice mix; stir well. Bring the chicken back to a boil in the rice mixture. Reduce heat to low, cover skillet, and cook for 40 minutes, or until chicken is no longer pink in the center and rice is soft. Serve the rice on a dish with the chicken on top.

Nutrition Facts

Per Serving:

400 calories; protein 27.3g; carbohydrates 41.9g; fat 14.2g; cholesterol 93mg; sodium 1750.6mg.

56. EASIEST ASPARAGUS RECIPE

Prep: 5 mins

Cook: 10 mins

Total: 15 mins

Servings: 5

Ingredients

- 2 tbsps butter, or more as needed
- 1 bunch asparagus, trimmed
- 1 tsp honey
- 1/8 tsp garlic powder
- 1/8 tsp cayenne pepper

Directions

1. In a pan over medium-low heat, melt 2 tbsps butter. Cook asparagus in heated butter for 6 to 8 minutes, stirring occasionally.
2. Season with garlic powder and cayenne pepper after drizzling honey over the asparagus.

Cook's Notes:

If the asparagus starts to stick to the pan, add up to 1 tbsp extra butter while cooking.

Use 2 tbsps extra-virgin olive oil instead of butter for a healthier alternative.

Nutrition Facts

Per Serving:

64 calories; protein 2.1g; carbohydrates 4.8g; fat 4.7g; cholesterol 12.2mg; sodium 34.6mg.

57. CRAB RECIPE

Prep: 10 mins

Cook: 6 mins

Total: 16 mins

Servings: 4

Ingredients

- ½ cup olive oil
- ½ cup butter
- ½ cup minced garlic
- 4 pounds Snow Crab clusters, thawed if necessary

Directions

1. Heat an outside barbecue to high temperatures. When the grate is hot, lightly oil it.
2. Brush the crab with a good amount of the olive oil, butter, and garlic mixture.
3. Cook crab over a hot grill, flipping once, for about 6 minutes, or until the shell begins to brown.

Nutrition Facts

Per Serving:

957 calories; protein 68.9g; carbohydrates 5.8g; fat 72.7g; cholesterol 394.5mg; sodium 1292.9mg.

58. CURRY MANGO CHICKEN

Prep: 15 mins

Additional: 2 hrs

Total: 2 hrs 15 mins

Servings: 6

Ingredients
Chicken:

- 3 ½ tbsps curry powder
- 2 tsps minced ginger
- 2 cloves garlic, minced
- 1 pinch crushed red pepper flakes
- ¼ tsp salt
- ¼ tsp black pepper
- 1 tsp thyme
- 10 skinless chicken thighs

Rice:

- 2 cups converted long-grain white rice, rinsed
- 2 cups mango - peeled, seeded, and chopped
- 1 onion, chopped
- 2 cloves crushed garlic
- 2 tsps minced fresh ginger root
- 1 tbsp curry powder
- 1 pinch red pepper flakes
- 1 tsp salt
- ¼ tsp thyme
- 10 whole allspice berries
- 3 tbsps brown sugar
- 1 cup water
- 2 cups chicken broth
- 2 tbsps lime juice
- ½ (14 ounce) can coconut milk

Directions

1. Combine the curry, ginger, garlic, red pepper flakes, salt, pepper, and thyme in a large mixing basin. Place the chicken in a mixing basin and season evenly. Cover and marinate for at least 2 hours.

2. Preheat the oven to 400 ° Fahrenheit (200 ° C).
3. Combine rice, mango, onion, garlic, and ginger in a large mixing basin. Curry, red pepper flakes, salt, thyme, allspice berries, and brown sugar are used to season. In a large mixing bowl, combine the water, broth, and lime juice. Place in a casserole dish and top with the marinated chicken. Then pour the coconut milk on top. Using aluminum foil, cover the dish.
4. Preheat the oven to 350°F and bake for 1 hour. Remove the foil and simmer for another 10 to 15 minutes. Before serving, take out the allspice berries.

Nutrition Facts

Per Serving:

769 calories; protein 35.5g; carbohydrates 83.9g; fat 32.7g; cholesterol 131.6mg; sodium 620.3mg.

59. DELICIOUS PIZZA SAUCE RECIPE

Prep: 10 mins

Cook: 10 mins

Total: 20 mins

Servings: 4

Ingredients

- 2 tbsps olive oil
- 1 (28 ounce) can crushed tomatoes
- 2 leaves basil, chopped
- 3 cloves garlic, chopped
- 1 pinch salt and ground black pepper to taste
- 1 pinch grated Parmesan cheese

Directions

1. In a saucepan, heat the olive oil. Place the smashed tomatoes in a saucepan over low heat. Bring the tomatoes to a simmer with the basil, garlic, salt, and black pepper. To serve, stir in the Parmesan cheese.

Nutrition Facts

Per Serving:

127 calories; protein 3.5g; carbohydrates 15g; fat 7.4g; cholesterol 0.2mg; sodium 263.1mg.

60. VERY OLD MEATLOAF RECIPE

Prep: 20 mins

Cook: 1 hr 30 mins

Total: 1 hr 50 mins

Servings: 8

Ingredients

- 2 pounds ground beef
- 2 tbsps water
- 1 tbsp milk
- 1 cup bread crumbs
- 1 onion, diced
- 1 carrot, diced
- 1 small Granny Smith apple, diced
- 1 egg

Directions

1. Preheat the oven to 375°F (190°C) (190 ° C).
2. In a large mixing basin, combine ground beef, water, and milk with your hands until the beef is equally moistened.
3. In a large mixing bowl, combine the bread crumbs, onion, carrot, apple, and egg.
4. Make a loaf out of the beef mixture.
5. Place the meatloaf in a deep baking dish and cover with aluminum foil.
6. Bake for 1 hour in a preheated oven; remove foil tent and bake for another 30 minutes or until center is no longer pink.

Nutrition Facts

Per Serving:

289 calories; protein 22.2g; carbohydrates 15g; fat 15.1g; cholesterol 94.4mg; sodium 181.3mg.

61. PATE RECIPE

Prep: 15 mins

Cook: 25 mins

Additional: 4 hrs

Total: 4 hrs 40 mins

Servings: 24

Ingredients

- 1 pound bacon strips, diced
- 3 medium onions, chopped
- 3 cloves garlic
- 1 pound chicken livers, trimmed and chopped
- 1 pound veal, trimmed and cubed
- 1 cup heavy cream
- ½ cup milk
- ¾ cup butter
- 1 pinch salt and pepper to taste

Directions

1. In a large skillet over medium-high heat, cook the bacon. Add the onion and whole garlic cloves when the spinach has wilted. Cook until the onion is tender, stirring regularly. Cook until the chicken livers and veal cubes are no longer pink in the skillet. Allow to cool before serving.
2. Set aside a 9x5 inch loaf pan or mold lined with waxed paper or sprayed with cooking spray. Place the meat mixture in a food processor container and pulse until finely minced. Do not purée the ingredients. In a large skillet over medium heat, melt the butter. Stir in the beef mixture, heavy cream, and milk. Cook until well heated. Season to taste with salt and pepper before pouring into the loaf pan or shape. Before serving, chill for at least 4 hours.

Nutrition Facts

Per Serving:

178 calories; protein 10.1g; carbohydrates 2.2g; fat 14.2g; cholesterol 155.3mg; sodium 214mg.

62. PINEAPPLE AND APRICOT SKILLET CHICKEN

Prep: 15 mins

Cook: 30 mins

Total: 45 mins

Servings: 4

Ingredients

- 2 fresh apricots, pitted and diced
- 1 (8 ounce) can crushed pineapple, with juice
- 1 tbsp olive oil
- 4 skinless, boneless chicken breast halves
- 1 tbsp lemon juice
- 1 tbsp butter
- 1 tsp orange zest
- ½ cup dark rum
- ¼ cup brown sugar
- 1 tbsp onion powder
- ½ tsp ground ginger
- 1 pinch ground white pepper
- salt to taste
- 1 yellow bell pepper, chopped
- 1 red bell pepper, chopped

Directions

1. In a blender or food processor, purée the pineapple, its juice, and the apricots until smooth.
2. In a large skillet, heat the olive oil over medium heat. Sprinkle the lemon juice over the chicken in the skillet. Cook for about 10 minutes, or until both sides are lightly browned.
3. Toss the butter and orange zest into the skillet, then pour in the rum once the butter has melted. Light the mixture with a match and let it burn until the flame goes out. Brown sugar, onion powder, ginger, salt, and pepper are added to the combined pineapple and apricot mixture. Reduce the heat to low and continue to cook for 5 minutes. Cook until the red and yellow bell peppers are hot but still crisp, about 5 minutes. Remove the pan from the heat and serve.

Nutrition Facts

Per Serving:

375 calories; protein 27.2g; carbohydrates 26.9g; fat 10.1g; cholesterol 79.6mg; sodium 88.9mg.

63. SPECTACULAR OVERNIGHT SLAW RECIPE

Prep: 10 mins

Cook: 5 mins

Additional: 8 hrs

Total: 8 hrs 15 mins

Servings: 16

Ingredients
Slaw:

- 1 head cabbage, shredded
- 1 red onion, thinly sliced
- ½ cup chopped green bell pepper
- ½ cup chopped red bell pepper
- ½ cup shredded carrots
- ½ cup sliced pimiento-stuffed olives

Dressing:

- ½ cup white wine vinegar
- ½ cup canola oil
- ½ cup white sugar
- 2 tsps Dijon mustard
- 1 tsp salt
- 1 tsp celery seed
- 1 tsp mustard seed

Directions

1. In a large mixing bowl, combine the cabbage, onion, green bell pepper, red bell pepper, carrots, and olives.
2. In a saucepan, combine the vinegar, oil, sugar, Dijon mustard, salt, celery seed, and mustard seed. Bring to a boil, then cook and stir for 1 minute, or until the sugar has dissolved. Toss the cabbage mixture gently with the heated dressing. Refrigerate for at least 8 hours or overnight after covering the bowl with plastic wrap.

Nutrition Facts

Per Serving:

121 calories; protein 1.3g; carbohydrates 12.5g; fat 8g; sodium 323.4mg.

64. MATT'S JERKY RECIPE

Prep: 15 mins

Additional: 1 day

Total: 1 day

Servings: 10

Ingredients

- 3 pounds beef top round
- 2/3 cup soy sauce
- ¼ cup Worcestershire sauce
- 1 tbsp brown sugar
- 2 tsps liquid smoke flavoring
- 2 tsps onion powder
- 2 tsps chili powder
- 2 tsps garlic powder
- 2 tsps cayenne pepper
- 2 tsps finely ground black pepper

Directions

1. Freeze the beef for about 20 minutes to make it easier to slice. Cut the beef into 1/4-inch thick strips against the grain.
2. In a large mixing bowl, combine soy sauce, Worcestershire sauce, brown sugar, liquid smoke, onion powder, chili powder, garlic powder, cayenne, and pepper. Toss in the meat strips. Cover and marinate in the refrigerator for 18 to 24 hours, stirring at least twice.
3. Arrange the beef strips on the trays of the dehydrator. Dehydrate for 8 hours at 160 ° F (70 ° C) until completely dry.

Cook's Notes:

A Nesco(R) dehydrator is what I use.

For an additional kick, lightly season the meat with coarsely ground black pepper or red pepper flakes before placing it in the dehydrator.

Nutrition Facts

Per Serving:

180 calories; protein 26.9g; carbohydrates 5.5g; fat 5g; cholesterol 67.7mg; sodium 1084.2mg.

65. CARIBBEAN FISH SOUP

Prep: 35 mins

Cook: 1 hr

Additional: 30 mins

Total: 2 hrs 5 mins

Servings: 8

Ingredients

- 2 whole fish, scaled and cleaned, or more to taste
- 1 lemon, juiced
- 8 cups water
- 4 green bananas, chopped
- 1 pound pumpkin, cut into 1-inch pieces, or more to taste
- 2 potatoes, chopped
- 2 ears corn, cut into 1-inch pieces
- 4 ounces carrots, cut into 1/2-inch pieces
- ½ cup chopped okra
- 4 scallions, chopped
- 1 hot chile pepper
- 2 cloves garlic, chopped
- 1 tsp salt
- 1 tsp ground black pepper
- 4 sprigs fresh thyme, leaves stripped

Directions

1. Drain the fish after rinsing it with lemon juice.
2. In a large mixing bowl, bring water to a boil. Add the salmon and cook for about 30 minutes, or until it is soft. Remove the fish from the soup and set aside. Allow the fish to cool. Remove bones while attempting to preserve huge portions of fish.
3. To make the broth, bring it to a boil. Green bananas, pumpkin, potatoes, maize, carrots, okra, scallions, chile pepper, garlic, salt, pepper, and thyme should all be added to the saucepan. Bring the water back to a boil. Reduce heat to low and cook for about 10 minutes, or until potatoes are almost tender. Add the fish and mix well. Cook for another 5 minutes, or until the flavors have melded.
4. Remove the soup from the heat and let it aside for 30 minutes before serving. Remove the chile pepper and toss it out.

Cook's Notes:

If you don't want a lot of heat, don't slit the chile pepper.

When reheating leftovers, do not boil; this will cause the fish to break down.

Nutrition Facts

Per Serving:

203 calories; protein 11.6g; carbohydrates 35g; fat 3.3g; cholesterol 25.5mg; sodium 338mg.

66. CARIBBEAN CRABMEAT SALAD

Prep: 20 mins

Cook: 10 mins

Additional: 1 hr

Total: 1 hr 30 mins

Servings: 4

Ingredients

- 3 cups uncooked rotini pasta
- 1 (8 ounce) package imitation crabmeat, flaked
- 1 red bell pepper, julienned
- 1 mango - peeled, seeded, and cubed
- 2 tbsps chopped fresh cilantro
- 1 jalapeno pepper, seeded and minced
- 1 tsp lime zest
- 3 tbsps fresh lime juice
- 2 tbsps olive oil
- 1 tbsp honey
- ½ tsp ground cumin
- ½ tsp ground ginger
- ¼ tsp salt

Directions

1. A big saucepan of lightly salted water should be brought to a boil. Cook for 8 to 10 minutes, or until the pasta is al dente; drain and rinse under cold water.
2. In a large mixing bowl, combine the pasta, crabmeat, red pepper, mango, cilantro, and jalapeño.
3. Whisk together the lime zest, lime juice, olive oil, honey, cumin, ginger, and salt in a small bowl. Pour dressing over salad, toss to coat, and chill for at least one hour before serving.

Nutrition Facts

Per Serving:

304 calories; protein 9.8g; carbohydrates 50.1g; fat 7.9g; cholesterol 11.2mg; sodium 629.3mg.

67. CARIBBEAN BREEZE

Prep: 5 mins

Total: 5 mins

Servings: 1

Ingredients

- ice
- 1 fluid ounce orange vodka
- 1 fluid ounce raspberry vodka
- ½ fluid ounce coconut-flavored rum
- 2 fluid ounces orange juice
- 2 fluid ounces pineapple juice
- 1 dash grenadine
- 1 orange wedge, for garnish

Directions

1. Ice should be added to a tall glass. Over ice, combine the orange vodka, raspberry vodka, rum, orange juice, pineapple juice, and grenadine. Serve with an orange slice as a garnish.

Nutrition Facts

Per Serving:

230 calories; protein 1.3g; carbohydrates 17.7g; fat 1.3g; cholesterol 8.5mg; sodium 11.1mg.

68. CARIBBEAN NACHOS

Prep: 20 mins

Cook: 20 mins

Total: 40 mins

Servings: 4

Ingredients

- 1 (16 ounce) package multigrain tortilla chips
- 1 red bell pepper, diced
- 1 orange bell pepper, diced
- 1 bunch green onions, chopped
- 1 avocado - peeled, pitted, and diced
- ½ pineapple, peeled and cut into 1/2-inch dice
- 8 thick slices bacon
- ¾ cup Caribbean jerk marinade
- 1 pound cooked shrimp, peeled and deveined
- ½ pound shredded Monterey Jack cheese
- 1 bunch fresh cilantro, chopped

Directions

1. Preheat the oven to 400 ° Fahrenheit (200 ° C).
2. On a pan or cookie sheet, layer the chips. On top of the chips, arrange the red pepper, orange pepper, onion, avocado, and pineapple.
3. In a big, deep skillet, cook the bacon. Cook until equally crisp over medium-high heat; drain on a platter lined with paper towels. Bacon should be chopped and sprinkled over the nachos.
4. In a saucepan over medium heat, pour the jerk marinade. Cook, stirring constantly, for 3 minutes, or until the marinade has thickened to a sticky consistency. Stir in the shrimp and simmer until they are thoroughly heated. Top the nachos with the shrimp and Monterrey Jack cheese, as well as cilantro.
5. Place the nachos in the oven for about 7 minutes, or until the cheese has melted.

Nutrition Facts

Per Serving:

1268 calories; protein 59g; carbohydrates 108.4g; fat 68.9g; cholesterol 299.4mg; sodium 2808.9mg.

69. CARIBBEAN BARLEY SALAD

Prep: 20 mins

Cook: 25 mins

Additional: 20 mins

Total: 1 hr 5 mins

Servings: 4

Ingredients

- 3 cups water
- ½ tsp salt
- ½ cup barley
- 1 large mango, peeled and diced, divided
- 3 tbsps lime juice
- 2 tbsps olive oil
- ½ tsp ground cumin
- ½ tsp salt
- 1 ½ cups cooked black beans
- 1 cup grape tomatoes, halved
- ½ cup diced red onion
- ¼ cup chopped fresh cilantro
- 1 tbsp minced jalapeno pepper

Directions

1. In a saucepan, bring water and 1/2 tsp salt to a boil. Cover and cook for 20 minutes, or until barley is soft but firm to the bite. Allow 20 to 30 minutes to cool completely after draining any extra cooking liquid.
2. Using a fork or a potato masher, mash 1/4 of the mango against the side of a large bowl. Lime juice, olive oil, cumin, and 1/2 tsp salt are whisked in. Toss together the barley, leftover mango, black beans, grape tomatoes, red onion, cilantro, and jalapeño.

Cook's Notes:

If you prefer, use one 15-ounce can of black beans, drained.

If you want, mint can be used instead of cilantro.

Nutrition Facts

Per Serving:

294 calories; protein 9.4g; carbohydrates 49.8g; fat 8g; sodium 942.9mg.

70. SORREL TEA

Prep: 5 mins

Cook: 5 mins

Additional: 8 hrs

Total: 8 hrs 10 mins

Servings: 4

Ingredients

- 9 ounces dried red sorrel buds
- 3 tsps grated ginger
- 3 strips dried orange zest
- 1 white clove
- 1 quart water
- 2/3 cup white sugar
- ice cubes

Directions

1. In a mixing dish, combine the sorrel, ginger, dried orange zest, and clove.
2. In a pot or kettle, bring water to a boil; pour over sorrel mixture. Stir in the sugar until it is completely dissolved. Allow 8 hours to overnight for the mixture to steep at room temperature.
3. Strain the sorrel mixture into a pitcher using a fine-mesh strainer; remove the particles. Serve with ice cubes.

Nutrition Facts

Per Serving:

177 calories; protein 0.9g; carbohydrates 44.7g; fat 0.5g; sodium 12.2mg.

71. BANANA SPLIT

Prep: 10 mins

Cook: 8 mins

Total: 18 mins

Servings: 4

Ingredients

- 1 tbsp unsalted butter
- 2 bananas, cut in half crosswise then lengthwise
- ¼ cup dark rum
- 1/8 tsp ground nutmeg
- 1/8 tsp ground cinnamon
- 2 tbsps lime juice
- 1 quart vanilla ice cream
- ¼ cup chocolate syrup
- ½ cup whipped cream

Directions

1. In a large nonstick skillet, melt butter over medium-high heat. Cook bananas in butter for about 1 minute, or until they are caramelized and softening. Remove the pan from the heat and mix in the rum, cinnamon, and nutmeg. Carefully ignite the liquid in the pan with a long match or lighter. Allow 15 to 30 seconds for the fire to burn out; if required, extinguish with a lid on the pan.
2. Cook for another 2 to 3 minutes, or until the sauce has reduced by half. Cook for an additional minute after adding the lime juice.
3. Divide the ice cream among the four serving bowls. Warm bananas and rum sauce mixture on top of each. Drizzle chocolate sauce over each sundae and top with whipped cream.

Nutrition Facts

Per Serving:

450 calories; protein 6g; carbohydrates 58.5g; fat 19.5g; cholesterol 71.4mg; sodium 130.1mg.

72. WHITE BEANS

Prep: 25 mins

Cook: 40 mins

Total: 1 hr 5 mins

Servings: 6

Ingredients

- 1 tbsp olive oil
- ½ onion, chopped
- ½ green bell pepper, chopped
- ½ cup water
- 1 (15.5 ounce) can small white beans
- 1 (6.5 ounce) can tomato sauce
- 1 ½ tsps minced garlic
- 1 sprig cilantro, coarsely chopped
- ¼ cup calabaza (pumpkin-like squash), peeled and medium diced
- 1 (.18 ounce) packet sazon with coriander and achiote
- 1 cube chicken with tomato flavored bouillon
- 1 pinch salt
- 1 pinch black pepper
- 1 pinch ground cumin

Directions

1. In a large saucepan, heat the olive oil over medium-high heat. Stir in the onion and green pepper and simmer for 5 minutes, or until the onion begins to brown. Fill the pot halfway with water, then add the white beans, tomato sauce, garlic, cilantro, and calabaza. Stir well to mix the sazon packet, bouillon cube, salt, pepper, and cumin.
2. Bring to a boil, then lower to a low heat, cover, and cook for 20 minutes, or until the calabaza has softened. Remove the lid and simmer for another 10 minutes, or until the sauce has thickened.

Nutrition Facts

Per Serving:

121 calories; protein 6.1g; carbohydrates 19.3g; fat 2.6g; cholesterol 0.1mg; sodium 483.4mg.

73. BANANA MUFFINS

Prep: 15 mins

Cook: 20 mins

Total: 35 mins

Servings: 12

Ingredients

- 2 cups all-purpose flour
- 1 tsp baking soda
- ½ tsp baking powder
- ½ tsp salt
- ½ cup butter
- 1 cup brown sugar
- 2 large eggs
- 3 medium bananas
- 1 tbsp rum extract
- 1 cup shredded coconut
- ½ cup chopped dried pineapple

Directions

1. Preheat the oven to 350 ° Fahrenheit (175 ° C). Using paper liners, line 12 muffin cups.
2. In a mixing basin, sift together the flour, baking soda, baking powder, and salt; set aside. Cream the butter and sugar together in a large mixing basin until light and creamy. After that, beat in the bananas and rum extract one at a time, mixing well after each addition. Combine the flour and baking soda in a mixing bowl. Mix just enough to evenly distribute the shredded coconut and pineapple. Divide the batter evenly among the muffin cups that have been prepared.
3. Cook for 20 to 25 minutes in a preheated oven, or until a toothpick inserted in the center comes out clean.

Nutrition Facts

Per Serving:

322 calories; protein 4.3g; carbohydrates 46.8g; fat 13.9g; cholesterol 51.3mg; sodium 297.3mg.

74. POTATO CURRY

Prep: 20 mins

Cook: 30 mins

Total: 50 mins

Servings: 6

Ingredients

- 1 tsp ground cumin
- ½ tsp ground turmeric
- ½ tsp curry powder
- ½ tsp ground allspice
- ½ cup olive oil
- 1 tbsp grated fresh ginger root
- 1 small onion, chopped
- 4 cloves garlic, minced
- 2 potatoes, cut into small cubes
- ½ cup chopped red bell pepper
- ½ cup chopped broccoli
- 1 cup chopped bok choy
- 1 plantains, peeled and broken into chunks
- 1 cup water, or as needed
- salt to taste

Directions

1. In a small bowl, combine cumin, turmeric, allspice, and curry powder.
2. In a skillet, heat the olive oil over medium-low heat. In the heated oil, cook and stir the ginger and cumin combination until aromatic, about 5 minutes. Cook and toss the onion and garlic into the ginger mixture for 1 to 2 minutes, or until the onion is heated. Cook for 1 to 2 minutes, stirring occasionally. In a large mixing bowl, combine the potatoes, red bell pepper, broccoli, bok choy, and plantains. Fill the skillet with water until it is about half-full.
3. Cook, covered, at a low heat until the potatoes are cooked, about 20 to 25 minutes. Season with salt and pepper.

Nutrition Facts

Per Serving:

190 calories; protein 2.7g; carbohydrates 25.8g; fat 9.4g; sodium 19.1mg.

75. CARIBBEAN CHICKEN SALAD

Prep: 30 mins

Cook: 15 mins

Additional: 2 hrs

Total: 2 hrs 45 mins

Servings: 4

Ingredients

- 2 skinless, boneless chicken breast halves
- ½ cup teriyaki marinade sauce
- 2 tomatoes, seeded and chopped
- ½ cup chopped onion
- 2 tsps minced jalapeno pepper
- 2 tsps chopped fresh cilantro
- ¼ cup Dijon mustard
- ¼ cup honey
- 1 ½ tbsps white sugar
- 1 tbsp vegetable oil
- 1 ½ tbsps cider vinegar
- 1 ½ tsps lime juice
- ¾ pound mixed salad greens
- 1 (8 ounce) can pineapple chunks, drained
- 4 cups corn tortilla chips

Directions

1. In a mixing bowl, combine the chicken and the teriyaki marinade sauce. Refrigerate for at least 2 hours before serving.
2. Combine the tomatoes, onion, jalapeno pepper, and cilantro in a small bowl. Refrigerate the salsa after covering it.
3. Combine the mustard, honey, sugar, oil, vinegar, and lime juice in a small bowl. Refrigerate the dressing after covering it.
4. Preheat the grill to medium-high.
5. Grease the grill grate lightly. Remove the chicken from the marinade and place it on the grill. Cook for 6–8 minutes per side, or until juices run clear.
6. On plates, arrange a mixture of salad greens. Sprinkle 1/4 of the pineapple chunks over each salad and top with some salsa. Toss salads with tortilla chips broken into big bits. Place a few grilled chicken strips on top of each salad. Finally, sprinkle each salad with dressing and serve.

Note

The full amount of marinade ingredients is included in the nutrition facts for this dish. The amount of marinade eaten will vary according on marinating time, ingredients, cook time, and other factors.

Nutrition Facts

Per Serving:

443 calories; protein 18.9g; carbohydrates 68.8g; fat 11.3g; cholesterol 33.6mg; sodium 1561.1mg.

76. CURRIED PEAS (LENTILS)

Prep: 25 mins

Cook: 50 mins

Total: 1 hr 15 mins

Servings: 4

Ingredients

- ¼ cup canola oil
- 1 large onion, diced
- 2 carrots, peeled and diced
- salt and ground black pepper to taste
- ½ tsp white sugar
- 3 cloves garlic, minced
- 1 fresh chile pepper, minced
- 1 tsp grated fresh ginger
- 3 tbsps curry powder
- 2 (14 ounce) cans vegetable broth, divided
- 1 cup lentils
- ¼ cup chopped fresh cilantro, or more to taste

Directions

1. Cook and stir onion, carrots, salt, black pepper, and sugar in a Dutch oven over medium-high heat until onion is a deep brown color, 15 to 20 minutes. Reduce to medium heat and stir in the garlic, chile pepper, ginger, and curry powder. Stir regularly for about 5 minutes to ensure complete incorporation.
2. Raise the heat to medium and add 1 can of vegetable broth to the onion mixture. With a wooden spoon, scrape off any veggies or curry powder clinging to the bottom of the pot. Cook

for 30 minutes, or until lentils are cooked, with the remaining 1 can of vegetable broth. Before serving, stir cilantro into the lentils.

Cook's Note:

Although this is a vegetarian recipe, when frying the onions, you can add pork or lamb. Any dried beans, such as black-eyed peas and garbanzo beans, work well in this dish (chick peas). We serve this over rice as a main course.

Nutrition Facts

Per Serving:

373 calories; protein 15g; carbohydrates 44.9g; fat 15.8g; sodium 432.9mg.

77. GRILLED CRAB CAKES

Prep: 20 mins

Cook: 10 mins

Additional: 30 mins

Total: 1 hr

Servings: 16

Ingredients
For Crab Cakes:

- ¾ pound crabmeat
- 1 cup plain bread crumbs
- ¾ cup mayonnaise
- 1 egg, beaten
- 2 green onions, minced
- Hot sauce, to taste
- Salt and pepper, to taste

For Mango Salsa:

- 1 mango, peeled, pitted and diced
- 1 red onion, diced
- 3 tbsps chopped fresh basil
- 3 tbsps chopped fresh cilantro
- 1 lime, juiced
- Minced jalapeno, to taste

- Salt and pepper, to taste
- 2 tbsps vegetable oil

Directions

1. Drain the crabmeat and set aside. Mix the crabmeat, bread crumbs, mayonnaise, egg, green onions, spicy sauce, and salt and pepper in a large mixing bowl until well blended. Make 16 little cakes out of the mixture. Refrigerate for 30 minutes before serving.
2. Meanwhile, combine the diced mango, onion, basil, cilantro, lime juice, jalapeño (if using), salt, and pepper in a small mixing bowl. Keep it refrigerated until you're ready to use it.
3. Grilling Instructions: Preheat the grill to medium heat and brush the grate or grill basket gently with oil. Grill for 8 minutes on each side, flipping once.
4. To pan-fry, in a large skillet over medium heat, heat 2 tbsps vegetable oil. Cook crab cake patties on both sides until crisp and golden brown, about 4 minutes per side.
5. Enjoy your crab cakes with mango salsa on top.

Nutrition Facts

Per Serving:

157 calories; protein 6.4g; carbohydrates 8.9g; fat 10.9g; cholesterol 31.7mg; sodium 195.4mg.

78. CARIBBEAN PASTA WITH SHRIMP

Prep: 40 mins

Cook: 20 mins

Total: 1 hr

Servings: 4

Ingredients

- 4 cloves garlic, minced
- ¼ cup minced shallots
- 1 tbsp minced fresh ginger root
- 3 tbsps olive oil
- 1 green bell pepper, seeded and chopped
- 1 ½ cups tomato - peeled, seeded and chopped
- 2 tsps curry powder
- ½ tsp whole allspice berries
- ½ cup chicken stock
- ¼ cup brandy-based orange liqueur (such as Grand Marnier®)
- 2 tbsps soy sauce

- 1 tbsp brown sugar
- 2 tsps cornstarch
- 2 tbsps chile paste
- 8 ounces rotini pasta
- 1 ½ pounds medium shrimp - peeled and deveined
- ½ cup fresh cilantro, chopped

Directions

1. Combine the garlic, shallots, ginger, and oil in a small bowl. Combine the green pepper, tomato, curry powder, allspice, chicken stock, Grand Marnier, soy sauce, brown sugar, cornstarch, and chile paste in a separate small bowl. Both should be covered and kept refrigerated until ready to use.
2. A big saucepan of lightly salted water should be brought to a boil. Cook for 8 to 10 minutes, or until pasta is al dente; drain.
3. Over high heat, heat a large saute pan. When the pan is hot, add the garlic-oil mixture. Cook until the garlic starts to sizzle but does not brown. Pour the tomato mixture into the saute pan after stirring it. Bring to a fast boil and simmer for 3 minutes, or until it thickens.
4. Toss in the shrimp and cook for 2 minutes, or until they become pink. Add the spaghetti right away. Stir and toss until everything is fully blended and the spaghetti is hot. Seasonings, especially salt, should be tasted and adjusted.
5. Sprinkle the cilantro on top and transfer to a hot dish. Serve right away.

Nutrition Facts

Per Serving:

482 calories; protein 39.9g; carbohydrates 42.6g; fat 14.9g; cholesterol 258.8mg; sodium 785.4mg.

79. QUICK CARIBBEAN QUESADILLAS

Prep: 10 mins

Cook: 12 mins

Total: 22 mins

Servings: 8

Ingredients

- ¼ cup honey mustard
- 2 tbsps pineapple preserves
- 8 (10 inch) flour tortillas
- 1 ½ cups shredded Swiss cheese
- 2 tbsps butter
- 2 cups chopped cooked chicken
- ½ cup cooked crumbled bacon
- 1 ½ cups unsweetened pineapple tidbits, drained

Directions

1. Combine the honey mustard and pineapple preserves in a small bowl. Distribute the mixture evenly across the four tortillas. To within 1 inch of the edges, spread evenly. To make quesadillas, evenly distribute the Swiss cheese, chicken, and bacon over the pineapple mixture; top with the remaining tortillas.
2. Preheat oven to 250 ° Fahrenheit (120 ° C).
3. Over medium heat, heat a large skillet. In a small skillet, melt a tiny amount of butter, tilting the pan to coat the entire surface. Place one of the quesadillas in the skillet and cook for 1 1/2 minutes on each side, or until lightly browned and the cheese has melted. Keep the cooked quesadillas warm in the oven while you finish the rest.
4. Cut each quesadilla into 6 wedges and place on a dish with pineapple tidbits in the center to serve.

Nutrition Facts

Per Serving:

600 calories; protein 32.4g; carbohydrates 52.6g; fat 28.9g; cholesterol 88.6mg; sodium 898.4mg.

80. CARIBBEAN BBQ SAUCE

Prep: 10 mins

Cook: 15 mins

Total: 25 mins

Servings: 24

Ingredients

- 2 tbsps olive oil
- 1 cup minced onion
- 2 cloves garlic, minced
- 3 (1 inch) pieces fresh ginger root, minced
- 2 cups ketchup
- ½ cup brown sugar
- ¼ cup molasses
- ½ cup spiced rum, divided
- 3 tbsps hoisin sauce
- 2 tbsps tomato paste
- 2 tbsps sherry vinegar
- 1 tbsp chili powder
- 1/8 tsp cayenne pepper

Directions

1. In a saucepan over medium-high heat, heat the olive oil. Cook until the onion, garlic, and ginger are soft. Reduce the heat to a low setting. Ketchup, brown sugar, molasses, rum, hoisin sauce, tomato paste, vinegar, chili powder, and cayenne pepper should all be combined. Cook and stir for 5 minutes, or until thoroughly combined and heated. Pour in the rest of the rum.

Nutrition Facts

Per Serving:

73 calories; protein 0.6g; carbohydrates 12.7g; fat 1.3g; cholesterol 0.1mg; sodium

81. CALLALOO AND CRAB

Prep: 20 mins

Cook: 1 hr

Total: 1 hr 20 mins

Servings: 8

Ingredients

- 18 taro leaves
- 12 pods okra, finely chopped
- 1 large onion, chopped
- 4 sprigs fresh thyme
- 6 cloves garlic, crushed
- 4 ounces salted pig's tail (Optional)
- ½ cup peeled, cubed pumpkin
- 1 cup water
- 1 habanero pepper
- 3 cups coconut milk
- 4 blue crabs, cleaned and chopped
- salt to taste
- 4 green onions, chopped

Directions

1. Remove the skin off the stalks and the tip from the center rib to clean the taro leaves. Cut into bite-size pieces after rinsing.
2. In a large saucepan, combine the taro leaves, okra, onion, thyme, garlic, salted pig's tail, pumpkin, water, whole habanero pepper, and coconut milk. Cover and cook for 30 minutes on low heat.
3. Toss in the crab in the saucepan. Make sure the habanero pepper isn't punctured. Cover and cook for another 30 minutes on low heat. Remove the habanero pepper and season to taste with salt. Using an immersion blender, puree the soup until it is completely smooth. A blender might alternatively be used to purée the mixture in small batches. Over rice, if desired.

Nutrition Facts

Per Serving:

260 calories; protein 7.9g; carbohydrates 8.8g; fat 23.2g; cholesterol 22mg; sodium

82. CRAB SOUFFLE

Prep: 35 mins

Cook: 30 mins

Total: 1 hr 5 mins

Servings: 8

Ingredients

- ½ cup sweetened, flaked coconut
- 4 tbsps unsalted butter
- 1/3 cup celery tops
- 1 clove garlic, minced
- ½ tsp curry powder
- ½ tsp dried thyme
- ½ tsp red pepper flakes
- ½ tsp salt
- ground black pepper to taste
- 3 tbsps unbleached all-purpose flour
- 1 ¼ cups milk
- 4 egg yolks
- ½ pound crabmeat
- 6 egg whites, stiffly beaten
- ¼ tsp fresh lemon juice

Directions

1. Preheat the oven to 400 ° Fahrenheit (200 ° C). Using butter, grease an 8-cup souffle dish.
2. In a nonstick skillet, toast the coconut over low heat.
3. Melt the butter in a medium skillet over low heat, then add the celery, garlic, curry powder, thyme, red pepper flakes, salt, and pepper to taste. Cook for 3 minutes. For about 1 minute, stir in the flour until it is completely smooth. Pour in the milk and simmer, stirring frequently, until the mixture thickens and comes to a boil. Allow to cool slightly before serving. One by one, whisk the egg yolks into the sauce. Combine the coconut and crab meat in a mixing bowl.
4. In a medium mixing bowl, whisk together the egg whites and lemon juice until stiff but not dry. 1/4 of the egg whites should be added to the crab mixture. Fold in the remaining whites quickly and gently. Deflate the volume but do not deflate it. Place the souffle dish on a rack in the bottom of the oven and pour the mixture into it.
5. Bake for 30 minutes, or until brown and puffy on the inside but still moist.

Nutrition Facts

Per Serving:

174 calories; protein 12.2g; carbohydrates 7.7g; fat 10.5g; cholesterol 142.3mg; sodium 332.1mg.

83. SWEET POTATO SALAD

Prep: 30 mins

Cook: 30 mins

Total: 1 hr

Servings: 5

Ingredients

- 1 large russet potato, peeled and quartered
- 1 large sweet potato, peeled and quartered
- 1 cup corn
- 1 tsp prepared Dijon-style mustard
- 2 tbsps fresh lime juice
- 3 tbsps chopped fresh cilantro
- 1 clove garlic, minced
- 3 tbsps canola oil
- ½ tsp salt
- ¼ tsp ground black pepper
- 1 cucumber, halved lengthwise and chopped
- ½ red onion, thinly sliced
- ¼ cup finely chopped peanuts

Directions

1. Fill a big saucepan halfway with salted water and add the Russet potato chunks. Bring to a boil, then reduce to a low heat and cook for 10 minutes. Cook for another 15 minutes after adding the sweet potato. Remove a portion of each potato and chop it in half to check for doneness. Add the corn kernels once the potatoes are cooked; simmer for another 30 seconds. Using a colander, drain the liquid. Fill the pot halfway with cold water and drop the vegetables in. Allow to cool for 5 minutes before draining.
2. Whisk together the mustard, lime juice, cilantro, and garlic in a large mixing basin. Slowly drizzle in the oil. Add salt and black pepper to taste.
3. Cut cooled potatoes into 1 inch pieces and combine with cucumber and red onion in dressing. Toss thoroughly. Serve refrigerated or at room temperature. Just before serving, toss in the peanuts.

Nutrition Facts

Per Serving:

231 calories; protein 4.6g; carbohydrates 27.8g; fat 12.6g; sodium 290.4mg.

84. CRABMEAT SALAD

Prep: 20 mins

Cook: 10 mins

Additional: 1 hr

Total: 1 hr 30 mins

Servings: 4

Ingredients

- 3 cups uncooked rotini pasta
- 1 (8 ounce) package imitation crabmeat, flaked
- 1 red bell pepper, julienned
- 1 mango - peeled, seeded, and cubed
- 2 tbsps chopped fresh cilantro
- 1 jalapeno pepper, seeded and minced
- 1 tsp lime zest
- 3 tbsps fresh lime juice
- 2 tbsps olive oil
- 1 tbsp honey
- ½ tsp ground cumin
- ½ tsp ground ginger
- ¼ tsp salt

Directions

1. A big saucepan of lightly salted water should be brought to a boil. Cook for 8 to 10 minutes, or until the pasta is al dente; drain and rinse under cold water.
2. In a large mixing bowl, combine the pasta, crabmeat, red pepper, mango, cilantro, and jalapeño.
3. Whisk together the lime zest, lime juice, olive oil, honey, cumin, ginger, and salt in a small bowl. Pour dressing over salad, toss to coat, and chill for at least one hour before serving.

Nutrition Facts

Per Serving:

304 calories; protein 9.8g; carbohydrates 50.1g; fat 7.9g; cholesterol 11.2mg; sodium 629.3mg.

85. COCONUT CHICKEN

Servings: 4

Yield: 4 servings

Ingredients

- 4 skinless, boneless chicken breasts
- 1 tsp vegetable oil
- 1 ½ onions, chopped
- 1 red bell pepper, chopped
- 1 green bell pepper, chopped
- 1 tbsp chopped roasted garlic
- ½ (14 ounce) can coconut milk
- salt and pepper to taste
- 1 pinch crushed red pepper flakes

Directions

1. Preheat the oven to 425 ° Fahrenheit (220 ° C).
2. Cook chicken breasts in vegetable oil in a large skillet until they are just starting to brown.
3. Combine the onions, green bell peppers, and red bell peppers with the chicken in a skillet. Saute the onions until they are transparent. Stir in the garlic and coconut milk once the vegetables are transparent. Allow 5 to 8 minutes for the mixture to cook before removing the skillet from the heat. Salt, pepper, and red pepper flakes to taste.
4. Transfer the mixture to a 9x13-inch baking dish and bake for 45 minutes at 425°F (220°C), or until the veggies have softened and the chicken is tender.

Nutrition Facts

Per Serving:

272 calories; protein 29.4g; carbohydrates 9.2g; fat 13.3g; cholesterol 68.4mg; sodium 87.2mg.

86. CANADIAN GLAZED CHICKEN

Prep: 30 mins

Cook: 1 hr

Total: 1 hr 30 mins

Servings: 4

Ingredients

- ½ cup ketchup
- 4 tbsps unsweetened pineapple juice
- 4 tbsps molasses
- 2 tbsps dark rum
- 2 tbsps prepared Dijon-style mustard
- 2 cloves garlic, chopped
- salt and pepper to taste
- 8 chicken thighs

Directions

1. To make the glaze, whisk together the ketchup, pineapple juice, molasses, rum, mustard, and garlic in a medium mixing bowl. Season to taste with salt and pepper, and stir well.
2. Brush both sides of the chicken pieces with the prepared glaze, using about 1/2 of the glaze, in a lightly greased 9x13 inch baking dish. Refrigerate the dish for at least 2 hours or overnight to marinate. Also, keep the remaining glaze refrigerated.
3. Preheat the oven to 375 ° Fahrenheit (190 ° C).
4. Brush one side of the chicken pieces with some of the remaining glaze and bake uncovered for about 25 minutes in a preheated oven. Turn the pieces over and bake for another 25 minutes, or until the chicken is tender.
5. Preheat the broiler in the oven.
6. Place the chicken in the broiler for 2 to 3 minutes on each side to lightly brown. (Note: This 'sugary' glaze burns easily, so keep an eye on the chicken!)

Note

The full amount of marinade ingredients is included in the nutrition facts for this dish. The amount of marinade used varies depending on marinating duration, ingredients, cooking style, and other factors.

Nutrition Facts

Per Serving:

519 calories; protein 33.1g; carbohydrates 26.6g; fat 28.8g; cholesterol 157.9mg; sodium 672.6mg.

87. CARIBBEAN FUDGE PIE

Servings: 8

Yield: 1 - 9 inch pie

Ingredients

- ¼ cup butter
- ¾ cup packed brown sugar
- 3 eggs
- 2 cups semi-sweet chocolate chips
- 2 tsps instant coffee granules
- 1 tsp rum flavored extract
- ¼ cup all-purpose flour
- 1 cup chopped walnuts
- ½ cup walnut halves
- 1 recipe pastry for a 9 inch single crust pie

Directions

1. Preheat the oven to 375 ° Fahrenheit (190 ° C). Microwave chocolate chips in a microwave-safe basin until melted. Stir until the chocolate is completely smooth.
2. Sugar and butter or margarine should be creamed together. One at a time, beat in the eggs. Melt the chocolate, add the instant coffee, and the rum extract. Mix in the flour and walnuts that have been split up. Fill the pie shell halfway with the filling. In a beautiful pattern, top with walnut halves.
3. Preheat oven to 375°F (190°C) and bake for 25 minutes. Cool.

Nutrition Facts

Per Serving:

635 calories; protein 10.5g; carbohydrates 63.9g; fat 40.9g; cholesterol 85mg; sodium 190.4mg.

88. GRILLED CARIBBEAN CHICKEN BREASTS

Servings: 6

Yield: 6 servings

Ingredients

- ¼ cup fresh orange juice
- 1 tsp orange zest
- 1 tbsp olive oil
- 1 tbsp fresh lime juice
- 1 tsp minced fresh ginger root
- 2 cloves garlic, minced
- ¼ tsp hot pepper sauce
- ½ tsp chopped fresh oregano
- 1 ½ skinless, boneless chicken breasts

Directions

1. Blend the orange juice, orange peel, olive oil, lime juice, ginger, garlic, hot pepper sauce, and oregano together in a blender. To make a marinade, combine all of the ingredients in a blender.
2. In a nonporous glass dish or bowl, place the chicken breasts. Pour the marinade over the chicken, cover the dish or bowl, and marinate for at least 2 hours or up to 24 hours in the refrigerator.
3. Prepare the oven to broil or gently grease the grill grate and preheat the grill to medium high heat.
4. Remove the chicken from the marinade (and discard any leftover marinade) and grill or broil for about 7 minutes per side, or until cooked through and no longer pink inside, 6 inches from the heat source.

Note

The full amount of marinade ingredients is included in the nutrition facts for this dish. The amount of marinade used varies depending on marinating duration, ingredients, cooking style, and other factors.

Nutrition Facts

Per Serving:

60 calories; protein 7g; carbohydrates 1.8g; fat 2.7g; cholesterol 17.1mg; sodium 24.7mg.

89. CARIBBEAN JERK PORK CHOPS

Prep: 15 mins

Cook: 10 mins

Additional: 12 hrs 5 mins

Total: 12 hrs 30 mins

Servings: 6

Ingredients

- ¾ cup water
- 1/3 cup lemon juice
- 1/3 cup chopped onion
- 1 tbsp packed brown sugar
- 1 tbsp chopped green onion
- 1 tbsp canola oil
- ¾ tsp salt
- ¾ tsp ground allspice
- ¾ tsp ground cinnamon
- ¾ tsp ground black pepper
- ½ tsp dried thyme, crushed
- ¼ tsp cayenne pepper, or to taste
- 6 raw chop with refuse, 113 g; (blank) 4 ounces lean pork chops, 1/2 inch thick

Directions

1. In a blender or food processor, combine the water, lemon juice, onion, brown sugar, green onions, oil, salt, allspice, cinnamon, black pepper, thyme, and cayenne pepper. Blend until completely smooth. 1/2 cup is set aside for basting.
2. Pork chops should be placed in a shallow glass dish. Over the meat, pour the remaining marinade. Refrigerate for at least 12 hours, but no more than 24 hours, covered.
3. Preheat the grill to medium. Placing the grate 4 to 5 inches above the heat source is a good idea.
4. The grill grate should be oiled. Place the chops on a grate and toss out the marinade. Cover the grill and cook the chops for 10 minutes, flipping once, or until done to your liking.

Nutrition Facts

Per Serving:

235 calories; protein 31.4g; carbohydrates 5g; fat 9.3g; cholesterol 81.4mg; sodium 343.2mg.

90. VEGAN CARIBBEAN STEW

Prep: 30 mins

Cook: 1 hr 40 mins

Total: 2 hrs 10 mins

Servings: 6

Ingredients

- 1 cup uncooked brown rice
- water
- ½ pound collard greens, chopped
- 2 cloves garlic, peeled
- 1 (10 ounce) package frozen okra
- 1 (28 ounce) can whole peeled tomatoes, chopped, with liquid
- 1 chayote squash, diced
- 2 cloves garlic, crushed
- ¼ tsp ground ginger, or more to taste
- ¼ tsp dried dill weed, or more to taste
- ¼ tsp ground cumin, or to taste
- 1 tbsp chopped fresh cilantro, or to taste
- 1 (16 ounce) can kidney beans, rinsed and drained
- 1 (6 ounce) can tomato paste
- all-purpose flour, or as needed

Directions

1. In a saucepan over high heat, bring brown rice and water to a boil. Reduce heat to medium-low, cover, and cook for 45 to 50 minutes, or until rice is soft and liquid has been absorbed.
2. In a pot, combine collard greens and 2 whole peeled garlic cloves; cover with enough water to cover. Cook for 15 minutes or until collards are soft. Drain.
3. In a separate big saucepan, combine the okra, tomatoes, chayote squash, and 2 crushed garlic cloves; bring to a boil and cook for 5 minutes, or until the okra has thawed. Reduce the heat to low and season to taste with ground ginger, dill weed, ground cumin, and cilantro. Add the collard greens and cook for at least 40 minutes, until the flavors have melded (1 hour for best flavor).
4. In a bowl, combine kidney beans and tomato paste; add to the stew. Mix in the cooked rice thoroughly. If desired, thicken with a tsp of flour. Season with salt and pepper to taste.

Cook's Note:

Simmer the collard greens and veggies for an hour or longer if you have time for a richer flavor and thicker consistency.

Nutrition Facts

Per Serving:

235 calories; protein 10.5g; carbohydrates 48.8g; fat 1.5g; sodium 217.6mg.

91. RED QUINOA PILAF WITH CARIBBEAN FLAVORS

Prep: 30 mins

Cook: 20 mins

Total: 50 mins

Servings: 8

Ingredients

- 1 cup red quinoa, rinsed and drained
- 2 cups water
- 1 pinch salt
- 1 cup frozen shelled edamame, thawed
- 1 unripe mango, shredded
- 1 red bell pepper, diced
- 1 serrano chile pepper, minced
- 6 green onions, chopped
- ¼ cup sliced almonds
- ¼ cup dried cranberries
- ¼ cup fresh shaved coconut
- 3 tbsps chopped fresh cilantro
- ½ cup lime juice
- 2 tbsps balsamic vinegar
- 1 pinch salt and ground black pepper to taste

Directions

1. Toast the quinoa in a dry pan over medium-high heat, shaking the pan often, until the quinoa is dry and has a roasted aroma, 2 to 5 minutes. Bring the quinoa to a boil with a pinch of salt, then cover, reduce heat, and cook for about 10 minutes.
2. Stir in the edamame, mango, bell pepper, and serrano chile, then cover and continue to cook for another 5 minutes, or until the water has been absorbed and the quinoa is fluffy. Green

onions, almonds, cranberries, coconut, cilantro, lime juice, balsamic vinegar, and salt and pepper are added to the salad. Return the mixture to a low simmer and serve immediately.

Nutrition Facts

Per Serving:

178 calories; protein 7g; carbohydrates 27.9g; fat 5.4g; sodium 65.6mg.

92. SAVORY CARIBBEAN-INSPIRED SWEET POTATO CAKES

Prep: 20 mins

Cook: 33 mins

Total: 53 mins

Servings: 4

Ingredients

- 2 sweet potatoes, peeled and cut into 1-inch cubes
- 1 tbsp canola oil
- 1 fresh jalapeno chile, seeded and finely chopped
- 3 green onions with tops, thinly sliced
- 2 cloves garlic, minced
- 1 tsp brown sugar
- ¼ tsp allspice
- salt and pepper to taste
- ¼ cup canola oil

Directions

1. Fill a pan halfway with water and place the sweet potatoes in it. Bring to a boil, then reduce to a low heat and cook for 10 minutes, or until potatoes are easily pierced with a fork. Drain the potatoes and mash them in a mixing basin.
2. Meanwhile, in a skillet over medium-high heat, heat 1 tbsp canola oil. Combine the jalapeño pepper, green onions, and garlic in a mixing bowl. Cook and stir for 5 minutes, or until the vegetables are tender. In a mixing bowl, combine the veggies, brown sugar, and spices. Season with salt and pepper to taste.
3. Using your hands or big spoons, form the sweet potato mixture into 12 slightly flattened cakes measuring 2 to 2 1/2 inches in diameter. Place on a serving dish.
4. In a skillet, heat 1/4 cup canola oil over medium-high heat. Place four sweet potato cakes in the skillet at a time and cook, flipping once, for 6 to 8 minutes, or until golden brown on both sides. If necessary, add more oil.

Nutrition Facts

Per Serving:

289 calories; protein 2.6g; carbohydrates 31.6g; fat 17.6g; sodium 80.7mg.

93. CARIBBEAN-STYLE SOFRITO

Prep: 45 mins

Total: 45 mins

Servings: 96

Yield: 12 cups

Ingredients

- 2 green bell peppers, cut into 1/4 inch cubes
- 2 red bell peppers, cut into 1/4 inch cubes
- 1 orange bell pepper, cut into 1/4 inch cubes
- 1 yellow bell pepper, cut into 1/4 inch cubes
- 10 tomatoes, cored and coarsely chopped
- 1 bunch green onions, chopped
- 1 ½ bunches fresh cilantro leaves, chopped
- 6 fresh tomatillos, husks removed
- 1 cup chopped garlic

Directions

1. In a blender or the bowl of a food processor, combine the green, red, orange, and yellow bell peppers. Combine the tomatoes, green onions, cilantro, tomatillos, and garlic in a large mixing bowl. To make a chunky or smooth combination, blend or pulse according to your preference. Refrigerate for up to 5 days in an airtight container or freeze for up to 45 days.

Cook's Tip

Use as needed by freezing the sofrito in resealable plastic bags, or spoon into ice cube trays to freeze in parts.

Nutrition Facts

Per Serving:

8 calories; protein 0.4g; carbohydrates 1.7g; fat 0.1g; sodium 1.9mg.

94. GRILLED SPICED CHICKEN WITH CARIBBEAN CITRUS-MANGO SAUCE

Prep: 20 mins

Cook: 45 mins

Additional: 20 mins

Total: 1 hr 25 mins

Servings: 4

Ingredients

- 1 tsp ground ginger
- ½ tsp ground cinnamon
- ¼ tsp ground cumin
- ¼ tsp ground anise seed
- 1 dash cayenne pepper
- 4 skinless, boneless chicken breast halves
- 2 cups water
- 1 cup basmati rice
- 1 mango - peeled, seeded and diced
- ½ cup orange juice
- 2 tbsps fresh lime juice
- 2 tbsps honey
- 1 tsps cornstarch
- 1 ½ tbsps water
- 2 tbsps dark rum

Directions

2. Combine the ginger, cinnamon, cumin, anise, and cayenne pepper in a medium mixing bowl. Place the chicken in the bowl after rubbing it with the spice mixture. Refrigerate for 20 to 30 minutes after covering.
3. In a saucepan, combine 2 cups water and basmati rice and bring to a boil. Reduce heat to low, cover, and cook for 20 minutes, or until vegetables are soft.
4. Combine the mango, orange juice, lime juice, and honey in a small saucepan. Bring to a boil, then reduce to a low heat and cook, stirring periodically, for 5 minutes. Combine cornstarch and 1 1/2 tbsps water in a small cup and stir until the cornstarch is completely dissolved. Stir in the mango mixture and cook for one minute, or until the sauce has slightly thickened. Add the black rum and mix well.
5. Preheat a medium-hot outside grill. Brush the grate with oil once the grill is hot.

6. 6 to 8 minutes per side on the grill, or until no longer pink and juices flow clear. Serve over cooked rice with a dollop of mango sauce on top.

Nutrition Facts

Per Serving:

418 calories; protein 28.9g; carbohydrates 62.4g; fat 3.5g; cholesterol 67.2mg; sodium 66.2mg.

95. PUMPKIN SEED CAKE

Prep: 15 mins

Cook: 44 mins

Total: 59 mins

Servings: 8

Ingredients

- 1 cup all-purpose flour
- 2 ¼ tsps baking powder
- ¼ tsp salt
- 2 eggs
- ¾ cup pumpkin seeds
- ¼ cup ground flax seeds
- 1 cup butter
- ¾ cup white sugar
- 2 tsps vanilla extract
- ¼ cup milk

Directions

1. Preheat the oven to 350 ° Fahrenheit (175 ° C). An 8-inch circular cake pan should be greased and floured.
2. In a large mixing basin, sift together flour, baking powder, and salt.
3. Over medium heat, heat a skillet. Cook, stirring regularly, until pumpkin seeds are lightly browned and roasted, about 5 minutes. Fill a food processor halfway with the mixture. In a food processor, blend the toasted pumpkin seeds until they have a sand-like texture. Toss in with the flour mixture.
4. In the same skillet, add the ground flax seeds. Cook and stir for 4 minutes, or until toasted. Incorporate the wet ingredients into the flour mixture until thoroughly incorporated.
5. In a mixing bowl, cream together the butter and sugar with an electric mixer until light and fluffy. 1 at a time, add the eggs and vanilla extract, mixing thoroughly after each addition. In

batches, add the flour-seed mixture and milk, mixing briefly after each addition until the batter is well incorporated. Pour the batter into the pan that has been prepared.

6. 35 to 40 minutes in a preheated oven, or until a toothpick inserted in the center of the cake comes out clean.

Cook's Notes:

Cake flour can be substituted for all-purpose flour.

Water can be used instead of milk.

If you don't want to roast the seeds, that's fine.

There should be around 2 cups of ground seed and flour combination.

Nutrition Facts

Per Serving:

447 calories; protein 7.5g; carbohydrates 34.9g; fat 32g; cholesterol 108.1mg; sodium 361.7mg.

96. FLAN DE COCO (COCONUT FLAN)

Prep: 10 mins

Cook: 1 hr

Additional: 8 hrs

Total: 9 hrs 10 mins

Servings: 12

Ingredients

- 1 ½ cups white sugar
- 1 (14 ounce) can sweetened condensed milk
- 1 (12 fluid ounce) can evaporated milk
- ½ cup milk
- 6 eggs
- ½ cup fresh shredded coconut

Directions

1. Preheat the oven to 350 ° Fahrenheit (175 ° C).
2. 1 cup sugar 1 cup sugar 1 cup sugar 1 cup sugar 1 cup sugar 1 cup sugar 1 cup sugar 1 cup sugar 1 cup sugar 1 cup sugar 1 cup sugar 1 cup sugar 1 Cook, without stirring, until the sugar

has melted, shaking the pan regularly. Continue to simmer until all of the sugar has dissolved and turned golden brown. Fill a large glass baking dish halfway with the mixture. Set aside to cool for 15 minutes after spreading the caramel evenly over the bottom of the dish.

3. Pour the condensed milk, evaporated milk, milk, eggs, 1/2 cup sugar, and coconut into a blender once the caramel has solidified. Blend for 3 minutes, or until completely smooth. Pour over the caramel in the baking dish.

4. Bake for 45 minutes, or until set, in a preheated oven. Remove from oven and set aside to cool for 30 minutes. To separate the flan from the sides of the dish, run a knife over the edges. Refrigerate for at least one night.

Nutrition Facts

Per Serving:

297 calories; protein 8.3g; carbohydrates 47.1g; fat 9g; cholesterol 114.1mg; sodium 114.7mg.

97. BAKED COCONUT FRENCH TOAST WITH PINEAPPLE-RUM SAUCE

Prep: 20 mins

Cook: 30 mins

Additional: 8 hrs

Total: 8 hrs 50 mins

Servings: 8

Ingredients
French Toast:

- 6 large eggs
- 1 (13.5 ounce) can light coconut milk
- 2 tbsps white sugar
- 1 tsp vanilla extract
- ¼ tsp salt
- 16 (1 1/4-inch thick) diagonal slices French bread
- 1 cup packed sweetened flaked coconut

Pineapple-Rum Sauce:

- 1 (6 ounce) can unsweetened pineapple juice
- ½ cup packed brown sugar
- 4 ½ cups frozen pineapple chunks

- 2 tbsps butter
- 2 tbsps dark rum

Directions

1. Using parchment paper, line a 13x18-inch sheet pan. In a large mixing bowl, whisk together the eggs, coconut milk, sugar, vanilla, and salt until the sugar is dissolved. Submerge each slice of bread in the egg mixture, flipping it over several times until soaked, and then transfer to a sheet pan lined with parchment paper. Pour the remaining egg mixture over the bread and chill for at least 8 hours or up to 24 hours, covered in plastic wrap.
2. Preheat the oven to 350 ° Fahrenheit (175 ° C). Evenly press the coconut into the bread. 30 to 35 minutes in the upper third of the oven, until brown and cooked through.
3. Meanwhile, over medium heat, bring pineapple juice and brown sugar to a simmer, stirring constantly. Bring to a boil, stirring constantly, then cook for 10 minutes over medium-high heat, stirring regularly. Stir in the butter and rum until the butter has melted. Keep warm, covered, and away from the heat.
4. Warm pineapple-rum sauce is served with French toast.

Nutrition Facts

Per Serving:

521 calories; protein 11.2g; carbohydrates 84.1g; fat 15.3g; cholesterol 125mg; sodium 514.9mg.

98. MONTEREY JERK DOG

Prep: 8 mins

Cook: 10 mins

Total: 18 mins

Servings: 6

Ingredients

- 6 Ball Park Original Hot Dog Buns
- ¼ tsp garlic powder
- ½ cup mayonnaise
- 1 tbsp olive oil
- 2 cups finely chopped sweet onion
- 1 tsp jerk or Cajun seasoning
- 6 hot dogs
- 8 ounces Monterey Jack cheese, shredded
- 4 ounces crushed pineapple, drained (Optional)

Directions

1. Preheat the grill to medium.
2. Mayonnaise is mixed with garlic powder and smeared on Ball Park® Hot Dog Buns.
3. Warm a small skillet over medium heat with olive oil on the bottom.
4. Add the onion and cook, stirring constantly, until golden brown.
5. Remove from heat and season with jerk seasoning.
6. Split the hot dogs on one side while leaving the other intact, then grill split-side down until grill marks show (safe internal temp. 160 ° F).
7. After flipping the hot dogs, fill each split with jerk onions and cheese.
8. Each bun should be opened and lightly toasted on the opening side.
9. Place each hot dog in a toasted bun and top with pineapple or other toppings of your choice.
10. Any leftovers should be kept refrigerated.

Nutrition Facts

Per Serving:

594 calories; protein 19.3g; carbohydrates 33.9g; fat 42.3g; cholesterol 63.1mg; sodium 1106.5mg.

99. WEST INDIAN CURRIED CHICKEN

Prep: 25 mins

Cook: 35 mins

Total: 1 hr

Servings: 8

Ingredients

- 3 tbsps vegetable oil
- 1 (3 pound) chicken, cut into pieces
- 1 large onion, diced
- 6 cloves garlic, minced
- 4 large potatoes - peeled and cubed
- 2 tbsps salt
- ¼ cup Jamaican curry powder
- hot pepper sauce to taste

Directions

1. In a big pot, heat the oil over medium-high heat. Cook the chicken, onions, and garlic for about 5 minutes, or until the chicken has browned. Stir in the potatoes, salt, and curry powder, then cover the chicken halfway with water. Cover and cook for 30 to 40 minutes, or until the vegetables are soft. Hot pepper sauce can be used to taste.

Nutrition Facts

Per Serving:

574 calories; protein 36.1g; carbohydrates 36.6g; fat 31.4g; cholesterol 127.7mg; sodium 1907.9mg.

100. SWEET AND KICKIN' MANGO-HABANERO HOT SAUCE

Prep: 25 mins

Cook: 20 mins

Total: 45 mins

Servings: 128

Ingredients

- 2 tbsps extra virgin olive oil
- 1 large sweet onion, chopped
- 7 ripe mangoes, cored and chopped
- 1 fresh peach, chopped (Optional)
- 1/3 cup honey
- 15 habanero peppers, stemmed, or more to taste
- ¼ cup yellow mustard
- 2 ½ tbsps salt
- 2 ½ tbsps paprika
- 1 ½ tbsps ground white pepper
- 1 tbsp ground cumin
- 1/3 tsp ground allspice
- ¼ cup light brown sugar
- 1 ½ cups white vinegar
- ½ cup apple cider vinegar

Directions

1. In a skillet, heat the olive oil over medium heat. Cook, stirring frequently, until the onion is transparent, about 5 minutes.
2. In a food processor, combine the onion, mangoes, peach, honey, habanero peppers, and mustard. Blend in salt, paprika, white pepper, cumin, and allspice until smooth. Continue to process until the brown sugar is well mixed.
3. Fill a big saucepan halfway with the mango-habanero mixture. Bring the water to a boil. Stir in the white vinegar and apple cider vinegar until fully mixed. Cook for 10 to 12 minutes, or until the sauce has thickened. Fill jars or containers with the sauce.

Cook's Note:

The sauce can be refrigerated and consumed the next day after it has been placed in containers; however, I recommend canning it in small jelly jars in a warm bath.

Nutrition Facts

Per Serving:

13 calories; protein 0.1g; carbohydrates 2.8g; fat 0.3g; sodium 142.4mg.

101. CARROT RECIPE

Prep: 5 mins

Cook: 12 mins

Total: 17 mins

Servings: 4

Ingredients

- 4 cups grated carrots
- 2 cups milk
- 1 cup white sugar
- 1 tbsp butter
- ½ cup cashew halves
- ½ cup raisins
- 1 pinch ground cardamom (Optional)

Directions

1. Combine carrots and milk in a saucepan over medium heat. Bring to a boil, then reduce to a low heat and cook for 10 minutes, or until most of the milk has evaporated. Stir add the sugar and cook until the mixture is completely dry. To keep it from burning, keep stirring constantly. Remove the pan from the heat.
2. In a skillet over medium heat, melt the butter. Add the cashews and raisins to the pan and cook until the cashews are golden brown. Spread the carrot mixture on top. For a fragrant finish, sprinkle ground cardamom on top.

Note

Although some individuals purée their carrots, shredded carrots have a wonderful texture.

Nutrition Facts

Per Serving:

486 calories; protein 8.4g; carbohydrates 88.3g; fat 13.6g; cholesterol 17.4mg; sodium 258.3mg.

102. JAMBO (DUTCH ANTILLES OKRA SOUP)

Prep: 25 mins

Cook: 30 mins

Additional: 8 hrs

Total: 8 hrs 55 mins

Servings: 4

Ingredients

- 6 ounces salt beef, fat removed and diced
- 12 cups water
- Salt and pepper to taste
- 3 cups fresh okra, cut into 1/2 inch slices
- 1 cup medium shrimp, peeled and deveined
- 8 ounces cod fillets, cubed
- ¼ cup chopped fresh basil
- 1 tbsp lemon juice, to taste

Directions

1. To remove the salt from chopped beef, soak it in plenty of cool water overnight. Set aside after draining and rinsing.
2. Over high heat, bring 12 cups of water to a boil. Season with salt and pepper, then add the okra. Reduce the heat to medium-low and continue to cook for another 20 minutes. Stir in the meat, shrimp, and cod, and continue to cook for another 10 minutes. Before serving, season with chopped basil and lemon juice.

Nutrition Facts

Per Serving:

189 calories; protein 24.3g; carbohydrates 6g; fat 7.4g; cholesterol 95.7mg; sodium 601.3mg.

103. TRINIDAD SWEETBREAD

Servings: 12

Yield: 12 servings

Ingredients

- ½ pound butter, softened
- 4 ½ cups white sugar
- 4 eggs, beaten
- 1 cup evaporated milk
- 2 tsps almond extract
- 9 cups all-purpose flour
- 9 tbsps baking powder
- 1 tsp ground cinnamon
- 6 cups shredded coconut
- 1 cup chopped dried mixed fruit
- 1 cup raisins

Directions

1. Preheat the oven to 350 ° Fahrenheit (175 ° C). Set aside two 5x9 inch loaf pans that have been greased.
2. Combine the butter, sugar, eggs, evaporated milk, and almond extract in a mixing bowl.
3. Combine the flour, baking powder, and cinnamon in a sifter. Stir in the dry ingredients.
4. Combine the coconut, coarsely chopped dry fruit, and raisins in a mixing bowl. Combine the ingredients in a mixing bowl and pour into loaf pans that have been lined with parchment paper.
5. 30–35 minutes, or until a toothpick inserted in the center comes out clean. Remove the pans from the oven and cool on a wire rack.

Nutrition Facts

Per Serving:

1063 calories; protein 15.2g; carbohydrates 188.8g; fat 30g; cholesterol 108.8mg; sodium 1362.7mg.

104. STRAWBERRY-MANGO ICE CREAM WITH FRESH SPEARMINT

Prep: 40 mins

Cook: 10 mins

Additional: 13 hrs 10 mins

Total: 14 hrs

Servings: 8

Ingredients

- 3 cups half-and-half
- 1 cup white sugar
- 3 egg yolks
- ½ tbsp chopped fresh spearmint
- 1 tsp coconut extract
- 2 cups sliced fresh strawberries, pureed
- 1 medium mango, pureed

Directions

1. In a medium saucepan, combine the half-and-half and cook over medium heat. Stir in the sugar until it is completely dissolved. Continue to heat until the half-and-half is steaming hot, but not boiling.
2. In a separate dish, whisk the egg yolks till pale yellow.
3. Slowly whisk in roughly 1 cup of the half-and-half mixture to the egg yolks while constantly whisking. Rep with a second cup. Cook, stirring constantly, until the egg yolk mixture thickens and coats the back of a spoon in the saucepan with the remaining half-and-half mixture. Do not allow the mixture to come to a boil.
4. Take the pan off the heat and add the spearmint and coconut extract. Allow 30 minutes for the mixture to cool in a basin with a pour spout. Refrigerate for at least 8 hours or overnight.
5. Pour half of the ingredients into an ice cream machine and churn until it reaches a soft-serve consistency. Toss in the strawberry puree. Churn the ice cream until it has thickened. Clean out the ice cream maker with a rubber spatula and transfer the ice cream to a bowl. Put the strawberry ice cream in the freezer for a few minutes.
6. Fill the ice cream maker halfway with the remaining ice cream base and churn to a soft-serve consistency. Toss in the mango puree. Continue to churn the ice cream until it thickens.
7. Take the frozen strawberry ice cream out of the freezer. Using two big spoons, scoop a large scoop of strawberry ice cream into a 9-inch loaf pan. Add a huge dollop of mango ice cream on top. Fill the loaf pan to the brim, alternating flavors as you go. Place in the freezer for at least 4 hours, covered with plastic wrap.

Nutrition Facts

Per Serving:

266 calories; protein 4.1g; carbohydrates 36.7g; fat 12.3g; cholesterol 110.4mg; sodium 41.3mg.

105. CLASSIC CINNAMON ROLLS

Prep: 30 mins

Cook: 30 mins

Additional: 1 hr 45 mins

Total: 2 hrs 45 mins

Servings: 24

Ingredients
Rolls:

- 1 cup mashed potatoes
- 1 cup reserved potato water
- ¾ cup butter OR margarine
- ¾ cup sugar
- 2 tsps salt
- 1 cup hot water
- 2 envelopes Fleischmann's Active Dry Yeast
- ½ cup warm water (100 to 110 ° F)
- 2 eggs
- 8 ½ cups all-purpose flour, or more if needed

Filling:

- ½ cup butter OR margarine, softened
- 1 cup sugar
- 1 ½ tsps Spice Islands Ground Saigon Cinnamon

Icing:

- 3 cups powdered sugar
- 6 tbsps butter OR margarine, softened
- 1 tsp Spice Islands 100% Pure Bourbon Vanilla Extract
- 5 tbsps milk, or more as needed

Directions

1. In a large mixing bowl, add the potatoes, potato water, butter, sugar, salt and hot water. Stir until the butter is melted; set aside to cool. In a small bowl, mix the yeast and 1/2 cup of warm water. Enable 5 minutes to rest. Connect the potato mixture to the eggs, 2 cups of flour and the yeast mixture. Beat until it mixes well. Continue to add flour, until soft dough shapes, 1 cup at a time.
2. Knead until smooth and elastic (about 4 to 6 minutes) on a lightly floured surface, OR knead with an electric mixer using a dough handle. Put it in a greased bowl and turn to coat. Uh. Cover.
3. Let it rise for about 1 hour in a wet, draft free area, until doubled in size. Down with punch dough; cut in half.
4. Roll one dough part into a 12 x 18-inch rectangle on a lightly floured surface. Using half the butter to spread. Combine the sugar and cinnamon; brush over the surface with half of the mixture. Tightly roll up lengthwise, covering the edges. Split into slices of 12. Place it in a 13 x 9-inch greased pan. Repeat with the dough that remains. Uh. Cover.
5. Let it rise for 30 to 45 minutes before it almost doubles.
6. Bake for 25 to 30 minutes in a preheated oven at 350 ° F.
7. 15 minutes to cool. Combine the ingredients with icing and drizzle over the rolls.

Tips

2 medium potatoes yield approximately 1 cup of mashed potatoes.

Nutrition Facts

Every Serving:

404 calories; protein 5.7g 12% ; carbohydrates 65.4g 21% ; fat 13.5g 21% ; cholesterol 49mg 16% ; sodium 318mg 13% .

106. CLASSIC BRAN MUFFINS

Prep: 20 mins

Cook: 20 mins

Total: 40 mins

Servings: 12

Ingredients

- 1 ½ cups wheat bran
- 1 cup buttermilk
- 1/3 cup vegetable oil
- 1 egg
- 2/3 cup of brown sugar
- ½ tsp vanilla extract
- 1 cup of all-purpose flour
- 1 tsp baking soda
- 1 tsp baking powder
- ½ tsp salt
- ½ cup raisins

Directions

1. Preheat the oven to 375°F (190 ° C). Grease muffin cups or paper muffin liners with a line.
2. Mix the wheat bran and buttermilk ; leave to stand for 10 minutes.
3. Whip the oil, egg, sugar and vanilla together and add to the buttermilk/bran mixture. Sift the flour, baking soda, baking powder and salt together. Stir the mixture of flour into the buttermilk mixture until it's mixed. Into prepared muffin tins, fold in raisins and spoon batter.
4. Bake for 15 to 20 minutes, or until the muffin center comes out clean with a toothpick inserted. Cool, and enjoy yourself!

Nutrition Facts

Every Serving:

168 calories; protein 3.5g 7% ; carbohydrates 25.6g 8% ; fat 7.1g 11% ; cholesterol 16.3mg 5% ; sodium 262.2mg 11% .

107. EASY DECADENT TRUFFLES

Prep: 1 hr

Total: 1 hr

Servings: 60

Ingredients

- 1 (8 ounce) package cream cheese, softened
- 3 cups confectioners' sugar, sifted
- 3 cups semisweet chocolate chips, melted
- 1 ½ tsps vanilla

Directions

1. Beat the cream cheese in a big bowl until smooth. Beat in the sugar of the confectioners steadily until well blended. Till no streaks remain, stir in melted chocolate and vanilla. For around 1 hour, refrigerate. Shape the balls into 1 inch.

Notes

Roll truffles into ground walnuts (or any ground nuts), cocoa, coconut, sugar, sprinkles of candy, etc.

Omit vanilla in order to flavor truffles with liqueurs or other flavorings. Divide the mixture of truffles into thirds. To each mixture, add 1 tbsp of liqueur (almond, coffee, orange); blend well.

Nutrition Facts

Every Serving:

78 calories; protein 0.6g 1% ; carbohydrates 11.7g 4% ; fat 3.8g 6% ; cholesterol 4.1mg 1% ; sodium 12mg 1% .

108. EASY CHOCOLATE PUDDING

Prep: 5 mins

Cook: 15 mins

Additional: 3 hrs

Total: 3 hrs 20 mins

Servings: 6

Ingredients

- 3 cups whole milk, divided
- ¼ cup cornstarch
- 1/3 cup of white sugar, or more to taste
- 1 cup of semisweet chocolate chips
- 1 pinch salt

Directions

1. In a small bowl, mix 1/2 cup milk and maize starch. Whisk or stir with a fork until all lumps are smooth.
2. In a medium saucepan mix the remaining milk with sugar over low heat. Slowly whisk in the cornstarch mixture. Cook for 8 to 10 minutes, whisking as required to prevent lumps from forming, until the mixture starts to thicken. Add salt and chocolate chips. Continue to stir until the chips are fully melted and the pudding is thickened and smooth for about 7 more minutes.
3. Into 1 big bowl or 6 individual bowls, pour pudding. To prevent the skin from developing, place plastic wrap directly on top of the pudding; smooth it gently against the surface. Refrigerate prior to serving for at least 3 to 4 hours.

Nutrition Facts

Every Serving:

271 calories; protein 5.1g 10% ; carbohydrates 39.2g 13% ; fat 12.4g 19% ; cholesterol 12.2mg 4% ; sodium 78.2mg 3% .

109. SOUTHERN BOILED CUSTARD

Servings: 8

Yield: 8 servings

Ingredients

- 1 quart whole milk
- 5 eggs
- 1 cup white sugar
- 1 tsp vanilla extract

Directions

1. Add water to the lower pot of a double boiler. Add milk into the upper pot. Over medium sun, heat through.
2. Beat the eggs until it's light. Remove sugar and blend thoroughly. To warm this part and thin it, pour a small portion of hot milk into the eggs and sugar. Pour in the hot milk slowly.
3. Cook, stirring continuously, until the spoon is coated. Do not cook over it. Attach an extract of vanilla. Before serving, cool in the refrigerator.

Nutrition Facts

Every Serving:

216 calories; protein 7.9g 16% ; carbohydrates 30.8g 10% ; fat 7.1g 11% ; cholesterol 128.4mg 43% ; sodium 92.6mg 4%

110. BAKED OMELET

Prep: 15 mins

Cook: 40 mins

Total: 55 mins

Servings: 4

Ingredients

- 8 eggs
- 1 cup milk
- ½ tsp seasoning salt
- 3 ounces cooked ham, diced
- ½ cup shredded Cheddar cheese
- ½ cup shredded mozzarella cheese
- 1 tbsp dried minced onion

Directions

1. Preheat the oven to 350 ° Fahrenheit (175 ° C). Grease and put one 8x8 inch casserole dish aside.
2. The eggs and milk beat together. Apply the salt, ham, Cheddar cheese, Mozzarella cheese, and chopped onion to taste. Pour the casserole dish into the prepared one.
3. Bake for 40 to 45 minutes, uncovered, at 350 ° F (175 ° C).

Nutrition Facts

Every Serving:

314 calories; protein 24.8g 50% ; carbohydrates 5.9g 2% ; fat 21.2g 33% ; cholesterol 415.3mg 138% ; sodium 738.2mg 30% .

111. BAKED BEEF STEW

Prep: 20 mins

Cook: 2 hrs

Additional: 10 mins

Total: 2 hrs 30 mins

Servings: 8

Ingredients

- 2 pounds beef stew meat, cut into 1 inch cubes
- 1 (14.5 ounce) can diced tomatoes with juice
- 1 cup water
- 3 tbsps instant tapioca
- 1 tbsp beef bouillon granules
- 2 tsps white sugar
- 1 ½ tsps salt
- ¼ tsp ground black pepper
- 4 carrots, cut into 1 inch pieces
- Celery 2 strips, cut into 3/4 inch bits
- 3 potato, peeled and cubed
- 1 onion, chopped roughly
- 1 slice bread, cubed

Directions

1. Preheat the oven to 375°F (190 ° C). Lightly grease a baking dish measuring 9x13 inches.
2. Brown the stew meat over medium heat in a large skillet; drain and set aside.
3. Combine the tomatoes, water, tapioca, granules of beef bouillon, sugar, salt and pepper in a mixing bowl. Stir in the beef, celery, carrots, potatoes, onion, and cubes of bread. Pour the prepared baking dish into it.
4. Cover and cook until the meat and vegetables are tender, or for 2 hours.

Nutrition Facts

Every Serving:

425 calories; protein 33.1g 66% DV; carbohydrates 23.2g 8% DV; fat 21.4g 33% DV; cholesterol 98.8mg 33% DV; sodium 794.3mg 32% DV.

112. CRAB CAKES WITH REMOULADE SAUCE

Prep: 30 mins

Cook: 10 mins

Total: 40 mins

Servings: 6

Ingredients

- 8 Ball Park Hamburger Buns
- 1 tbsp butter, melted, or more as needed

Remoulade Sauce:

- ¾ cup mayonnaise
- 3 tbsps chopped green onion
- 1 tbsp grainy mustard
- 1 tbsp chopped fresh flat-leaf parsley
- 2 tsps ketchup
- 2 tsps white wine vinegar
- 1 tsp prepared horseradish
- 1 tsp garlic granules
- 2 dashes hot pepper sauce (such as Tabasco®), or to taste
- salt and pepper to taste

Crab Cakes:

- ¼ cup mayonnaise
- 1 large egg, beaten
- 1 ½ tsps minced red onion
- ½ tbsp minced Italian parsley
- 2 (6 ounce) cans crabmeat, drained, picked clean
- 2 cups fine bread or cracker crumbs, divided
- 3 tsps seafood seasoning (such as Old Bay®)
- ½ tsp sea salt
- 2 tbsps ground black pepper
- 1 pinch cayenne pepper
- 2 tbsps vegetable oil
- Trimmings to include lettuce, tomato and onion, as desired, plus lemon wedges

Directions

1. Combine all the ingredients in a medium bowl to make the sauce, and whisk well. Cover and store in the fridge.
2. Combine the mayonnaise, bacon, red onion and parsley in a large bowl to make crab cakes, stirring well with a fork.
3. Attach the crab, 1 cup of bread crumbs, salt, pepper, paprika, seafood seasoning and cayenne. Stir when combined; it will be somewhat loose and wet with the mixture.
4. Shape the mixture into 8 equally-sized patties. To make a crust, cover each patty with the remaining bread crumbs.
5. Heat oil over medium heat in a large skillet and cook patties for about 8 minutes, rotating just once, about halfway through cooking, until evenly golden brown.
6. In the meantime, clean hamburger buns at 400 ° F with melted butter and toast only before they start browning at the edges.
7. Place patty on each bun to serve, top with sauce remoulade and preferred trimmings. Serve on the table with additional sauce and lemon wedges.

Tip:

Refrigerate them for 30 minutes before placing them in your skillet to help the crab cake patties stay together during cooking.

Nutrition Facts

Every Serving:

707 calories; protein 25.1g 50% ; carbohydrates 62.7g 20% ; fat 41.2g 63% ; cholesterol 99.9mg 33% ; sodium 1440.5mg 58% .

113. BUFFALO CHICKEN WINGS

Prep: 15 mins

Cook: 15 mins

Additional: 1 hr 30 mins

Total: 2 hrs

Servings: 5

Ingredients

- ½ cup all-purpose flour
- ¼ tsp paprika
- ¼ tsp cayenne pepper
- ¼ tsp salt
- 10 chicken wings
- oil for deep frying
- ¼ cup butter
- ¼ cup hot sauce
- 1 dash ground black pepper
- 1 dash garlic powder

Directions

1. Mix together the rice, paprika, cayenne pepper and salt in a small cup. In a large non-porous glass dish or cup, place the chicken wings and sprinkle the flour mixture over them until they are evenly coated. Cover and refrigerate the dish or bowl for 60 to 90 minutes.
2. In a deep fryer, heat the oil to 375 ° F (190 ° C). The oil should be just enough to fully cover the wings, an inch or so thick. In a small saucepan over low heat, add the butter, hot sauce, pepper, and garlic powder. Stir and heat together until the butter is melted and the mixture is well mixed. Remove from the heat and set aside to serve.
3. Fry the coated wings for 10 to 15 minutes in hot oil, or until parts of the wings turn brown. Remove from the oven, put the wings in a serving bowl, add the mixture of hot sauce and stir. Just serve.

Nutrition Facts

Every Serving:

364 calories; protein 7.9g 16% ; carbohydrates 10.7g 4% ; fat 32.4g 50% ; cholesterol 44.2mg 15% ; sodium 496.5mg 20% .

114. KETO CHICKEN PARMESAN

Prep: 20 mins

Cook: 8 mins

Total: 28 mins

Servings: 2

Ingredients

- 1 (8 ounce) skinless, boneless chicken breast
- 1 egg
- 1 tbsp heavy whipping cream
- 1 ½ ounces pork rinds, crushed
- 1 ounce grated Parmesan cheese
- ½ tsp salt
- ½ tsp garlic powder
- ½ tsp red pepper flakes (Optional)
- ½ tsp ground black pepper
- ½ tsp Italian seasoning
- ½ cup jarred tomato sauce (such as Rao's®)
- ¼ cup shredded mozzarella cheese
- 1 tbsp ghee (clarified butter)

Directions

1. Set the oven rack approximately 6 inches from the heat source and preheat the broiler in the oven.
2. Slice the chicken breast from one side to within 1/2 inch of the other side horizontally across the middle. Open the two sides and like an open book, spread them out. Pound chicken flat to a thickness of around 1/2 inch.
3. In a tub, whip the egg and cream together.
4. Combine the crushed pork rinds, the Parmesan cheese, the salt, the garlic powder, the red pepper flakes, the ground black pepper and the bowl with the Italian seasoning.
5. Dip chicken into a mixture of eggs; coat entirely. Press the chicken into the bread; cover both sides thickly.
6. Over medium-high heat, heat a skillet; add ghee. Place the chicken in the pan; cook until the juices are clear, around 3 minutes on each side, until the middle is no longer pink. A center-inserted instant-read thermometer should read at least 165 ° F (74 ° C). Take care to keep the bread in place.
7. The chicken is moved to a baking sheet. Use tomato sauce to cover; top with mozzarella cheese.
8. Broil for about 2 minutes until the cheese is bubbling and barely browned.

Nutrition Facts

Every Serving:

442 calories; protein 46.5g 93% ; carbohydrates 5.8g 2% ; fat 25.3g 39% ; cholesterol 216.8mg 72% ; sodium 1604.7mg 64% .

115. EASY KETO ALFREDO SAUCE

Prep: 5 mins

Cook: 10 mins

Total: 15 mins

Servings: 6

Ingredients

- ½ cup unsalted butter
- 2 cloves garlic, crushed
- 2 cups heavy whipping cream
- ½ (4 ounce) package cream cheese, softened
- 1 ½ cups grated Parmesan cheese
- 1 pinch salt
- 1 pinch ground nutmeg
- 1 pinch ground white pepper

Directions

1. In a medium saucepan, melt butter. Cook the garlic for about 2 minutes, until it is fragrant. Heavy cream and cream cheese are added. Add the Parmesan cheese slowly, stirring continuously for 5 to 7 minutes until well absorbed and the sauce thickens. Add the cinnamon, nutmeg, and white pepper and stir.

Nutrition Facts

Every Serving:

531 calories; protein 10.3g 21% ; carbohydrates 3.8g 1% ; fat 53.8g 83% ; cholesterol 177.3mg 59% ; sodium 391.9mg 16% .

116. PRALINE PECAN FRENCH TOAST CASSEROLE

Prep: 15 mins

Cook: 30 mins

Additional: 8 hrs

Total: 8 hrs 45 mins

Servings: 8

Ingredients

- 1 ½ cups half-and-half
- 8 eggs
- 2 tbsps vanilla extract
- 1 tbsp dark brown sugar
- 8 slices French bread
- ¼ cup butter, or more if needed
- ¾ cup brown sugar
- ½ cup maple syrup
- ¾ cup of chopped pecans
- 2 tbsps confectioners sugar, or more to taste

Directions

1. In a big shallow bowl, mix half-and-half, eggs, vanilla, and 1 tbsp of dark brown sugar; add French bread. Cover the bowl with plastic wrap, then refrigerate overnight for 8 hours.
2. Preheat the oven to 175 ° C.
3. In a 9x13-inch casserole dish, put the butter. In the preheated oven, put the casserole dish and melt the butter for about 5 minutes. Butter swirls over the bottom of the dish.
4. Spread over the melted butter with brown sugar, maple syrup, and pecans. Set the soaked bread on top of the pecan mixture.
5. Bake in the preheated oven for 30 to 35 minutes until the French toast is cooked through. Sprinkle with sugar from confectioners.

Nutrition Facts

Every Serving:

460 calories; protein 12g 24% ; carbohydrates 50.2g 16% ; fat 23.9g 37% ; cholesterol 218mg 73% ; sodium 320.1mg 13% .

117. BBQ CHICKEN DRUMSTICKS

Prep: 10 mins

Cook: 1 hr

Total: 1 hr 10 mins

Servings: 3

Ingredients

- 6 chicken drumsticks
- ½ cup water
- 1/3 cup ketchup
- 1/3 cup white vinegar
- ¼ cup brown sugar
- 4 tsps butter
- 2 tsps salt
- 2 tsps Worcestershire sauce, or to taste
- 2 tsps dry mustard
- 2 tsps chili powder, or to taste

Directions

1. Preheat the oven to 200 ° C. In a baking dish, put drumsticks.
2. In a cup, whisk together water, ketchup, vinegar, brown sugar, butter, salt, Worcestershire sauce, mustard and chili powder; pour the drumsticks over the mixture. Aluminum foil cover.
3. Bake in a preheated oven until the bone is no longer pink and the juices run clear for around 1 hour, turning the chicken halfway through. 165 ° F can be read by an instant-read thermometer inserted near the bone (74 ° C).

Cook's Note:

I typically cook the chicken for 10 to 15 minutes to make the sauce thicken. I like to mix it with mashed potatoes and drizzle the potatoes with some of the chicken sauce. It's also perfect with any seasoned rice.

Nutrition Facts

Every Serving:

443 calories; protein 39.4g 79% ; carbohydrates 20.7g 7% ; fat 22.2g 34% ; cholesterol 142.3mg 47% ; sodium 2071.9mg 83% .

118. SWEET GREEN BEAN BUNDLES

Prep: 10 mins

Cook: 45 mins

Total: 55 mins

Servings: 6

Ingredients

- 3 (14.5 ounce) cans whole green beans, drained
- 1 pound bacon, cut in half
- ½ cup butter, melted
- 1 cup brown sugar
- 1 tsp garlic salt

Directions

1. Preheat the oven to 350 175 ° C. Grease a baking dish that is 9x13 inches.
2. Wrap the bacon with 7 green beans and put in the prepared oven. Using all the green beans and bacon, repeat.
3. Combine brown sugar with butter. Pour over the bundles of green beans and sprinkle with garlic salt.
4. Using foil to cover and bake for 45 minutes.

Nutrition Facts

Every Serving:

608 calories; protein 10.7g 21% ; carbohydrates 31.1g 10% ; fat 49.4g 76% ; cholesterol 92.1mg 31% ; sodium 1623.2mg 65% .

119. BEST CLAM CHOWDER

Prep: 25 mins

Cook: 25 mins

Total: 50 mins

Servings: 8

Ingredients

- 3 (6.5 ounce) cans minced clams
- 1 cup minced onion
- 1 cup diced celery
- 2 cups cubed potatoes
- 1 cup diced carrots
- ¾ cup butter
- ¾ cup all-purpose flour
- 1 quart half-and-half cream
- 2 tbsps red wine vinegar
- 1 ½ tsps salt
- ground black pepper to taste

Directions

1. Drain the juice from the clams over the onions, celery, potatoes and carrots in a large skillet. Add water to cover, and cook until tender, over medium heat.
2. Meanwhile, melt the butter over a medium heat in a big heavy saucepan. Whisk in the flour until it's tender. Whisk in the cream and whisk continuously until smooth and thick. Stir in the clam juice and vegetables. Hot it but don't boil it.
3. Just prior to serving, whisk in the clams. They get tough when they cook too much. Stir in the vinegar when the clams are heated, and season with salt and pepper.

Nutrition Facts

Every Serving:

501 calories; protein 23.9g 48% ; carbohydrates 28.4g 9% ; fat 32.7g 50% ; cholesterol 136.6mg 46% ; sodium 712.3mg 29% .

120. PUMPKIN CREAM CHEESE MUFFINS

Servings: 18

Yield: 18 muffins

Ingredients

- 1 (8 ounce) package cream cheese
- 1 egg
- 1 tsp vanilla extract
- 3 tbsps brown sugar
- 4 ½ tbsps all-purpose flour
- 5 tbsps white sugar
- ¾ tsp ground cinnamon
- 3 tbsps butter
- 3 tbsps chopped pecans
- 2 ½ cups all-purpose flour
- 2 cups white sugar
- 2 tsps baking powder
- 2 tsps ground cinnamon
- ½ tsp salt
- 2 eggs
- 1 ⅓ cups canned pumpkin
- 1/3 cup olive oil
- 2 tsps vanilla extract

Directions

1. Preheat the oven to 375°F (190 ° C). 18 muffin cups, grease and flour, or use paper liners.
2. To make the filling: beat the cream cheese until soft in a medium cup. Put the egg, vanilla and brown sugar together. Smooth beat until then set aside.
3. Mix the flour, sugar, cinnamon and pecans in a medium dish. Apply the butter and cut it until crumbly with a fork. Only set aside.
4. For the muffin batter: Sift the flour, sugar, baking powder, cinnamon and salt together in a big bowl. Add the eggs, pumpkin, olive oil and vanilla and make a well in the middle of the flour mixture. Beat until smooth, together.
5. Place the pumpkin mixture in approximately 1/2 full muffin cups. Right in the middle of the batter, apply one tbsp of the cream cheese mixture. Try to prevent the paper cup from hitting the cream cheese. Sprinkle the topping with streusel.
6. Bake for 20 to 25 minutes at 375 ° F (195 ° C).

Nutrition Facts

Every Serving:

304 calories; protein 4.3g 9% ; carbohydrates 45.2g 15% ; fat 12.2g 19% ; cholesterol 49.8mg 17% ; sodium 225.8mg 9%

The End

Printed in Great Britain
by Amazon

45788199R00156